INTRODUCTION TO
Home
Management

Bettye B. Swanson

Western Illinois University

INTRODUCTION TO
Home
Management

MACMILLAN PUBLISHING CO., Inc.
New York
COLLIER MACMILLAN PUBLISHERS
London

Macmillan Publishing Co., Inc.
866 Third Avenue, New York, New York 10022

Collier Macmillan Canada, Ltd.

Library of Congress Cataloging in Publication Data

Swanson, Bettye B
 Introduction to home management.

 Includes bibliographies and index.
 1. Home economics. I. Title.
TX167.S93   640   80–12072
ISBN 0–02–418500–0

Printing: 1 2 3 4 5 6 7 8   Year: 1 2 3 4 5 6 7

To

Dr. Karen Craig
Professor of Home Economics
University of Illinois

Dr. Anna Carol Fults
Professor of Home Economics
Southern Illinois University

Ms. Lillian Matthiesen
Home Economics Teacher, Retired
Freeport Senior High School

PREFACE

Individuals and families use home management principles and concepts throughout their daily life. How these are used often determines their success in attaining their desired *quality of life*. This introductory textbook written for the college student is intended not only to develop a knowledgeable awareness of these concepts but also to demonstrate through case studies and student activities the real and immediate implications of management to the daily lives of the students. The student is given the opportunity to undertake steps leading to self-examination, analysis, and evaluation of how the concepts of home management impact and affect his or her lifetime goals, value hierarchy, living patterns, decision making and future endeavors.

Included in this text are the management concepts of values, goals, decision making, the management system, and the identification and allocation of resources. Specific resources discussed at length include time, energy, money and communication. In addition to the management concepts, several chapters have been included which discuss the effects of the stages of the life cycle, the nuclear and non-nuclear family unit, and technology upon managerial behavior.

This text emphasizes two basic premises. The first is that although home management may be undertaken as an individual or as a member of a collective group, it is nonetheless initiated by and most directly affects the individual. Management, per se, produces, through interaction, input upon other systems. Introduced herein are the spheres of interaction within which the individual initiates and undertakes managerial behavior and through which the individual receives input that necessitates managerial behavior.

The second premise of this text is that effective managerial behavior does not occur until the individual is not only aware of, but actively utilizes the management concepts in a purposeful and meaningful manner. Thus, knowledge of management concepts does not automatically yield effective managerial behavior. Effective management occurs only when these concepts are based upon thoughtful, rational intent.

The objective of this text is to enable the student to study and apply the concepts of management to their own lives in a real and meaningful way. To further this objective, this text is written in the familiar rather than the impersonal third person style. Each chapter format introduces the various concepts through a series of self-examination questions which then become the salient discussion points throughout the chapter. Activities and case studies relating to the chapter topic are found at the end of each chapter. Each of these has been developed to correlate chapter discussion with a real life situation. Resolution of the case study questions necessitates that the student draw upon the current and previous chapters, and in so doing, demonstrates the interlinking of concepts. To further assist the student, a glossary of terms is found at the end of each chapter.

The author gratefully acknowledges the assistance provided by several individuals. The support given by my family, the home economics students at Western Illinois University and my colleagues is most appreciated. Mrs. Marilyn Eck devoted many hours to the secretarial tasks involved. A special acknowledgement is given to Professor Sumiye N. Onodera, California State University; Professor Imogen Whatley, Texas Christian University and Professor Judith Van Name, University of Delaware for their contributions in reviewing and critiquing the drafts of this text. A very special thanks and expression of appreciation must also go to Mr. John J. Beck, Senior Editor, Macmillan Publishing Company, Inc. for his assistance, guidance, and encouragement.

CONTENTS

CHAPTER THREE
Decision Making   37

CHAPTER FOUR
The Management Process   90

CHAPTER FIVE
Resources   112

CHAPTER TEN
Individual and Family Management

CHAPTER ELEVEN
Management of Other Family Units

CHAPTER TWELVE
Management and a Changing World

FIGURES

INTRODUCTION TO

Home
Management

INTRODUCTION

Specifically, what is individual and family management? More importantly, what does it mean to you? How does it affect your actions, behavior, and your daily life? Would it surprise you to learn that many of the home management principles and concepts you are going to be studying have made you the person you are today. They will also affect your future.

Before we begin to study individual and family management, let's look at the development of "home management" and why it has become an integral part of the home economics discipline.

The term *home management* was coined by Maria Parloa in 1880.[1] When she first used the term, it simply meant anything that needed to be accomplished within the household. It included ironing, cleaning, cooking, planning a party, social behavior and so forth. The study of home economics at this time included cooking, sewing, food preparation and so forth.[2]

As the discipline of home economics began to develop, the specific fields of study as we know them today began to emerge. With the passage of time, each field refined its area of study and identified its concepts. Scientific research has continued through these years to advance each field to the present.

Gross, Crandall, and Knolls have identified six stages of development. Home management has moved from the "dumping grounds" to the "holistic approach."[3] As the field progressed through these stages, the principles and concepts of home management began to emerge. The definition of what home management is and how it is used in daily life took on new directions and meaning.

The validity of these principles and concepts to daily living increased; new studies clearly demonstrated their importance. Today it is readily apparent that individual and family management involves more than completing the tasks of household operation and passing on to younger generations the mode of acceptable social behavior. Although home management still involves the household operational tasks; individual and family management encompasses a great deal more.

Every individual has values, goals, and standards. This same individual makes decisions; assumes roles; interacts within family, community, state and nation; and uses those resources that are available to him or her. The person you are today is a result of all of these. The choices you make among your alternatives now and in the future will be influenced by those individuals, agencies, and communities, with whom you interact. At the same time events will occur and demands will be placed upon you which may well affect not only your life but the lives of others as well. There will be times when you will experience a higher degree of freedom of choice than at other times. At some point you may well be forced to choose between alternatives, none of which are really desirable.

The future offers you much more latitude than it held for your parents. Careers, once highly restricted, are affording you greater opportunities than ever imagined. Technological advances are creating new demands for the individual and the family in business, industry, and government. Once clearly defined stereotyped roles are no longer valid. The society in which you live is continually undergoing changes.

The result is more individual freedom of choice concerning your career, your roles, and your life style patterns. Although you have far greater latitude than your parents to make these choices and to determine the person you aspire to be, the risk factors inherent within each must be recognized.

Each day of your life you and your family use management principles and concepts, although you may not be fully aware of them. Nor are you completely aware of the extent to which each affects your total process of daily living.

There are choices, events, and demands that will necessitate the continual and on-going use of management principles and concepts. How effectively you make these choices, analyze demand input and/or assess the impact of the event upon you, your life style, resources, and decision making will determine your degree of success in goal attainment and your desired quality of life.

Studying the management principles and concepts will give you better insight into your life patterns, behavior, and the choices you make. Increasing your skills in using these can enrich your life and give it greater meaning. Effective management:

1. Enhances your chances of reaching the goals you have set for yourself.
2. Increases your understanding of yourself and others.
3. Aids in making decisions.
4. Encourages you to make better use of your resources.
5. Give you the tools whereby you can better attain your desired quality of life.

Each of these means you are better able to take a more active and meaningful role in the world in which you live. Collectively they mean you are better able to direct your life: to manage your daily living through effective decision making rather than merely coping. You, rather than outside events and demands, will provide the greatest input into your management world.

Effective management for the individual and family means: recognizing your values and those of others; understanding not how decisions are made but also the factors which can effect them; determining your immediate and long-range goals and the needed action to achieve each; and allocating the use of resources within the management process to attain these goals. It involves studying these not only as individual components but also discovering how each is an integral part of management process. In other words individual and family management is more than theoretical knowledge. It is theoretical knowledge applied throughout every phase of daily life.

The use of management principles and concepts is not limited to individuals, families, and household operation. Most of these principles are used by governments, businesses, and industries. In fact, any group, large or small, private or public, commercial or noncommercial whose existence necessitates a continual flow of communication and organization structuring must use some, if not all, of the management principles and concepts to successfully reach the goals and objectives of the group.

The difference lies in where and how these principles are applied. Corporations and governments spend a great deal of time and effort in their management functions. An unwise decision or an inappropriate use of resources could have far reaching effects not only upon the corporation or government but also upon the economic structure.

A decision made by a corporation to market a new product or to change an existing one is done after months or even years of research. Involved are whether or not the public would purchase the new or changed product; the extent and amount of resources which could or should be expended to develop and market the product; the cost of marketing the product; what should be the consumer's price for the product; and how and when to introduce the product to the consumer market. The corporation uses the management process to determine the probability of success. This ultimate decision is based on research, the weighing of alternatives, and the making of many decisions. In reaching this final decision the corporation has used many of the principles and concepts of management. Such decisions take place on a daily basis as corporations contribute goods and services to the economic marketplace; governments function in a similar manner.

Individuals and families also have goals. In order to achieve these goals, they follow much the same pattern. Resources must be identified and allocated, decisions must be made, and planning takes place. Choices must be made as goals are given priorities. Resources are assessed and analyzed to ascertain which combination will produce the highest degree of success. Just as with the corporation, the decisions made by a family or an individual could have a far reaching effect.

Management techniques used by families and individuals are just as important as those used by corporations or governments. The decisions made concerning goal priorities and attainment through resource allocation can affect not only today, tomorrow, and next week but the future.

The extent to which individuals and families use management principles and concepts will determine to a great extent how effective each is in achieving his or her desired quality of life. In the succeeding pages we will be exploring these management principles and concepts.

Although the principles and concepts of home management are universal, each individual undertakes managerial action on the basis of his or her individuality. Although families may perform managerial action as a collective group, the perception and implementation of management concepts produce feedback which becomes input upon each individual within the group.

The use of home management principles and concepts is an individual endeavor. For this reason this textbook is addressed to you, the individual. Because you use the principles and concepts of home management in your daily life, this textbook is designed to increase and enhance your home management knowledge and skills through an in-depth study of each concept that can enable you to achieve a more satisfying life.

REFERENCES

1. Irma H. Gross and Elizabeth Walbert Crandall, *Management for Modern Families*, 2nd ed. (New York: Appleton-Century-Crofts, 1963), p. 525.
2. Ibid.
3. Irma H. Gross, Elizabeth Walbert Crandall, and Marjorie M. Knoll, *Management for Modern Families*, 3rd ed. (New York: Appleton-Century-Crofts, 1973), p. 669.

CHAPTER ONE

Spheres
of Interaction

Before examining the separate components of individual and family management, you need to be aware of how the society in which you live is a source of input upon you and the management you undertake. At the same time, your characteristics and input have a part in shaping the continual changes taking place in society. You need to become aware of the influence kinship networks, role perceptions, and reference groups have upon you. Each of these has had a great deal of influence upon the person you have become, the decisions you have made, and the directions you plan to take in the future.

Very few of us live in a society where we have complete and utter control. Rather each one of us is influenced by and influences the society in which we live.

Every individual lives and functions within a system. To ascertain the extent of these influences, let's look first at the basic components of a simple system as shown in Figure 1.1.

There are two basic types of systems. The one shown in Figure 1.1 is a closed system. Feedback from the output goes back into the system. At no time is input received from outside the system. Thus a closed system is totally self-contained. At times your use of the management principles and concepts will represent a closed system.

The system shown contains four major components. The first component is *input*. Input can best be described as those facts or factors being "fed into" the system. The square in the center of the system can be called the *action* or *analysis* phase. The action or analysis phase is the area in which the analysis of the input occurs, decisions are made, and implementation through action takes place. The *output* is the end result of the action or analysis. It is here that you attain satisfaction through having succeeded in attaining the goal or objective you desired. Within this phase you measure the degree of success you have achieved and look at the resources which have been used to achieve this goal or objective. *Feedback* is the last part of the system. This phase of the system represents new goals, input, and objectives that have developed as a result of the output.

Undoubtedly you have many tasks you hope to accomplish today, one of which is reading this textbook. In a closed system your input would be to set priorities for your tasks and to determine a course of action. The analysis or action would be to undertake the course of action. Output would occur when each task had been completed. Through feedback you would assess how successfully you had completed each one. One portion of the feedback would be the extent to which you understood the information given in the textbook.

However, the society in which you live is an open system. It does not

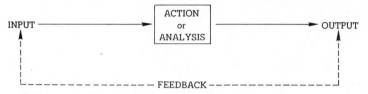

FIGURE 1.1. *Basic Systems.*

afford you the opportunity to function totally devoid of external input. As you identified the tasks you needed to accomplish today, inputs other than your own were also being fed into the system. These inputs may have accrued from other events taking place: demands being made upon you by peers, faculty, friends, family, and/or resource availability. These external factors have an impact upon you, the choices you make, and the action you take. The output resulting from your action produces feedback not only upon you and your future actions but also upon the world around you.

What do you anticipate accomplishing this coming weekend? Assume that one goal you have is to complete at least half of the research needed for a term project. If you had access to all of the research in your room, lived alone, and no other demands were placed upon you, this could be accomplished within the framework of a closed system.

In an open system, as shown in Figure 1.2, many other events and demands are sources of input upon you. Since you do not have research available in your room, you will need to use the library, but your use of the library is dependent upon when it is open.

You are also experiencing the demands being placed upon you by friends, peers, faculty, other careers, and your family. For instance, your friends may want you to spend the weekend with them rather than at the library. Your family wants you to come home for the weekend. An instructor might have given you a special assignment that entails either attending a special lecture or lengthy reading in the reference library. Other events may be taking place. Perhaps there is a concert, a field trip, or a tennis tournament scheduled on campus. If you are a member of an athletic team, your coach might schedule an extra practice or your team will be competing away from the campus.

As you determine your specific course of action, this input will affect how and in what manner you allocate your resources. The output attained and the feedback produced will impact not only upon you but upon others as well. This feedback will also create new demands. Your feedback then becomes input into other systems.

Using Figure 1.2, identify specific inputs you might receive in a similar situation. Assuming you had formulated and implemented a course of action, what do you anticipate would be the outcome you achieved? Identify the inputs you and others would receive as feedback from your anticipated outcome. Would this feedback received as input by others have varying degrees of impact? Why or why not?

Neither individuals nor families live and function in a vacuum; there is daily contact and interaction with each other and with other phases of society. This interaction occurs through employment, education, social and recreational activities, participation in the marketplace, and in the roles each assumes within the family, reference groups, agencies, and organizations. Each time interaction takes place, two inputs are received. A family, either collectively or individually, provides input into the household and into the society which exists outside the home. At the same time, the family and/or individual receives input from outside the home. Just as your decision can be expressed as a system, so can the interaction of a family with society.

Many different system structures have been developed to diagram the society in which you live to indicate the continuous and on-going input and output. Gross, Crandall, and Knoll's system incorporates the use of three environments: household, near and larger.[1] Deacon and Firebaugh's uses the macro and micro habitats as the basis for their system.[2] The basic system illustrates how an individual manages in a single situation. However, it is readily apparent that although you make individual decisions, the resulting feedback from your decision affects others as well as creating new demands.

Individuals and families do not live in a totally self-contained world apart from society; nor does the managerial action each takes remain solely and completely devoid of input from others. Individuals and families receive input from society and the output of their managerial action becomes input into society. This input-output between individuals, families, and societies means that a continual flow of interaction is taking place. Through the mediums of communication, this interaction occurs throughout life. These mediums of communication are the expression of input and output between the individual and his or her spheres of interaction.

Spheres of Interaction

Every individual has a series of *spheres of interaction*. Each of these spheres represent a specific level of interaction between the individual and society. Separately and collectively they are a source of input upon individual management. Located within each of these spheres of interaction are potential resources the individual can draw upon. At the same time, these spheres create demands upon the individual that necessitate action.

The individual's resulting managerial action and output occurring from these demands (input) in turn formulate the input into the various spheres. Thus there is a continual flow of interaction between the various spheres and the individual. The continual flow of interaction between the individual and each sphere varies. Some spheres are a stronger source of input than others. The strength of the input will affect the degree of interaction between the individual and the various spheres. Figure 1.2 illustrates all of the spheres that surround you.

In Figure 1.2 you will note that each sphere forms a circle around you. Each of these represent part of the society in which you live. Connecting the spheres are overlapping subsystems. Each subsystem has distinct characteristics common to all of the spheres. For example, the economic subsystem has characteristics common to each of the different spheres. These subsystems connect the different spheres to provide a cohesive and unified society. Each also is a source of specific input upon you and the society. Within each of these can be found specifically identifiable resources which you can draw upon.

Just as some spheres are a stronger source of input upon you than others, output from your managerial action will be felt more in some spheres than it will in others. In order to ascertain how each of these spheres affect you and your managerial action, you need to examine each separately.

Individual Sphere

At the center of the spheres of interaction is you, the *individual*. Over the years you have grown and matured to become who you are today. Throughout your life, you have undertaken many managerial actions; in the years ahead, you will undertake many more. Much of this managerial action has resulted from the input you have received from the spheres of interaction surrounding you.

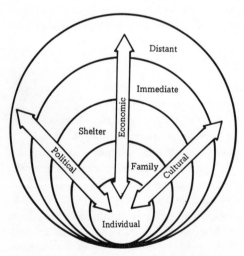

FIGURE 1.2. Spheres of Interaction.

Your managerial action has resulted from decisions you have made. The basis for those decisions is your value structure—a continual major influence upon your life. The input you receive from each of these spheres is decoded in terms of your value structure and acted upon by you. This can be expressed as the basic system discussed earlier. Your output then becomes input into the sphere where the process repeats itself over and over again.

No two people have identical value hierarchies. Thus each person is distinctly different from the other. These differing value hierarchies mean each person receives and decodes input from the spheres of interaction. In other words, you may decode the input received from the family sphere differently than your sister, mother, brother, or father.

Within the individual sphere, you undertake managerial action. This action may occur as a closed system. It may occur from input received from one of the other spheres. This input may have come through the channel of one or more of the subsystems. A demand or event taking place in one of the spheres may be a source of input into the individual sphere.

The inputs you receive are decoded within the individual sphere. This decoding is done on the basis of your values, the goals you have set, the standards you have established, and the roles you have assigned to yourself. On the basis of the decoded input you determine a specific course of action. As the action is undertaken you use resources within your individual sphere. There are times when you will also use some part or all of the resources in the remaining spheres too. If the latter is true, this resource utilization in and of itself becomes input into another sphere.

The outcome of your managerial action provides feedback into your individual sphere and it may also produce input into the other spheres and subsystems as well. As the feedback occurs new goals, objectives, demands, or events may result. This will be felt in the individual sphere and possibly in others too.

In order to clarify this, let's look at an example. Judy received a letter from her parents which contained a $20.00 check. In their letter, her parents told her to use the money for something she needed. Judy decoded her parent's letter to mean she should purchase a personal item for herself. Upon decoding the message, she thought about all of the things she could purchase but couldn't make a decision.

Judy asked her roommate to go shopping with her. After spending several hours looking, Judy decided to put the money in her checking account for use at a later date.

The input into Judy's individual sphere was the letter and the $20.00 check from her parents. As she determined and implemented a course of action she used not only her resources but others as well. The output of her managerial action was to put the $20.00 in her checking account. This in turn became input into several other spheres.

Thus, although you undertake managerial action within your individual sphere, the output of this action can and often is input into other spheres. Just as Judy drew upon the resources of other spheres to undertake her individual managerial action, so do you.

Family Sphere

The *family sphere* is composed of the individuals who reside in the housing unit. It is with these individuals that you interact most frequently. There is a continual and on-going flow of interaction between you and the others.

During your lifetime this interaction has provided you with the opportunity to develop, establish, analyze, and refine your values. As you have grown into adulthood, the interaction between you and this sphere has changed. As a very young child, the degree of input upon you was much greater than yours was upon this sphere. However, as you grow older your input increases. As it increased, you could observe its influence upon the other members of the family sphere.

Within the family sphere goals are established and standards are observed. As an individual you have goals and standards; the family sphere serves to reinforce and enhance these. Currently, one of your goals is to complete your college education.

Located within this sphere are resources that you have and will continue to draw upon as the years pass. The exact nature of these resources will be dependent upon the given time and situation. The use of resources of the family sphere available to you as a young child were much different than they are today. As a baby you used the resources of your parent's knowledge, skill, time, energy, money, and so forth in a totally different manner than you do now. Although these same resources are still available to you, their use is quite different today. As you have grown and matured, other resources within the family sphere have emerged. At the same time, some resources within the family sphere may have diminished in availability or you may no longer use them in quite the same manner as before. For instance, how has your use of your parent's time and energy changed from when you were a small child to the present time?

You interact with the family sphere in many ways. Just as it represents a potential source of resources for you, you in turn, serve as a potential source of resources for it. Just as you draw upon the other members of the family sphere for resources, there are times when this sphere or members of the sphere draw upon you as a source of resources. Your interaction within the family sphere may well result in defining individual or family goals, making group decisions, providing assistance in arriving at a single individual's decision, or establishing standards for using collective resources to attain a desired goal.

This family interaction will continue throughout your life. The interaction between you and your family sphere will affect your managerial action.

As you receive and decode the input from the family sphere, you will make decisions. These decisions and the resulting managerial actions will serve as input into the family sphere. The observation of your input into the family sphere acts as a source of feedback for you. You, in turn, use the feedback in your future interaction within the family sphere.

Shelter Sphere

You and your family sphere live within a *shelter sphere*. It is here that household operations take place, the evidences of managerial action are more observable, and resources are drawn upon and utilized most frequently.

This sphere serves as a control in that you and your family are able to establish limits as to who or what provides input into the sphere. As such it acts as a partial cushion or barrier between the family and remaining spheres. The family as a collective group determines the extent of interaction from beyond the shelter sphere in numerous ways; for instance the selection of communication media, social involvement, participation in community activities, and so forth.

In most instances, the shelter sphere incorporates interaction with individuals other than the family membership. These may include individuals who compose your kinship network, or friends of the family members. Each of these individuals interact with you and other members of the family. As such they affect your managerial action.

Within the shelter sphere standards are observed, resources are allocated, and goals are sought. Each of these takes place as a result of your managerial action and the interaction of others. The various subsystems which link the spheres together also provide a source of specific input.

Your managerial action and/or interaction with the shelter sphere can take many different forms. It may be evident in tangible forms such as completing the various household operational tasks. You may assist in the financial planning of the family's money resources or you may use your time and energy in child care tasks. Less tangible forms might include contributing your potential resources, assisting in finding a solution to a problem, or acting efficiently in a crisis situation.

It is within this sphere that you and your family interact not only with others as individuals but also as a collective group. A group decision made here becomes input into one or more of the remaining spheres. Decisions concerning allocation of family resources can have far reaching effects upon both the outer spheres and the subsystems linking them together as well as the inner spheres.

Demands initiated from this sphere can affect both you and the family sphere. Goals established in the family sphere may be accomplished within this sphere. Standards established in the other inner spheres are often most observable here. The very nature of the sphere itself provides a form of control over the interaction taking place. Input from the outer spheres can often be assessed and acted upon as a collective group. The extent of interaction with other individuals beyond those of the family membership is governed by the choices of the individual members.

The shelter sphere serves many functions in the interaction taking place. You, your family, and those who regularly enter the shelter sphere interact. As such it can be a control on the extent to which input is received and acted upon. At the same time the shelter sphere can serve to facilitate and possibly initiate interaction.

The confines of the shelter sphere encourages interaction. Don't you and your roommate frequently discuss your daily activities together? When a group of your friends get together in your room or apartment interaction again takes place. In either case, as interaction takes place, you are receiving input. This input in turn initiates your interaction.

Unlike the remaining outer spheres, the shelter sphere has clearly defined boundaries. Both tangible and intangible evidences of managerial action can be observed. It is here your managerial action may occur as the combined effort of a collective group or as an individual. As a cushion between the family and remaining spheres, the shelter sphere allows both the individual and the family to place some limitations on input being received.

Immediate Sphere

The *immediate sphere* is composed of that part of society outside your shelter sphere with which you interact on a regular basis. This sphere, then, includes both individuals, reference groups, organizations, agencies, and the community surrounding you. The input from each of these will have an impact upon your managerial action. The extent of their impact will be determined by the degree of importance you attach to each.

Individuals with which you interact on a regular basis would be faculty members, other students, your employer, and others who live in the same building you do. You interact with these people but not to the same extent as those which compose part of your shelter sphere. Nonetheless, this interaction serves as input upon you and the other spheres around you. These individuals also represent possible sources of resources. They affect the decision making taking place and provide an opportunity for you to analyze your value structure.

Your reference groups constitute those groups with which you identify yourself as being a member. One of your reference groups is being a member of the student body of your particular university. There are many others such as social clubs or fraternal organizations, dormitory floors or wings, political affiliations, or your college major. These reference groups provide you with many different sources of input. Your use of leisure time may well be influenced by one or more of these groups.

Each of these reference groups have a direct bearing upon your managerial action. When you identify yourself as being a part of a group, you also assign yourself the characteristics and behavioral patterns you associate with that group. After assuming the identifying characteristics and behavioral patterns, you then assign yourself a role within the reference group.

One of your reference groups is as a student on your particular college campus. Since you have identified yourself as such, you have adopted the mode of dress common to the majority of students. The activities you engage in are associated with this reference group. Listen to the comments made by yourself and other students and you will readily see the degree to which this reference group has input upon your managerial action.

In addition to adopting the characteristics and behavioral patterns of the college student, you have also assigned yourself a role within this group. Although you may not be aware of it, this role is expressed in many different ways. Comments concerning your college major, academic standing, or involvement in student activities clearly indicate your perception of your role within this reference group. This group is only one of many you belong to and actively interact with on a regular basis. Take a moment and think of all of your individual reference groups and the input each has upon you. Now examine your input into each of them.

Reference group membership not only serves as a source of input but also provides you with a self-identification as a member of the society in which you live. Through this self-identification you derive a sense of belonging, a feeling of self-worth, and an enhancement of your own self-esteem. Reference group membership enables each person to assume roles within a particular group as well as providing an avenue for self-expression and a sense of belonging.

Inherent within your immediate sphere are organizations, agencies, and such which act as an additional source of input. These include the university you are attending, the community in which you live, and the geographical location around you. You interact with each of these on a regular basis. The flow of input-output between you and each of these spheres may not be as readily observable. At times you may feel their input upon you is greater than yours is upon them.

Your interaction with this sphere may occur in many different ways. It may occur as direct interaction, a delayed interaction, or as an initiator for interaction between other agencies or groups within the sphere.

When you participate in the business meeting of a club or organization, direct interaction takes place. You may be asked to evaluate a course, make recommendations concerning a textbook, or give suggestions about changing graduation requirements. In each of these instances, your interaction may not be evident for a prolonged period of time. In this case, delayed interaction has taken place. Your interaction within this sphere might initiate input into other spheres. You are a consumer in the economic marketplace and as you assume this role, you want specific products with desired sets of criteria. Assume that the product being offered for sale does not meet your set criteria, therefore you refuse to purchase it. Other consumers also do not purchase this product. When retail merchants determine consumers will not purchase the product, they refuse to stock the product. Your refusal to purchase the product has become an initiator for the retail merchant.

The degree and extent of your interaction with the immediate sphere is governed not only by your reference groups but also by your own role perception and the validity you feel your input has. Each individual has a role perception of him or herself. Through this role perception, you have identified your "worth" to yourself and others. As such you have identified your reaction to others, your daily life patterns, the manner in which other people react and perceive you, and your ability to make meaningful contributions to society.

As you identify and define your role, you also identify and define roles for others around you, such as your parents, friends, and teachers. As you define these roles, you anticipate these individuals will act within the confines of the roles you have identified for each of them. For example, you expect teachers to give lectures and grade tests. The roles you assign to others provide you with a frame of reference and your actions and behavior will be based upon these roles.

Your own role perceptions and the roles you assign to others will have a direct bearing upon your interaction within all of the spheres. How you define your role within the immediate sphere will determine not only the impact you anticipate your input will produce but also the impact of this sphere upon you.

The individual who views his or her role as having little if any impact upon the immediate sphere may feel this sphere has a tremendous impact upon him or her. You have met individuals who feel they contribute little if anything to the society. Thus their role perceptions allow others to direct their thinking and their daily life patterns. At the same time, you have also met individuals who think and act as though the entire world revolves around them. Each of these individuals have different views of their interaction with the immediate sphere. This difference in role perceptions has an effect upon how input is decoded and interaction takes place. For the first person, the immediate sphere had a great deal of strength and impact upon his or her daily life patterns. The second person feels he or she has the capability of controlling the sphere.

The self-perceptions of each of these individuals are extremes. In each case the input is received and decoded, but in totally different terms. The importance and impact of the input is also different, as is the managerial action taken and the output produced. One individual might well feel his or her managerial action was controlled by others and therefore, undertake little or no active participation. However, the strong role perception of the second person could result in extensive managerial action.

Role perceptions and their effect upon managerial action are factors in every sphere of interaction. However, they are more readily observable with the immediate sphere. For instance, the individual whose role perception does not include extensive involvement with the immediate or distant sphere may well not "bother" to vote in elections, be concerned with current governmental issues, or participate in community activities.

The immediate sphere does not have defined parameters as do the other spheres previously discussed. The parameters for this sphere are established by your own role perceptions, reference groups, organizations, agencies, and communities. Other factors are the stage in the life cycle and the family composition. Each of these will, in its own way, shape and mold the outermost parameters of your immediate sphere.

As an individual you interact with not only your own reference groups but with reference groups of other members of your household. Your parents have interacted with one or more of your college reference groups. This will probably be true as long as these reference groups form a part of your daily life. Your communication with your parents includes these groups. Consequently, these groups have been included in the immediate sphere of your parents.

The immediate sphere encompasses more than your college activities. It also includes your employment, social activities, and community participation. In fact any intereaction taking place on a regular basis outside the shelter sphere is included in your immediate sphere.

Potential resources are available for your use within this sphere. Some are provided by the community. These may be used for the purpose of leisure-time activities such as parks and recreational areas or they may be tax supported services such as police and fire protection. Other community resources might include public agencies, school systems, churches, and citizens of the community.

The business community is another source of potential resources. In addition to making goods and services available for your consumption, they may be a place of possible employment. Through employment other resources such as money, fringe benefits, and social security may be made available.

Your interaction within this sphere will be dependent upon your life patterns at any given time. With the passage of time and changes in your life patterns, your membership in some reference groups will disappear, some will remain the same, and new ones will be added. Throughout your life you will draw upon the resources found here while engaging in a continual flow of input-output.

As this occurs, the parameters of your immediate sphere will be modified. The input you receive from this sphere will be accessed. Your input into this sphere will be governed by the parameters you recognize. Thus the immediate sphere will be an important part of your daily life outside the shelter sphere as well as being a source of input for the managerial action that takes place in the two inner spheres.

Distant Sphere

The parameters of the *distant sphere* encompasses any interaction you have with individuals, organizations and agencies, and geographical locations on an infrequent, irregular, and remote basis. This interaction will be governed by your self-perceptions and the extent to which you feel the interaction has a viable effect upon your managerial action.

As you interact with this sphere you designate its parameters. How you view this interaction will be the determinant factor in your assessment of these parameters and the impact this sphere has on your managerial action.

The parameters are formulated by the furthest extension of input you recognize as having an effect upon you. To determine your own distant sphere, think for a moment of the most distant input you receive which could, even in the most remote way, have an impact upon your managerial action. These then become the exterior boundary parameters of your distant sphere.

Although this sphere is also a source of potential resources, these may not be as readily available, as clearly delineated, or occur in the same form as those of the other spheres. Their allocation will be to all rather than specific individuals within the sphere. Resources here might include tax supported public services such as national defense or federally assisted student loans; private services such as national foundations and educational institutions; or corporations offering employment, consumer information, and consumer goods and services.

Since resources within this sphere are available primarily to segments of the population rather than specific individuals, some may not be as readily available as others. For instance, in order to utilize resources available from welfare assistance agencies you must meet certain criteria. The resources found in this sphere are available primarily for the general well-being of the total population.

Just as in the other spheres, there is a continual flow of communication necessitating managerial action. Although initially input originating from this sphere applies to many individuals, this input is received by each individual and decoded with reference to his or her life patterns.

Input initiated within this sphere, for the most part, affects individuals equally. One example of input originating from the distant sphere would be income taxes. Although this input affects the majority of the population, its impact occurs on an individual basis and necessitates individual managerial action.

The nature of this sphere denotes that the output of your managerial action will be different than that of the other spheres. Any controls you exert will be accomplished as a collective action with other individuals. Examples of these controls would be voting in elections, paying taxes, or writing to a congressman concerning current issues. In other spheres you could, for the most part, readily observe the impact of your managerial action. This may not necessarily be true here; in many cases, the impact of your managerial action may not be immediately evident. In other instances, your managerial action will have an impact only when similar action is taken by a large number of individuals such as in an election.

Although many people feel so removed from the distant sphere that there is little if any actual flow of communication eminating from them to this sphere, such is not the case. As with the other spheres, there is a continual and on-going flow of interaction. This interaction between you and your distant sphere is a necessary part of your spheres of interaction.

Subsystems Within the Spheres of Interaction

In Figure 1.2, you noted three subsystems linking the different spheres together. Each has special characteristics and has a direct effect upon your managerial action. These subsystems provide a direct channel for input and output between you and the spheres of interaction. They have distinct characteristics that set them apart from each other. Within each, however, there are characteristics common to each sphere.

Each subsystem has a unique function which affects your managerial action. Resources are allocated and goals are achieved primarily through the economic subsystem. The political subsystem provides guidelines and an ordering for life patterns. Traditions, heritage, social customs, and behavior are directed and reinforced through the cultural subsystem.

In linking your spheres of interaction together, they give you a sense of belonging and well-being. They also aid you to achieve and measure your desired quality of life.

Economic Subsystem

Of the three subsystems, the managerial action occurring from the *economic subsystem's* input is probably more evident than for the other two. One reason is the tangible evidences observed in measurable terms. Interaction also takes place on a continual, and often times, daily basis. It is through this component subsystem that decisions are made concerning resource allocations.

As an individual, you experience a continual flow of communication from this subsystem. Advertising is a prime example. Each of the spheres provides a continual flow of communication channelled through this subsystem and directed toward you. At the same time, your decisions concerning resource allocation radiate outward. These decisions are input into the managerial action of various groups within each sphere.

Many individuals denote the economic subsystem as being synonymous with the economic marketplace. Although in many instances, interaction between the economic marketplace and the individual is a major function of this subsystem, the primary interaction involves resource allocation. As you allocate your resources you are seeking to achieve your desired quality of life. Thus you seek to maximize your resource allocation in a manner that will enable you to achieve as many of your goals as is possible.

The major resources involved in the input-output of this subsystem are time, energy, and money. Through this subsystem you allocate resources by transferring, exchanging, producing, or conserving them. You may exchange one resource such as your time for another of money paid to you as a salary. You might transfer your money resource for the resource of a train ticket to go home for the weekend. At the moment, you are using your resources of time and energy to produce a new resource of a college degree. In order to achieve your goal of a college degree you may have saved (conserved) part of your summer wages to pay for your college expenses.

Many of your goals may involve the economic subsystem. Your desired quality of life may, in part, be reflected in your anticipated participation within the economic subsystem.

Some individuals very often tend to measure their degree of success in terms of their capabilities to actively participate in the economic subsystem. How viable this measure is depends upon the individual's value hierarchy. Needless to say, your participation in the economic subsystem is a real and on-going interaction throughout all the spheres of interaction.

Political Subsystem

The *political subsystem* that links the spheres of interaction together involves the rules, regulations, and governance inherent within each sphere. Perhaps through examining the input of the political subsystem into each of the spheres, a clearer distinction of how this subsystem affects you and your managerial action will become more evident.

Input within the distant sphere of this subsystem often takes the form of rules and regulations. Laws are passed, regulations are established, and directives are given. These may be initiated by governments, agencies of governments, or the prime administrative offices of a corporation. As such these provide a sense of stability and apply equally to all individuals.

Evidence of input from the political subsystem within the immediate sphere would be the "chain of command" within corporations or your university's policies and procedures. The policies governing class attendance, registration for new courses, and graduation requirements are examples of input from your immediate sphere through the political subsystem.

Evidences of the political subsystem within the shelter sphere often involve task assignments. The standards established for completion of a specific task are but one example. Role perceptions may designate not only the task assignment within the shelter sphere but also provide evidence of the political subsystem which is operable within the family sphere as well. For instance, meal preparation may be an assigned task to a specific member of the household on a regular basis; or the task of meal preparation may be completed by the first person to arrive home following employment.

Other evidences of the political subsystem within the family sphere are the divisions of authority or the power structure. Most households have established rules and regulations concerning the expectations of various members. You and your roommate have established these as you live and work in your apartment or room. You have also probably set certain standards and you are expected to meet these standards. Each of these are evidences of the operation of the political subsystem within your family sphere.

Collectively these represent evidences of the political subsystem. This subsystem acts as a control to some extent and yet at the same time provides a sense of security. As each individual moves through the various stages of the life cycle, he or she becomes cognizant of the components at each level of the political subsystem. These components, in turn, provide a kind of ordering. This ordering is a set of guidelines. Each individual uses these guidelines to establish an order for life patterns. At the same time, they assist the individual in identifying risk, allocating resources within other subsystems, and making decisions.

Cultural Subsystem

As indicated earlier, your interaction within each of these subsystems has and will continue to shape and direct you as an individual. Interaction with the *cultural subsystem* has a definite purpose too. It is from this interaction that your values are continually analyzed and refined, guidelines of acceptable social behavior are examined and restructured, traditions are observed and reinforced, and our heritage is revered. This interaction assists you in establishing and defining your role perceptions as well as creating your unique life style.

Within each sphere your interaction enables you to "test" your value hierarchy, to examine your role perceptions, and to carry on previous traditions while developing new ones for the future. As a result of this interaction you may discard a previous life pattern and devise a new one. At the same time, you may refine and modify an existing one. The interaction taking place within each sphere results in a continually evolving society. Although you are probably not aware of it, many aspects of the cultural subsystem have changed during your lifetime.

The cultural subsystem enables each individual to measure the present against the past. This in turn brings about a slow, gradual change in society. As you measure the past against the present, you determine your future direction and the possible changes you might make. This process provides you with a sense of continuity and belonging.

The controls operable within this subsystem are not necessarily clear cut, well defined, or written down. They vary among societies. Nonetheless they are present and often center around acceptable modes of behavior, observation of traditions, and conformity to certain social customs. As your life patterns change and emerge these serve as input and ultimately as controls for this subsystem.

Although many young people would like to discount and perhaps discard much of the input from the cultural subsystem upon their life patterns, it does have an effect upon their managerial action. The cultural subsystem is a definite part of the managerial action taken by each individual. Even when the managerial action undertaken is not acceptable to the majority of the population, it forces the population to examine the implications of the input upon their own lives.

Interaction within each of the subsystems has a meaningful effect upon your managerial action. Each one is uniquely different from the other. As you interact within each subsystem and the spheres of interaction, managerial action takes place. At the same time, you as an individual are continually changing. These changes taking place initiate changes in each of the spheres and in the subsystems. This process will continue throughout your life.

Summary

Managerial action begins with you. Every individual, young or old, continually interacts with the individuals, groups, organizations, and agencies composing his or her spheres of interaction. This interaction necessitates managerial action. Thus, you initiate managerial action as a result of the interaction taking place between you and your spheres of interaction.

You live within four spheres of interaction. Each of these spheres is a continual source of input upon you. This input is received and decoded by you. As you decode the input you undertake managerial action. The managerial action you take becomes the input into one or more of the spheres of interaction.

Operable within the spheres are three subsystems. These subsystems are connecting links between the various spheres. Each serves a unique function. Through the economic subsystem resources are allocated and goals are sought. The ordering of your life through rules and regulations has its derivation from the political subsystem. Your values, social behavior, heritage, social customs, and traditions comes from the cultural subsystem.

Since you originate managerial action, all of these play a major role in your life. The interaction taking place between you, your spheres of interaction and the subsystems have done much to make you the person you are today and will become in the future.

Thus far you have undertaken managerial action without being fully aware of this interaction nor of its implications for you. In developing an awareness of this interaction, you are better able to recognize and assess the point of origin of the input. Through recognition and assessment of this input, you will in the future, make more viable decisions and take more meaningful managerial action.

ACTIVITIES

1. Using a simple system and a decision you have recently made
   a. Identify the input you received.
   b. Outline the analysis you made of the input.
   c. Describe the action steps you took.
   d. Indicate the feedback you received from the output.
   e. List the new decisions or demands which resulted from the outcome.
2. Draw your spheres of interaction and identify the boundaries of your immediate and distant spheres. Using these two spheres
   a. Describe at least three inputs from each of the subsystems upon these spheres.
   b. Describe three inputs you have received from each of the subsystems.
3. Select one of the spheres of interaction and describe the interaction taking place between you and this sphere. In so doing, include the following:
   a. Demands from the sphere.
   b. Evidences of your input upon the sphere.
   c. The effects of input you receive upon your management.
   d. New decisions or demands resulting from the sphere's input upon you.
4. You are a member of several reference groups. Do the following:
   a. Identify your reference groups within each of the spheres of interaction.
   b. The effect of one reference group found in each of the spheres upon your management.
   c. Two decisions you have made which have been influenced by a reference group within each sphere.
   d. Your role within a reference group found in each sphere.
5. You are assuming a number of different roles within the various spheres of interaction. Identify your roles and indicate the effect these roles have upon your management for each of the following:
   a. Your family unit within the community.
   b. Your family unit on the collegiate campus.
   c. Within the immediate sphere.
   d. Within the distant sphere.
6. Identify six inputs you have received from your distant sphere of interaction. Indicate how three of these have directly affected your managerial action. Describe how your managerial action became input into the other spheres of interaction. Did the managerial action you took become a direct input upon the distant sphere? If so, how?

7. Using the resources of education, money, and energy, describe your input into the economic, political, and cultural subsystems. What inputs are you receiving from each of these subsystems? How is this input evidenced in your management?
8. Select a current newspaper headline. Trace the inputs of this event through all of your spheres of interaction. Describe the effects of this input within each of the spheres and its specific impact upon your management.
9. Write a short paper describing your desired quality of life. Turn in the paper to your course instructor in one week.

JULIE AND MAUREEN

Julie and Maureen are daughters of Mr. and Mrs. Johnson who live on a 300-acre farm five miles from a predominately rural midwestern community of about 20,000. One son, older than either of the girls, is married and lives on the adjoining farm with his wife and small son. Another older brother is completing his senior year in the School of Medicine at the same university Maureen is attending. Their youngest sister is a senior in high school.

Julie is a freshman in a small midwestern university where she is majoring in English education. In high school she was a slightly above average student who followed her brothers and Maureen, all of whom were class valedictorians. Although her parents wanted her to attend the same university as Maureen and her brother, Julie decided to enroll at her present university and then possibly transfer in her junior year. She lives on the third floor of one of the dormitories. Her close friends are her roommate and the girl who lives in the next room. Because she rode the school bus, she was seldom a member of any high school organization. Although quite pretty, Julie has seldom dated. Her only friend in high school married shortly after graduation. Most people would describe Julie as a ''loner'' who spends most of her time studying.

Maureen is a junior at a large metropolitan university where she is majoring in Interior Design. In high school she was a cheerleader, Homecoming Queen, and active in nearly all of the organizations as well as student council president her senior year. Although only a junior, she is president of her sorority and vice president of the student government association. She has been a member of the varsity cheerleading squad since her freshman year and her name consistently appears on the Dean's List for academic excellence. Maureen lives in the sorority house but plans to move to her own apartment as soon as her term of office is completed at the end of the year. Although she is often seen out with different men, she tends to date one on a fairly regular basis. Maureen and Julie closely resemble each other in appearance and are often mistaken for one another by people who do not know either of the girls well. Unlike Julie, Maureen has a large number of friends who either call or drop by to see her frequently.

Discussion Questions

1. Both Julie and Maureen have spheres of interaction. What are the similarities and differences in the spheres of each girl? What has created these differences?
2. What is Julie's self-perception? Compare this role perception to Maureen's. What has created the differences in the role perceptions? If Maureen were asked to describe her sister's role perception, how would she respond?

3. Compare Julie's reference groups to those of Maureen. Which girl would have the greatest number and why?

4. How would Julie's role perception affect her reference groups? What reference groups would both girls share? What would be their roles within the reference groups they share?

5. Both girls have made the decision to attend a specific university. Using a simple system, identify the inputs each received, the factors each considered in the analysis phase, the feedback each is receiving from their output, and the satisfaction each might possibly be achieving.

GLOSSARY

Action or Analysis The system phase in which the input is analyzed, implementation of the plan takes place, and resources are used.

Closed System A totally self-contained system which receives no external input.

Cultural Subsystem A subsystem linking the various spheres of interaction where traditions, customs, heritage, and social behavior are evidenced, and influences of the value system are observed.

Distant Sphere The farthest extension of the individual's interaction beyond the immediate sphere.

Economic Subsystem A subsystem linking the various spheres of interaction where resources are allocated and used to bring about satisfaction.

Family Sphere The sphere of interaction composed of all members of the family unit who reside within the housing unit.

Feedback The evaluative phase of a system which produces new goals, demands, or objectives which become input into the current system or a new system.

Immediate Sphere The sphere of interaction outside the shelter sphere where regular and frequent interaction takes place. This sphere is composed of reference groups, organizations, agencies, employment endeavors, and communities.

Individual Sphere The center of the spheres of interaction where managerial action and the management process are used by the individual to achieve the desired quality of life.

Input Any information, demand, event, resource, fact, value, or factors that are entering the system.

Open System A system in which external input is being received and from which output affects other systems.

Output The outcome, results, or product yielded from the analysis or action of a system.

Political Subsystem A subsystem linking the various spheres of interaction where rules, regulations, policies, and guidelines are established and enforced.

Reference Group The groups which an individual recognizes himself or herself as belonging to or holding membership in on a regular and on-going basis and from which behavioral actions are influenced.

Role An individual's self-determination of a specified manner of behavior. It is the identification of the self-established relationship between the individual and reference groups, and the self-created ranking of the individual within a given social structure.

Shelter Sphere The sphere of interaction composed of the boundaries established by the housing unit.

Spheres of Interaction The levels of interaction between an individual and society which produce a continual input-output flow within and among the levels.

REFERENCES

1. Irma H. Gross, Elizabeth Walbert Crandall, and Marjorie M. Knoll, *Management for Modern Families,* 3rd ed. (New York: Appleton-Century-Crofts, 1973), p. 10.
2. Ruth E. Deacon and Francille M. Firebaugh, *Home Management Context and Concepts* (Boston: Houghton Mifflin Company, 1975). p. 18.

CHAPTER TWO

Values, Goals, and Standards

I n your daily life both external and internal input mold and shape your existence. The strength of this input is determined by the point of origin and by the individual recognition given. Some of this input originates in the outermost spheres of your interaction. Others come from within you. The validity and strength of this input has a bearing on the kind of person you are and will become in the future.

How you interpret this input and the action you take will be determined, to a great extent, by your values, goals, and standards. To demonstrate how the latter have an affect upon your management, we can compare them to the construction of a house. Values are the foundation of the house. From these you derive your goals or the walls of the house. You use values to identify your desired quality of life or the roof of your house. The support walls of the house which hold up the roof and add strength to the walls are your standards.

Each of these is dependent upon the other. When one part of the house is missing, the house cannot stand nor can it withstand the winds of life. The same is true for you. Your values are used to identify your desired quality of life. Your desired quality of life then determines the goals you have set for yourself. As you achieve these goals, you measure your degree of success in terms of your standards. These same standards, used to measure your success, also mirror the relative strength of your values. Without goals, your life has no direction. Without standards, you don't know when you have achieved your goal nor the degree of success you have attained. Lacking values, you cannot set goals. Your perception of your capabilities reflects the knowledge and your awareness of your values, the exactness and your willingness to strive to attain your goals, and the establishment of acceptable and realistic standards. Thus values, goals, and standards have and will continue to be an integral part of your life. Considering their importance to you, you should be aware not only of their existence but also of the role each has played in your development and will play in your future.

Values

What is a value? In order to explore and define the role and scope of values in your life, let's begin by examining statements made by others concerning values. Riebel states the following in relationship to the effect of values upon the individual.

Values furnish the guiding compass for everyone's life, providing the basis for deciding what is more worthwhile and what is less so. They are the "why" guideposts, the "why" we decide to do the things we do. They help us judge our actions. Values are very important to the individuals and are at the root of human motivation; they give meaning to our life.[1]

In *Creative Life,* Moustakas states:

Value refers to worth as an ingredient of being as well as to an ingrained human condition that is infinite and enduring.

A value system refers to beliefs, expectations, and preferences that offer direction and influence choice. But value is an integrating or unifying dimension of the self. It is the quality that renders the person whole in the concrete moments of life.[2]

To quote Raths, Harmin, and Simon:

Persons have experiences, they grow and learn. Out of experiences may come certain general guides to behavior. These guides tend to give direction to life and may be called values. Our values show what we tend to do with our limited time and energy.

Since we see values as growing from a person's experiences, we would expect that different experiences would give rise to different values and that any person's values would be modified as his experiences accumulate and change. . . . Values may not be static if one's relationship to his world are not static. As guides to behavior, values evolve and mature as experiences evolve and mature.[3]

We therefore see values as constantly being related to the experiences that shape and test them. They are not, for any one person, so much hard and fast verities as they are the results of hammering out a style of life in a certain set of surroundings. After a sufficient amount of hammering, certain evaluating and behaving tend to develop. Certain things are treated as right, or desirable, or worthy. These tend to become our values.[4]

A value then is a belief, conviction, or an expectation so strongly held that it has become an integral part of existence. It motivates your behavior, influences your interaction with others, guides your actions, and directs your path throughout your life. Perhaps by identifying some values held in common by a majority of individuals this concept will be clearer. Examples of these would be truth, honesty, and friendship. Throughout your life these values along with many others have been a part of you. Your values determine what you want from life, what is important to you, what you expect from other people, and how and to what extent you participate in the spheres of interaction.

The concept of values is not only a complex but often a nebulous one; no two individuals would define a value in identically the same terms. Although each person can establish loosely drawn boundaries, an exact parameter does not and cannot exist. When you speak of the value of truth do you mean that you always tell the whole truth regardless of the situation or individual involved? How would you define the boundaries of truth?

As an individual you have numerous values that have developed over the years. As you have grown and matured, you have refined and evaluated the values you have until they have become an integral part of you.

How do values develop? Your values began their development as you began to comprehend the meaning of words. Your parents, through their actions and words, demonstrated their values. As a young child you were told to: "tell the truth," "it is wrong to steal," "do not lie or cheat," or "respect other people's property." These and similar statements made by your parents developed into such values as honesty, truthfulness, and respect for others. As you grew older, your interaction with your friends and your school environment provided you with an opportunity to see other people's values. This interaction helped you to identify and determine your individually held values.

The society in which you lived as a child and now as an adult has also played an important part in shaping and molding your values. Some originated from your cultural heritage while others came from the neighborhood and community in which you live. These values have their origin in the immediate and distant spheres of interaction. Some examples of these would be the values of marriage, kinship, and the Puritan work ethic. Just as these experiences and interactions have helped to develop your values, they also helped you in establishing a value structure.

Your interaction and experiences in the spheres of interaction were sources of input upon you. From this input, you weighed and analyzed each value to determine its validity and relative importance. The output was a value structure which is uniquely your own. This value structure means you have rank ordered all of the values you hold in order of their importance to you.

This rank ordering is your value hierarchy. This means some values are more important to you than others. However, this does not mean that once values are placed in a rank order, they will always remain exactly the same. Your value hierarchy is not static.

In Chapter 1 you saw the continual fluid movement of the boundaries of the immediate and distant spheres of interaction. As these boundaries flow outward and inward, you are continually interacting with individuals and events. Your interaction, resource allocation, decision making, communication, and the actions you undertake mirror your values and their hierarchy. Your role perception and the roles you project on others are also reflections of your value structure.

Inherent in the interaction taking place is still another factor affecting your value structure. The input of interaction enables you to examine and further refine your individually held values and their value hierarchy.

Your involvement in college activities and campus life is but one example of this process of value examination and refinement. In your academic career you have interacted with many individuals who have different value hierarchies from yours. Although you may not have been aware of it, this interaction has forced you to examine and redefine some of your values. This process means you also analyze your value hierarchy. You may have discovered that some of your values, which you felt were very important, are not as important now as they once were. Then, too, you may have discovered that although you and your parents hold the same value, your definition of this value is quite different from theirs.

Your value hierarchy will be dependent upon many factors. The input you receive from the spheres of interaction, the experiences you have, and your interaction will necessitate a continual assessment of the hierarchy. Situations that affect you either directly or indirectly will also bring about a reordering of your value structure. The location of a specific value within the total hierarchy will be somewhat dependent upon the given situation and the interaction taking place.

Since you are enrolled in college courses it is obvious that education and intelligence are two of your values. Currently, each has a high priority.

In order to ascertain how an individual value could fluctuate within a value hierarchy, assume that the value of education is one of your top ten values. As a college student, using a point scale of one to ten (with ten being the highest), what number would you assign to the value of education? Would you have assigned the same number to it as a high school freshman? As a sixth-grader? Ten years after your college graduation would you still assign the same number as you did today?

Although those values which are now important to you will remain important in the future, their degree of importance will be dependent upon the current situation, your stage in the life cycle, your occupation, your role perception, input from the spheres of interaction, and your degree of successful attainment of your desired quality of life.

In defining a value, Rath, Harmin, and Simons developed the following criteria.

1. Choosing freely. If something is in fact to guide one's life whether or not authority is watching, it must be a result of free choice. If there is coercion, the result is not likely to stay with one for long, especially when out of the range of the source of that coercion. Values must be freely selected if they are to be really valued by the individual.
2. Choosing among alternatives. This definition of values is concerned with things that are chosen by the individual and, obviously, there can be no choice if there are no alternatives from which to choose. It makes no sense, for example, to say that one values eating. One really has no choice in the matter. What one may value is certain types of food or certain forms of eating, but not eating itself. We must all obtain nourishment to exist; there is no room for decision. Only when a choice is possible, when there is more than one alternative from which to choose, do we say a value can result.
3. Choosing after thoughtful consideration of the consequences of each alternative. Impulsive or thoughtless choices do not lead to values as we define them. For something intelligently and meaningful to guide one's life, it must emerge from a weighing and an understanding. Only when the consequences of each of the alternatives are clearly under-

stood can one make intelligent choices. There is an important cognitive factor here. A value can emerge only with thoughtful consideration of the range of the alternatives and consequences of choice.

4. Prizing and cherishing. When we value something, it has a positive tone. We prize it; esteem it, respect it, hold it dear. We are happy with our values. A choice, even when we have made it freely and thoughtfully, may be a choice we are not happy to make. We may choose to fight in a war, but be sorry circumstances make that choice reasonable. In our definition, values flow from choices that we are glad to make. We prize and cherish the guides to life that we call values.

5. Affirming. When we have chosen something freely, after consideration of the alternatives, and when we are proud of our choices, glad to be associated with it, we are likely to affirm that choice when asked about it. We are willing to publicly affirm our values. We may even be willing to champion them. If we are ashamed of a choice, if we would not make our position known when appropriately asked, we would not be dealing with values but something else.

6. Acting upon choices. When we have a value, it shows up in aspects of our living. We may do some reading about things we value. We are likely to form friendships or to be in organizations in ways that nourish our values. In short, for a value to be present, life itself must be affected. Nothing can be a value that does not, in fact, give direction to actual living. The person who talks about something but never does anything about it is dealing with something other than a value.

7. Repeating. Where something reaches the stage of a value, it is very likely to reappear on a number of occasions in the life of the person who holds it. It shows up in several different situations, at several different times. We would not think of something that appeared once in a life and never again as a value. Values tend to have a persistency, tend to make a pattern in a life.[5]

The question often arises as to what is the difference between values and attitudes. Rath, Harmin, and Simons indicate that unless your value can meet all of these criteria, it is a notion, feeling, or attitude.[6] Indicators of your values can be seen, according to Fitzsimmons and Williams, in

1. The goals and purposes which give your life direction.
2. Aspirations which indicate or point to the possibility of something you value.
3. Your expressions of attitudes toward others.
4. Your interests.
5. Your expressions of feelings.
6. Your beliefs and convictions.
7. Your behavior and activities.
8. Your worries and the things you perceive to be obstacles.[7]

Values play an important role in all aspects of your mangement. They influence the decisions you make, motivate your behavior, direct the goals you set, determine your role perceptions and your interaction with others, and guide your daily life. Those values which have become a part of you over the years will continue throughout your life. Your management will continually be influenced by them. Your input and output within the spheres of interaction will be guided and directed by your values as they exist within a hierarchy.

Value Classification

Individually held values can be classified in a number of different ways. In exploring the various classifications of values, it must be remembered that a single value may well be classified in a number of different ways at any given point in time. Values may be classified by clusters, as intrinsic or extrinsic, or according to human needs. Thus a single value, although it may be a part of a cluster on occasion, may also be either intrinsic or extrinsic. In addition it may be classified as satisfying a specific human need.

Each person is different and unique; no two people have identically the same value hierarchy. Therefore, the determinant factors in classifying a value is dependent upon the individuality of the person, the given situation, and the relationship of one value to another at that point in time.

Why then is it important to learn how values are classified? How you classify a value will be a motivational and/or behavioral factor. If you classify a specific value as being an intrinsic one, your course of action may well be quite different than if you had classified it as being extrinsic. A closer examination of the various classification of values will demonstrate this.

Value Clusters

Due to their similarity, certain values will tend to form groups or clusters. Truth, fairness, and honesty is one example of a value cluster. These values are interrelated. Their interrelationship often means they all tend to be operable at the same time in a given situation. However, this does not mean that they cannot and do not function as separate values in similar or single situations. Nor does this mean that as individually held values they cannot come into conflict with each other.

Think about your own values. Which of your values would you group together in a cluster? When you make decisions you often find several values clustered together which guide and direct your final choice.

Sometimes values are used as clusters. At other times these same values will be treated as separate and distinct from one another. Frequently only part of the cluster is used to direct your thoughts and actions. The ultimate determination as to whether one, part, or all of the cluster will serve as a motivational force will be determined by the input you receive and its interpretation.

Value clusters aid in making choices. You, like everyone else, have value clusters and knowledge of these clusters will enable you to make decisions more effectively. Value clusters evolve depending upon you and your value hierarchy.

Extrinsic and Intrinsic Values

This classification divides values into two categories. Intrinsic values stand alone and represent strong values that are important for themselves. Extrinsic values may also be strong values but they help, aid, or assist an intrinsic value. Intelligence is an intrinsic value. The value of education is the helping or assisting value for the intrinsic value of intelligence.

A value may exist as an intrinsic one, as an extrinsic one, or it may be extrinsic in some instances and intrinsic in others. There are some values that could be generally classified as being either intrinsic or extrinsic. Yet at the same time, there are some values in which the given situation and the demands being placed upon you determine whether they would be classified as extrinsic or intrinsic.

Assume your three high priority values are friendship, truth, and honesty. In most circumstances, the friendship value would be classified as being intrinsic. The values of truth and honesty might, in some instances, be extrinsic. At other times, one would be intrinsic to the other. However, when a situation arises where all three are involved, two might well become intrinsic to the third. Can you think of an experience you have had where your values of truth and honesty were intrinsic to your value of friendship?

Extrinsic values enable you to better utilize your intrinsic values in attaining your desired quality of life. As such they play an important part in your enjoyment of life and the fullfillment you receive from the world around you.

Human Needs Values

Values may also be classified according to their ability to satisfy human needs. The most widely known method of classifying values by human needs was developed in Maslow's hierarchy of needs.

Maslow's hierarchy of needs divide values into five categories or needs. These are (1) physiological, (2) safety, (3) love and belonging, (4) self esteem, and (5) self actualization. These categories encompass the physical, psychological, and emotional needs for human well being. Satisfaction of these needs occurs in a chronological ordering. The physical need for shelter must be satisfied before self-esteem can be attained.[8]

Maslow's hierarchy can be used not only to catagorize values but also to identify more fully the shape of the value as you define and establish boundaries. This definition is mirrored in your desired quality of life. Using the value of shelter, as shown in Figure 2.1, let's examine this concept.

Maslow's hierarchy allows each person to not only identify individually held values but also to examine the extent to which each is a motivating factor. By looking at your values, their slope and definition, you can measure how successful you are in achieving your desired quality of life. Conversely, you measure your success in attaining your desired quality of life by how well you are satisfying your human needs.

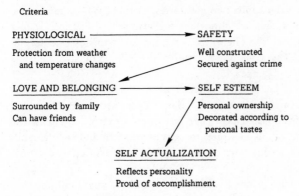

VALUE – SHELTER

Criteria

PHYSIOLOGICAL ————————————→ SAFETY

Protection from weather   Well constructed
  and temperature changes   Secured against crime

LOVE AND BELONGING ————————→ SELF ESTEEM

Surrounded by family   Personal ownership
Can have friends   Decorated according to
                                                 personal tastes

                          SELF ACTUALIZATION

                          Reflects personality
                          Proud of accomplishment

FIGURE 2.1.   *Shelter, Human Needs Value.*

Unfortunately many people are not truly aware of their own value hierarchy nor the extent to which their value structure affects their lives. As you study these different classifications and the concept of values you become more aware of your values. This increasing awareness of your values, your value structure, and scope of valuing enables you to better understand your own actions and the actions of others. As you become more aware of how your values influence and motivate your own actions, decision making, and behavior you can better understand the actions of other people. Throughout your life you will continue to evaluate and refine your own values. This process of examination and refining is enhanced by a knowledge of individually held values and the role they play in your life. Knowledge of your values will also help you when value conflicts arise.

Value Conflict

Throughout your life you have and will continue to experience value conflicts. Some of these conflicts will be minor ones that you may well resolve without a great deal of thought or concern. Others may be major ones in which the process of resolution is stressful, frustrating, or even quite painful. How you view and resolve these value conflicts has an effect upon your perception of yourself. Successful resolution enhances your self-image and your feelings of self-worth. Uncertain or inadequate success may yield self-doubts concerning your ability to really manage your life.

A value conflict occurs when two or more values come into opposition with each other. An example of a value conflict you may well have experienced might occur during a test when a friend asks you to give him or her a correct answer to a test question. Your value of friendship would be in opposition to your value of honesty.

Although your values of honesty and friendship are in conflict with each other, there are a number of different factors which might well affect your decision. For instance, how close a friend is the person who asked you to cheat? Has this person asked you to do this before? Is the test a minor quiz, a major test, or a final examination? How good a friend has this person been in the past? Do you really want to retain this friendship? How strong is your fear of being caught? What will be the consequences? As these questions arose in your mind, you were seeking to resolve your value conflict.

In resolving the conflict, you were basically weighing your value of honesty against your value of friendship. You took action on the basis of the decision you made. The feedback resulting from the consequences of your decision and the action taken provided input, first, for your own self-image and your feeling of worthiness and, second, for future situations.

In order for value conflicts to exist certain things must occur. First, you must recognize that the conflict does exist and second, you must attach a degree of importance to the conflict. The degree of importance will help you to decide how necessary it is to resolve the conflict. Finally, you must determine whether you want to resolve the conflict at all.

A value conflict does not really exist until you recognize it as a reality. You have many values. Assume that two of your values are honesty and friendship. Suppose your best friend asks for your honest opinion concerning a specific situation. You respond giving your honest reaction, unknowing that your response reflects back upon your friend. In this instance, your values are not in conflict. However, if you know your response will endanger your friendship, this awareness results in a value conflict. The value conflict did not exist until you recognized these values were in opposition to each other.

Undoubtedly you have experienced several value conflicts over a period of time. If all your value conflicts were placed on a continuum, some might occur at the lower end, these are minor ones. Some might be in the middle; the others, major ones, would be at the opposite end. As you placed each one on the continuum, you assigned each a specific degree of importance.

Combined with the recognition that a value conflict exists is the necessity to resolve the conflict in an acceptable manner. How and in what manner this is achieved will be dependent upon three factors. (1) How you view the conflict, (2) the degree of importance you attach to the conflict, and (3) the demand upon you to resolve the conflict.

These factors are both interrelated and yet separate. Although you may be aware a value conflict exists, your perception of the conflict is a vital factor in determining your need for resolution. If you view the conflict as a minor one, your desire for resolution is also minor. Also important is your perception of the relative strength of each of the opposing values. If one value is stronger than the other, the conflict is considered to be a minor one. If, on the other hand, the two opposing values have equal strength the conflict is very likely to be viewed as a major one.

The degree of importance or emphasis is another factor governing your desire for resolution. Just as you have determined your perception of the conflict, so have you attached a degree of importance to the resolution. As you attach a degree of importance, you are recognizing your value hierarchy and the individual values within it, indicating the relative importance of the conflict, and analyzing whether the conflict is a major or minor one. You are identifying the strength of each opposing value, determining how soon the conflict needs to be resolved, and indicating the amount of stress or frustration brought about by the conflict.

The easiest value conflicts to resolve are those viewed as being minor ones. These might occur when one value is stronger than the other, where little or no stress exists, or in the absence of a strong need to resolve the conflict. When this occurs, the conflict is resolved and your life goes on with little or no apparent disruption.

However, this does not always happen. Some value conflicts involve stress, opposing values of equal strength, and a strong need for resolution. How did you view the value conflicts that occurred the first time you went to a party where alcoholic beverages were served but you were too young to legally drink? For some people this was a value conflict, for others it was not. Do you have "open visitation" or co-ed dorms? Did either of these present value conflicts for you? What degree of importance did you attach to these value conflicts? How much stress did you experience? How soon did you have to make a choice concerning your own life style?

As you assigned a relative degree of importance to resolving the conflict, you also determined how important it was for you to resolve the conflict. In the dormitory you have seen other students who have had to resolve value conflicts that affect their life styles. You may recognize that should you face a similar situation a value conflict would exist. However, until you are actually experiencing the conflict, there is no necessity to resolve the conflict.

The third factor is the demand placed upon you for resolution. Although interrelated to the other two, it is still operable as a separate factor. The demand for resolution may be an internal one, or it may be an external demand from one of your spheres of interaction. The demand may also occur within a time frame.

One or all of these factors may exist. Each one may create stress and/or frustration. You may need to resolve the conflict to alleviate the internal stress you are experiencing. This would be particularly true if the opposing values are of equal strength. In other words, resolution is necessary for your own "peace of mind." The demand for resolution may originate from one or more of your spheres of interaction. A friend might be exerting pressure upon you to "make up your mind."

The conflict may need to be resolved in terms of a time deadline. This time deadline may be one you imposed upon yourself or one imposed from your spheres of interaction. When the demand for resolution is accompanied by a time deadline, additional stress is created.

Each of these are separate factors governing your need to resolve the conflict, yet they are also interrelated. Your perception of the value conflict is directly related to how important you feel the conflict really is and the demand for resolution. Each of these, however, occurs only after you recognize the existence of a value conflict. In looking at value conflicts, it is important to realize that everyone, young or old, experiences them.

Evidences of Values

Your facial features, the color of your hair, and your speech patterns set you apart from other individuals. The same can also be said for both your values and your value conflicts. Values make you uniquely you. Because they exist your interaction within the spheres of interaction follow an established pattern. To emphasize again, the evidences of your values can be seen in the goals and standards you set for yourself, in your desired quality of life, and in your worries and problems.

Value conflicts, although often stressful experiences, also serve a useful purpose. When a value conflict occurs, you are eventually forced to make a choice. As you make that choice, you are evaluating and redefining each of the opposing values. As this process occurs you are continuing to refine individual values and your value hierarchy. If you had absolutely no values your life would have no direction. You would simply exist. An individual without values would be living in a void and would have no purpose for existence.

Fortunately this does not happen. Every individual has some values. The question is not whether or not you have values but rather how well each of your values is defined and how aware you are of their existence. You need to be aware not only that your values do exist but also of their strengths and their location within a hierarchy.

Goals

What do you plan to get done by the end of next week? What do you plan to accomplish before you go to sleep tonight? What do you anticipate you will be doing ten years from today? As you answer these questions you are indirectly stating your goals.

Goals, like values, play an important role in your life. Values give meaning to your life. Goals, on the other hand, point the direction you want your path to follow. Thus values and goals are interrelated. Values are the vehicles, and goals are the highways you use to attain your desired quality of life.

But what is a goal? Where does it originate? Does everyone have goals? Goals are what you are striving to attain or achieve. Right now your goals are to successfully complete your courses, to graduate from college, and to obtain a job in your chosen profession. As you achieve each of these goals, new ones will emerge which will lead you down still other highways.

You might well define a goal as an objective, condition, or something you desire to attain or achieve at any given point. In determining your goals, you have chosen a path or direction you intend to follow.

These goals have originated from your value system. Thus your values are the vehicles which determine your goals. Because you value intelligence and education one of your goals is to graduate from college. As you achieve this goal, your values of intelligence and education will serve as vehicles to determine other goals.

Everyone has goals. We may not be fully aware of these goals nor are they always clearly defined or thought out, but they do exist.

Classification of Goals

To identify your own goals, start by listing your goals for the coming month. Then list the goals you intend to achieve by the close of the academic year. Now list the goals you are planning to achieve in the next five years. Look back over your list. Did you find as you wrote down your goals for one period of time, others for the same or different periods of time came to mind? Prior to this, did you realize how many goals you had? Beside each of your goals identify your value(s).

Unfortunately a great many people don't take the time to specifically identify their individual goals. Have you ever taken the time to list your goals? The goals you have listed for yourself can be divided into the categories of short range, intermediate, and long range. Each of these categories have distinct characteristics and serve a useful purpose in your life pathway. Let us examine them.

Short-range Goals

The characteristics of short-range goals make them uniquely different from the other two. A short-range goal represents an objective, condition, or something you intend to achieve in the immediate future. An example of one of your short-range goals would be to successfully complete this course.

Since the achievement is anticipated in the near or immediate future, short-range goals usually involve a time period of six months or less. In all probability you have some goals that would involve a single day, a week's duration, or a semester. How often have you thought or said: "I'm going to get such and such done today" or "I have to have my term project completed by ——"? In reality, these are short-range goals.

Short-range goals tend to be more clearly defined and identified than either of the remaining categories. Being clearly defined, they tend to evolve around a single objective, condition, or item.

Since these goals are, for the most part, well defined, you have established a process or procedure that will enable you to achieve them. For instance, in order to achieve your goal of completing this course, you will have to undertake certain action. In all probability, this means you will read the textbook, study and pass examinations, and complete any other class assignments. These represent the procedure you have established to achieve the goal of completing the course.

The purpose of short-range goals is to help you plan your immediate future. They serve as highways for short periods of time. Short-range goals often serve as the beginning or initiating point to achieve an intermediate and long-range goal. Figure 2.2 illustrates this: your long-range goal is to enter your chosen profession. In order to do so, you must achieve your intermediate goal of a college graduation. Thus your short-range goal of completing this course represents the beginning of the achievement of an intermediate and ultimately a long-range goal.

A third function of short-range goals is to help you to evaluate and assess your intermediate and long-range goals. It may well be as you are achieving your short-range goal you discover some of your intermediate goals need modification. The direction taken by these goals may need to be changed. Others may no longer be as important as they once were.

Short-range goals perform still another function. They may assist you in identifying other goals. These newly emerging goals may or may not have been a part of your initial plan.

When you enrolled in college you had a specific profession in mind. As you have completed courses, this choice may have changed or modified to incorporate a different career direction than you originally intended. Although you may have planned to be a teacher of a specific subject, as you took classes, you may have found you want to teach that subject to a specific target popula-

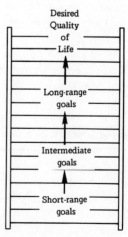

FIGURE 2.2. Progression of Goal Attainment.

tion such as special education students. This new goal has emerged from your achievement of a short-range goal.

These same goals also help you to more clearly define your intermediate and long-range goals through the process of achievement. Short-range goals, in addition to having specific characteristics, also serve many functions in your life plan. These goals are an important part of your management. They originate from your values and serve as a directional pathway for your immediate future.

Intermediate Goals

In general, intermediate goals might well be thought of as the link connecting your short-range and long-range goals. They, too, have definite characteristics and serve a purpose in your lifetime management.

The time frame involved in intermediate goals is longer. Achievement of these goals is often measured in terms of several months or even years. How soon will you achieve your intermediate goal of graduation?

Although they are identified and clarified to some extent, there remains a certain degree of vagueness. Are you aware of all the particular courses by title that you will need to complete for graduation? Do you know specifically when you will enroll in each course? Although you may well know the number of hours and possibly the specific courses required for graduation, in most cases, you are not fully aware of which ones will be taken each year nor the specific semester for each one. You usually do not make out a class schedule for the entire four years. The same holds true for intermediate goals. Although they may be identified and have some depth of definition, they are not as completely and clearly defined as your short-range goals.

Intermediate goals often tend to form clusters directed toward an overall objective, condition, and so forth. Your graduation is an example of this clustering effect. Although it may appear to be a single goal, clustered around this are other goals such as completing required courses, having recommendations that will help you to secure the job you want, and many others. These goals and their clusters also mirror your value hierarchy.

Although not as completely outlined as short-range goals, you have established a general process that will lead to attainment. How actively you pursue this general procedure will be dependent upon a number of factors.

The first factor is the importance of the goal. When a high ranking goal is being sought you will expend more of your resources and deliberately implement procedures which will enable you to attain that goal. You will also more actively pursue the steps which will lead toward attainment of your high priority goal than for one of lesser importance.

Another factor is the immediacy of goal attainment. Although you may have several goals which are classified as intermediate, those which are closer to attainment will have a more clearly defined procedure. The close proximity means you will implement and more actively pursue this goal than one which has a more distant completion date.

The requirements of goal attainment will also affect the amount of time spent in pursuing the goal. The attainment of some intermediate goals necessitates regular and frequent activity in order to achieve them. This may not be true with others. Your graduation goal means you must actively pursue this goal on a regular basis. However, your goal of having good recommendations for your placement papers does not require the same degree of action involvement.

When the achievement of one intermediate goal is dependent upon another, you will actively pursue this goal in order to achieve the next. This is particularly true in two different situations. The first instance is when the more distant goal has a higher priority. The more immediate goal is viewed as a means to achieve a more distant and desirable goal. This more distant and desirable goal would bring about a high degree of satisfaction and increase your feelings of self-worth. Thus the first goal is actively sought not for itself alone but as a means to ultimate achievement of the distant and more desirable goal.

The second involves the clustering effect of intermediate goals. Achievement of the entire cluster may be deemed necessary. In this instance, a "stair step" effect may be observable. You rank order all the goals within the cluster. Achievement of one or more goals leads to the next one until all goals comprising the clusters are attained. In both instances, implementation of the procedure is done in order to attain the anticipated satisfaction. This satisfaction will only be realized when completion of the entire cluster is achieved rather than a single or major goal.

Still another factor in goal attainment is the degree of interest you have in achievement. There are times when your goal may have been established partly by you and partly by others. Although it is one of your goals, it may not be as important to you as it is to someone else. When this occurs, you work at the goal but your major interest may lie in other directions and goals. If on the other hand, you have a deep interest in achieving this goal, you may place other goals in a lower rank. Although this does involve priority ranking, a difference does exist. Your concern, interest, and involvement acts as an additional motivational force to encourage the achievement of the goal. The satisfaction you anticipate by completion of the goal is an additional motivating factor.

Input from the spheres of interaction may also influence the degree to which you actively pursue a goal. This input might occur as encouragement or discouragement from one or more spheres. Undoubtedly your parents have and will continue to encourage you to complete your college studies. This input acts as a motivational device for you. However, if you receive adverse input from one or more of the spheres of interaction, this input may act as a motivational device to "show them you can do it." Or it could lead to self-doubt which would in turn, impede rather than encourage further pursuit of the goal.

Each of these factors will play a part in your pursuit of your intermediate goals. Although they are separate factors, as you look over your intermediate goals, one is related to the other. Intermediate goals serve many functions. They give direction to the future. Since they originate from your values, they indicate what you feel is your role in society and your future direction. As in the case of short-range goals, intermediate goals may assist you in attaining long-range goals. As you saw in Figure 2.2, attainment means you are a step closer to achieving one or more of your long-range goals.

Intermediate goals also involve the analysis and evaluation of other intermediate goals and long-range goals. Because they tend to form clusters, intermediate goals act as a check and balance system upon each other. In achieving part of the cluster, you may pause to analyze the validity of other goals within the cluster. At the same time you evaluate your long-range goals. As you achieve some of your intermediate goals you may identify and formulate other goals. These may be future, intermediate, or long-range goals you have not identified prior to this time.

The attainment of intermediate goals may also assist you in more clearly identifying the specific components of some of your long-range goals. This is still another function of intermediate goals.

Long-range Goals

Classification of long-range goals differs from the other two in regard to the time period involved, the degree of specificity, and the extent of active implementation involved in attainment. Long-range goals are those you have set for yourself in the distant future. This time span is often thought of in terms of years rather than months.

Long-range goals are not always clearly defined. Since achievement is not anticipated at any time in the immediate future, there remains a certain aspect of vagueness about these goals. Your long-range goals may well include one or more of the following: getting a good job in your chosen profession, getting married, raising a family, or owning your own home. At the present time, how clearly are these goals defined? Do you know who will be your employer? Where you will live the majority of your lifetime? How many children you intend to raise? What kind of house you intend to buy in the future? Although these are your general long-range goals, a vagueness remains. These goals cannot be as clearly defined as your intermediate goals nor as completely as your short-range goals.

The implementation of procedures to achieve these long-range goals will be dependent upon a number of factors. It could be you cannot achieve your long-range goals until you have first achieved your intermediate and short-range goals. In this instance, you are not pursuing your long-range goals indirectly but directly. Since these goals are not clearly defined, you probably cannot establish an exact procedure which will lead to attainment. Thus the indefiniteness of the goal is still another factor. The degree of specificity of the goal will determine how actively and effectively the achievement of the goal can be done.

In other cases, the progress toward achievement will be measured by events and time. It may be that progress is accomplished in a sporadic manner. Situations and events may govern the extent of active pursuit toward attainment. Some of your long-range goals require a slow steady pacing of action; evidence of this progress will at times be barely discernable. Progress at other times may be a sporadic burst of action. In these instances you might actively pursue your long-range goals for infrequent intervals. During these times, a great deal of thought and action is directed toward goal attainment. At other times, attainment activities are almost dormant. Examples of both of these might well be seen in your pursuit of a good job in your chosen profession. Your slow steady pacing of activities to achieve this goal can be seen in your academic studies. The sporadic bursts of action could be seen in different instances. You might well seek employment in occupations leading to this profession during summer vacation periods. You might also periodically examine the growth potential of prospective employers as you undertake academic studies. Periodically you examine and further refine your resumé and professional portfolio while you are still engaged in your academic studies.

Long-range goals serve many functions. Since they represent the things, situation, or conditions you are striving to attain, they reflect your desired quality of life. These goals give meaning to your short-range and intermediate goals. As you strive to attain long-range goals the short-range and intermediate goals are often a part of the striving. Although short-range and intermediate goals may be important for themselves, they take on an additional importance when they are lead to the attainment of a long-range goal.

In essence, your long-range goals reflect the direction you intend your life to take in the future. Thus they mirror your values and your future image as well as your desired quality of life.

Evidence of Goals

You have many goals. Each of these goals, regardless of their classification, originated from your values, self-concept, and input from the spheres of interaction. If you were to classify each of these goals today, they would not appear in the same classification two, five, or ten years from now. As you attain some of your short-range goals, an intermediate goal change replaces it. When an intermediate goal becomes a short-range one, it is replaced by a long-range goal. This long-range goal is then replaced by a newly emerging goal. Thus as you attain goals, others emerge to replace them. Through this process, you are continually striving to move your life forward.

There are many other evidences of goals in your life. Although you may not have been aware of them prior to this time, your actions and verbalization often indicated your goals. When you indicated your college major, in a sense you were verbalizing your goals for the future. Talking about your future plans is still another evidence of your goals.

Goals are also evident in your daily routine and the decisions you make. Why are you enrolled in certain college courses? Why do you study for tests, read textbooks, or go to classes? Why are you in college rather than working full time? The answer to each of these questions lie in the goals you have set for yourself.

In order for you to have a goal it must be realistic. You may have a number of dreams about what your life could become. For instance, someday you are going to write the greatest American novel, or you are going to develop a medical cure for the common cold or a rare disease, or you are going to be the greatest actor or actress in the world, or whatever your own personal dream might be. Unless these are real goals and something you are actively seeking, they are merely dreams and will remain so. Although you may state your dreams as being just that, they may represent long-range goals which you may either not be willing to tell others or are long-range goals you have not consciously recognized.

Your behavior, the decisions you make, and the actions you take are evidences of your values. They are also evidences of your goals.

Goals represent the life plan you have developed for yourself. As you attain these goals, they reflect and enhance your self-image. A person who is achieving their desired goals conveys this to those around him or her. These individuals exude a sense of self-worth. Think about yourself and your feelings of self-worth as you have attained some of your goals. Didn't you feel confident about your abilities? As you continue to attain other goals, this image of self-confidence and your ability to partake in your spheres of interaction increases.

Goals and values are interrelated. Values are the primary source of your goals. At the same time, goal setting helps you to refine and more clearly identify your values.

Setting goals is not something that just happens. It is an art which must be learned. You are continually receiving input from your spheres of interaction. This input can be a valid source to aid you to set goals. As you determine your goals you must weigh the input you are receiving in terms of your value hierarchy.

Goals, if they are to be attained, must originate from you. They must be realistic. They must be based on your values. A goal which does not meet any of these criteria is not really your goal. Instead it is a goal that has been set for you.

You probably know students who are seeking to enter professions selected by their parents. These individuals may or may not want to actually enter this profession. They may be pursuing their own goal or a goal set by their parents. If it is the latter, how happy and satisfied are they with the choice? Do you think they will find happiness and fulfillment in their professions in the future?

Goals reflect your life plan for yourself. For this reason they must be realistically developed on a sound basis: your value system. Unless based on your value system, your goals provide little direction to your life. If they are actually attained, they will produce a limited degree of satisfaction.

Short-range, intermediate, and long-range goals serve as highways for your life pattern. When they are realistically identified, built upon a firm foundation, and actively sought, they give meaning and direction to your life. They help you to achieve your desired quality of life. As you achieve these goals, they enhance your self-image, feelings of self-worth, and bring about satisfaction.

Standards

If values are the vehicles and goals are the highways of your life plan, then standards are the sign posts along the highways. As you set your goals, you establish "clues" that will indicate your progress. These "clues" are your standards. As you measure your progress by standards, you are doing two other things. You are analyzing your values as they exist within a hierarchy. You are also examining your goals and their priority.

Standards are the criteria you set for your actions or operations. They indicate the degree of accomplishment you find acceptable. Just as your values and goals are uniquely your own, so are your standards.

Some of your standards have originated from the society in which you live. Many of these standards have been handed down from one generation to another over the years. As such, they have become a part of your cultural heritage. Several traditions observed in society are actually standards which have been established in this manner. One example is wearing wedding rings on the third finger of the left hand. You can probably think of many other examples.

Some standards seldom change; however, many others are changing as society continues to evolve. The standards of acceptable dress for males and females is changing. So, too, are the changing roles of males and females within the family structure, as well as the emerging role of women, in general. You can probably think of other standards within society that are in the process of change.

Your standards also developed from the input you received through the spheres of interaction. As your knowledge increases, it is reflected in your standards. The increasing boundaries of your spheres of interaction provide additional input which impacts upon your standards. The feedback you receive from the standards you have taken also becomes input upon your standards. This feedback enables you to analyze the validity of your standards.

Thus your standards are derived from your value hierarchy, input from your spheres of interaction, your cultural heritage, your goals, aspirations, and your role perception. Your standards are a self-analysis criteria. As you define your role perception, you set certain standards for yourself. The degree of success you feel you are attaining and your perception of other's success is expressed in terms of standards. For example, you have probably indicated to yourself and others which faculty members are good instructors. In so doing, you were indicating your standards for a good instructor based upon your perception of the role of a good teacher.

Standards are important. Through these you have identified what is acceptable and what is not acceptable for yourself. You use standards to measure your degree of success in achieving your goals, your daily living patterns, and your role perceptions.

Classification of Standards

Standards, like values and goals, can be classified. There are many different ways of classifying standards. Classification involving household operations are proposed by Deacon and Firebaugh.[9] Walker's classification involves housekeeping standards.[10]

Although both of these apply directly to home management, some of the other courses you have taken within the educational system have produced other classifications such as the standards for food products, work production standards, product marketing standards, and so forth. Although these apply to specific activities or items, they are nonetheless classifications of standards.

Just as there are many ways of classifying standards within other fields of study, so, too, are various methods being used within the field of home management. Gross, Crandall, and Knoll's classification applies most directly to you and your individual management. These are qualitative vs. quantitative and conventional vs. nonconventional.[11] As you will see most standards could be generally identified under these two broad catagories.

Quantitative vs. Qualitative Standards

Quantitative standards might also be called objective standards.[12] These standards have an element or capability of measurement. Standards that are set in order to achieve a passing test score, or the requirements for graduation are quantitative standards. These are probably the easiest standards to identify and apply since they are readily observable. They can be measured and a method of successful attainment can readily be determined. The risk factor is known.

Qualitative standards are just the opposite: They are subjective standards.[13] As such no specific measure can readily be identified. Each individual may, therefore, have a different criteria established to indicate the degree of successful attainment. Qualitative standards are often the adjectives you use to describe tangibles and intangibles. When you describe someone as a "good" friend, you are expressing your qualitative standards. These are subjective standards that have emerged from your value system, input from your spheres of interaction, past experience, and the feedback you have received through your own management actions.

Qualitative standards may not be as clearly defined and identified; nor are they as readily observable as quantitative ones. Since they are subjectively developed by you, they may or may not be comparable to those of others.

Although there may be certain aspects of these standards that are common to other individuals, the actual refinement and definition is uniquely yours alone. You may have more control over the qualitative standards than you have over your quantitative ones.

You have and use both quantitative and qualitative standards. They serve many functions in your life. Each is used to measure your progress in goal attainment. They also serve as reflectors of your value hierarchy. Each can be used as evaluative devices for value refinement and goal setting. At the same time, they assist in determining your self-image and feelings of self-worth. These same standards are also the criteria you used to identify your desired quality of life. You use them as an evaluative measure of the input being received from your spheres of interaction.

Conventional vs. Nonconventional Standards

The concept of conventional or nonconventional standards refers to what is generally recognized as socially acceptable by the society in which you live.[14] These standards may involve social behavior, mode of dress, social customs and mores, life style patterns, and many other aspects of daily living. Although most do not appear in written form, these standards represent the rules and regulations that influence much of your life.

For the most part, you adhere to these conventional standards as a way of life. For instance, you take notes in class, do not talk when the instructor is lecturing, dress in the same manner as other students, and live your life in much the same manner as do other college students throughout the nation.

Many of your conventional standards have their origin in customs and traditions.[15] They also originate from input received from your spheres of interaction. Other students had an input upon your standards as a college student. At the same time your parents, too, have had an input. All of this input has helped you to establish your standards of a college student.

How do you feel and react when you meet someone whose life style and actions are different from the conventional, socially acceptable standards? Could you adopt this behavior and life style for yourself?

Nonconventional standards are the opposite of conventional standards. Whenever an individual elects to adopt nonconventional standards, he or she must recognize and accept the accompanying potential risk factor. The risk involved will be dependent upon the degree to which the standard(s) deviate from conventional standards. An individual who elects to adopt a different mode of dress may be considered an eccentric. In this instance, the risk factor may not be great. However, an individual who elects to adopt a life style that greatly differs from the conventional one may find the risk factor is greatly increased. The extent to which the standard is nonconventional will determine not only the degree of risk involved but also the extent and form in which society in general reacts.

Conventional standards are derived from your society or culture. These standards serve as a common link or foundation upon which society is built and functions. The conventional standards of our country serve as the basis for much of our governmental structure, daily life patterns, and interaction among individuals. You use these as a basis upon which to analyze and adopt your own. Thus they serve not only as a link between people but also as a starting point for the development of individual standards.

Standards also serve as a point of reference against which you can measure and analyze yours. Where are the commonalities and differences between your standards and the conventional ones? Many times the degree of difference between the two will identify the risk factors involved. As you do this, you are identifying your potential risk factor. As the extent of the risk factor becomes known, you can make a valid decision concerning the reliability of the standard and the anticipated reactions which may occur should you elect not to observe a conventional standard.

As society evolves, conventional standards serve as a point of reference to indicate changes are taking place. For example, one conventional standard that is changing concerns the role of females within society. Over the years, these standards have undergone a dramatic change as more and more women enter and remain in the labor force. There are many other instances of standards being changed or modified as social evolution takes place.

Nonconventional standards also serve a useful purpose in your life. As you interact within the various levels of the spheres of interaction you encounter individuals having nonconventional standards. This interaction enables you to examine and analyze both their standards and yours. During this process you may reinforce or modify your standards.

In some instances, current nonconventional standards serve as indicators of the direction in which society is moving. Our nation's history illustrates this. The right of women to vote, the freeing of the slaves, and the Equal Rights Movement are only three instances of where a change of standards was sought to bring about more conventional standards for all.

Sandards are a part of your life and your management. You have some standards which are rigid and inflexible. You are not willing to modify these, nor will you fail to observe them. On the other hand, you have some standards which are somewhat flexible. These are the ones you are willing to forgo or to modify from time to time.

You have certain standards for your personal appearance, your grade point average, the things you do for fun, the amount of time you spend studying, and many others. In thinking about these standards, which ones are rigid and inflexible? Which ones are flexible? Why are some rigid and others flexible?

Of those that are rigid and inflexible, how many directly relate to your high priority values? Aren't the flexible ones closely associated with lower ranking values? How many of your rigid standards are related to your goals? Aren't these same standards also directly related to your desired quality of life?

Standards like values and goals are a part of your daily life. Standards serve as a measure of your values and at the same time provide "clues" to your progress in goal attainment.

Interlinking of Values, Goals, and Standards

Although the concepts of values, goals, and standards have thus far been discussed individually, they are closely interlinked. Your values are the foundation of your management. As such they are a source of input upon the goals you set and the standards you established. Without values you would have no goals. Therefore, you would have no need to establish standards.

Values produce goals. However, unless you establish standards, you have no way of assessing your progress toward goal attainment nor will you know specifically when you have achieved the goal. Standards are used not only to measure progress and attainment, but also to indicate how successful you are in achieving the goal.

Everyone has standards that are a set of criteria by which you judge your success in your various endeavors. Standards are also used to determine the satisfaction you achieve.

Each of these separately and collectively are sources of input upon decision making and the management process. As you make decisions in order to maximize resource utilization, values, goals, and standards become valuable input sources. These same concepts are a vital part of the management process.

Because they are so closely linked it is difficult to separate one from the other. Assume for a moment you are trying to determine which of two cars you will purchase. Each has several options and attributes you want but neither has both. As you make the final choice, can you totally separate individual values, goals, and standards in this decision? The same is true for other decisions made during use of the management process.

Values, goals, and standards because of their close interrelationship also tend to act as a check and balance system upon each other. In setting your goals you are indirectly examining, reinforcing, and/or strengthening your values. At the same time you are assessing the validity of the standards you have established.

The combination of these three also enables you to assess the probability and the extent of any risk factors in your actions. Upon assessing the risk factor, values, goals, and standards in combination will assist you in determining whether you desire to undertake or maintain the action.

Values, goals, and standards are separate concepts. Yet they are so closely linked that one cannot exist without the other. Each in its own way has been a source of input upon you. Separately and collectively their input has enabled you to become a unique person. Throughout your life their input will motivate, guide, and direct your management.

Summary

Every individual has values, goals, and standards. Each of these is interrelated. Although separate and distinct concepts, they are interlinked. You use your values to establish the meaning and purpose for your life. From these you determine your desired quality of life. Using your values you identify the goals that will enable you to achieve your desired quality of life. As you set goals and seek them, your standards act as indicators of your progress toward attainment.

Your values help you to establish your goals and standards. As you pursue your goals, your values aid in examining the validity of the goals. During this process, your standards enable you to identify your progress and assess your future goals. As this occurs, your goals and standards aid in the process of refining your values. Values and goals work together to help you establish your standards. They help you to determine which standards are rigid and inflexible and which ones are not.

Although values are the vehicle you use to give your life meaning, you must have goals to give direction to your life. These goals are the life pathways you travel. Both of these, however, are to no avail if you do not have standards against which you measure your progress.

No two individuals have the same values, goals, and standards. Thus the input being received from the various spheres of interaction and each individual's output into these spheres is uniquely his or hers. The process of input-output between you and your spheres of interaction is derived from your own values, goals, and standards. These same values, goals, and standards affect not only the role and scope each is to play in your life but also the management process you employ and the decisions you make now and in the future.

ACTIVITIES

1. What are your five highest values? Describe how these values are shown in your interaction within your family sphere. Using two of these values, trace their development within your family unit by showing how each is a part of the value hierarchy of one or both of your parents.
2. Select one of your values and trace its development from your early childhood until today. Describe how you have modified and refined this value from its point of origin to the present time.
3. Select one person you know very well and identify his or her values and their rank order. Cite experiences or situations you have observed which indicate these are the values held by the individual.
4. Apply the seven criteria listed for a value given in Chapter 2 to ascertain which of the following are your personal values.

      Friendship   Truthfulness
      Knowledge   Beauty
      Personal Appearance   Religion

5. Describe how your values have influenced the following:
   a. A recent decision.
   b. A goal.
   c. A Standard.
6. Identify one of your value clusters. List all the values which are found in the cluster and the dominate value. In a value cluster there are intrinsic and extrinsic values. Identify which values are intrinsic and which are extrinsic.
7. You have experienced value conflicts. Describe one in which one of the opposing values was strong and the other was not. How did you resolve the conflict? Describe another value conflict in which both values were of equal strength. How did you resolve this conflict?
8. List five short-range, intermediate, and long-range goals. Indicate the values which influenced the establishment of each, the inputs received, and the standards which will indicate when each goal is attained.
9. Identify the standards you have set for each of the following:
   a. Your personal appearance.
   b. Your academic career.
   c. Your role as a college student.
   d. A close friend.
10. In question 9, you have listed a number of standards. For each standard, identify which of the following are present.
    a. Quantitive.
    b. Qualitative.
    c. Inflexible
    d. Flexible.
    e. Conventional.
    f. Nonconventional.

LARRY AND ROGER

Larry and Roger are roommates in the dormitory. They are planning to move off campus for their junior and senior years. Larry wants to find a small house between the university and where he works in the evening so he will be able to walk to both since he does not have a car. Larry is one of four children from a rural community. As the oldest he has helped quite a bit around the house with most of the household chores as well as the cooking. Although he knows a house will require more work and probably cost more, he thinks with two other men they will be able to manage. One reason Larry wants to move off campus is to get away from the "closed in" feeling he has in the dorm. He also thinks that by doing their own cooking, he will be able to save money. He is looking forward to the freedom of being able to sit outside and study without having to use the elevator or being disturbed by people walking by or playing baseball.

Roger is from a suburban community where his father runs his own highly successful business. He is the youngest child with two older sisters. His mother felt housework was not to be done by the "men of the house." Roger had enough trouble learning to do his laundry and doesn't do it now unless he can't talk one of his many "girl friends" into doing it for him. Although he is not a "slob" he doesn't really do much to keep their room clean with the exception of picking up his clothes, when everything becomes cluttered with his belongings or when Larry really yells at him. Roger wants to rent an apartment close to the university so he can be "near the action." Larry's lack of transportation won't be a problem since he can always use Roger's car. Then too, Roger doesn't want other roommates feeling "they will just get in the way." Although he is more knowledgeable about taking care of his clothes now and can cook to some extent (as long as its hamburgers or hot dogs), he doesn't want the bother of the extra work that would have to be done if they rented a house. Roger is a rather outgoing person who has an active social life. He is looking forward to the parties he plans to have as soon as they get their stuff moved in and unpacked.

Discussion Questions

1. Identify Larry and Roger's values. Where are there similarities and differences? What has created these? Identify the differences between their spheres of interaction.
2. Compare Larry's standards with Roger's. Why are these different? What would you anticipate would be Larry's standards for their off campus housing? Would there be a difference between his and Roger's? Why or why not?

3. If you were asked to identify Roger's future goals, what would they be? What evidence is given to indicate these are his goals?

4. Assuming you are going to help these two men find a place to live off campus, what do you think you would show them and why?

5. On the basis of the information given, describe the life style of Larry, including his values, goals, and standards. What evidences do you have to support your conclusions?

GLOSSARY

Conventional Standard Standards that are generally recognized as socially acceptable by the society and culture.

Extrinsic value An assisting value that must be combined with an intrinsic value.

Flexible Standard A standard that the individual is willing to modify or adjust in relationship to the specific situation, event, or demand.

Goal An objective, condition, or something desired or sought by an individual; its attainment is anticipated to yield satisfaction.

Goal Cluster A grouping of goals directed toward similar objectives, conditions, or desires sought by the individual which is anticipated to bring about satisfaction when attained.

Human Needs Value A classification of values based upon the psychological and emotional needs of the individual.

Inflexible Standard A rigidly held standard from which the individual does not or will not allow a deviation or modification to occur.

Intermediate Goal An objective, condition, or something sought by the individual that is anticipated to be obtained or secured in the future.

Intrinsic value An independently strong value having importance for its own sake and which may or may not require the assistance of an extrinsic value.

Long-range Goal An objective, condition, or something desired or sought by the individual that is anticipated to be obtained or secured in the distant future.

Nonconventional Standard A standard that deviates from the socially accepted standard, the observance of which yields a potential risk factor.

Qualitative Standard A subjective standard that has no objective evaluative measure.

Quality of Life The tangible and intangible component parts of a life style, mode of living, and personal satisfaction that the individual deems to be necessary to achieve self-fulfillment.

Quantitive Standard A standard having an objective, readily identifiable numerical or quantity evaluative measure.

Risk The probability or chance of loss.

Short-range Goal An objective, condition, or something desired or sought by the individual that is anticipated to be obtained or secured in the immediate future.

Standard The criterion set for the actions, behaviors, operations, goals, or conditions by which the individual assesses the degree of accomplishment.

Value Individual beliefs so strongly held they motivate behavior, influence interaction with others, direct the choices made, and provide direction to daily life and management.

Value Cluster The grouping of values that are related to each other by content and role.

Value Conflict A situation in which two or more values are in opposition to each other.

Value Hierarchy The rank order of values from the highest to the lowest priority; the importance of each individually held value in relationship to other values.

REFERENCES

1. L. Jean Riebel, "Philosophy of Management," *Journal of Home Economics* (January 1969), 16.
2. Clark E. Moustakas, *Creative Life* (New York: D. Van Nostrand Company, 1977), p. 76.
3. Louis E. Raths, Merrill Harmin, and Sidney B. Simon, *Values and Teaching: Working with Values in the Classroom* (Columbus, Ohio: Charles E. Merrill Publishing Company, 1966), p. 27.
4. Ibid., p. 28.
5. Ibid., pp. 28-29.
6. Ibid., p. 28.
7. Cleo Fitzsimmons and Flora Williams, *The Family Economy, Nature and Management of Resources* (Ann Arbor, Michigan: Edwards Brothers, Incorporated), 1973. pp. 43-45.
8. Abraham H. Maslow, *Motivation and Personality* (New York: Harper, 1954). p. 80.
9. Francille Maloch and Ruth E. Deacon, "Proposed Framework for Home Management," *Journal of Home Economics* (January, 1966), 31-35.

10. Florence S. Walker, "A Proposal for Classifying Self-Imposed Housekeeping Standards," *Journal of Home Economics* (June 1968), 457.

11. Irma H. Gross, Elizabeth Walbert Crandall, and Marjorie M. Knoll, *Management for Modern Families,* 3rd ed. (New York: Appleton-Century-Crofts, 1973), p. 129.

12. Ibid. p. 130.

13. Ibid. p. 131.

14. Ibid. p. 134.

15. Ibid.

CHAPTER THREE

Decision Making

Have you ever thought about the decisions you make? Why are some easier to make than others? What kind of decisions are easier to make in a group and which ones do you prefer to make alone? Is it a valid choice not to make a decision?

How many decisions have you made today? How many do you anticipate making the rest of the day or tomorrow? What motivates you to make certain decisions? How far reaching are the decisions you make?

Everyone makes decisions every day. Some decisions are easier to make than others. Some can be made easily and quickly; others take a great deal of thought and time. If you are like most people, you have some decisions you are very proud you made. At the same time, there are others that you wish you had the opportunity to change. This is particularly true in cases where you have more knowledge now than when the original decision was made.

Some of the decisions that you make will have a long lasting effect upon your life. Others will not. But what is decision making? Why is the study of decision making important? What factors affect decision making? Are there different kinds of categories of decisions?

Role and Scope of Decision Making

To understand the components of decision making, you need to be aware of what is involved in decision making, who makes decisions, where and when decisions are made, and how decision making affects your daily life. Effective decision making does not just happen but takes place when your choice among the alternatives is done in a rational, thoughtful, logical, and reasonable manner rather than by impulse. It is therefore a learned skill. It must be continually practiced day after day.

It should be remembered, however, that a decision reached after thoughtful consideration of the alternatives does not automatically guarantee that the decision is an effective one. No one can have such a guarantee. Yet, the probability is increased that the best possible decision was made when based upon known facts.

Every decision has an element of risk. By examining alternatives in a thoughtful, logical, and reasonable manner you are reducing the risk factor. The purpose is to reduce risk to a point where it can be recognized and assessed.

Think about the decisions you have made thus far today. You made a decision to do the assigned reading in the textbook. Other decisions you have made today include what to wear, when to study, how to spend your day, whether or not to eat lunch and so forth. From the time you awaken until you return to sleep at night, you make decisions. Input received from the subsystems within your spheres of interaction motivate some decisions; others are motivated by the levels of the spheres of interaction. Still others originate from your values, goals, and standards.

There are certain times in your life when the decisions you make have a direct bearing upon both the present and the future. These decisions may be so important that once made, they become difficult if not impossible to reverse. They often center around your lifetime goals such as your major in college, anticipated employment, when or if you decide to become a parent.

You also make other decisions that can be easily and readily changed. For instance, a consumer product purchase can, in most cases, be returned to the retail merchant. A decision concerning when to study can probably be altered.

As you make decisions, certain factors affect not only how you make decisions but why you select one alternative and not another. Just as your values, goals, and standards are different from other individuals, so is your decision making. Each person makes decisions on the basis of knowledge, skills, past experiences, values, goals, standards, input from the spheres of interactions, and the decoding of this input. Thus each person's decision-making is uniquely different from the other.

Decision-making plays a definite role in your life. You use decision-making to achieve your goals, to assess your standards, and as an aid in attaining your desired quality of life. The decisions you make reflect your value hierarchy. It is conceivable that two individuals faced with making the same decision will approach the decision from different aspects, identify different alternatives and then select totally different alternatives as their final choice. The underlying reason for this is the difference in individual values, goals, and standards.

As you progress through life you make decisions. Almost any decision you make leads to another one. The decisions you are making now will affect those you will make in the future. Decision-making has an important role in your management. As you make decisions you allocate resources and determine courses of actions. This process also affects your input into the levels of the spheres of interaction.

Thus decision-making serves many different purposes in your management. You use decision-making to set your goals and their priorities; to determine which resources should be used, or whether one resource will be used instead of another. The courses of action you take result from your decisions. The habits and routines you follow on a regular basis have come about from earlier decisions you made. In addition to these, your input into the spheres of interaction is based upon single and collective decisions.

Have you ever thought of the effect of your decisions upon other people and your spheres of interaction? Although you may not be aware of it, a decision you make can have a far reaching effect not only upon you but upon other people as well. Just as decision making serves a viable role in your life, the scope or extent of your decisions encompass more than your individual sphere of interaction.

The decision you make in the marketplace will be important not only to you but to others. Each time you make a consumer decision, it affects not only your own spending patterns but also the overall consumption of goods and services. Your decision concerning the university and your major had a far reaching effect. Thus the scope of your decisions may be input into several levels of the spheres of interaction as well as within the subsystems.

Decision making encompasses two different aspects: the inputs you receive and the output received within the spheres of interaction from the decision and action you undertake. This input and output can be expressed as a model. Figure 3.1 represents the extent of the decision you made to enroll in the university you are now attending. The inputs in Figure 3.1 represents part of the input you have received. Figure 3.1 also identifies some of the output resulting from your decision and action. Together they compose the scope of your decision.

As you approached your high school junior or senior year, you began to receive input from differing levels of your spheres of interaction as shown in Figure 3.1. In all probability you can add others not listed here. As you received this input, you decoded and applied it to your self-concept, desired

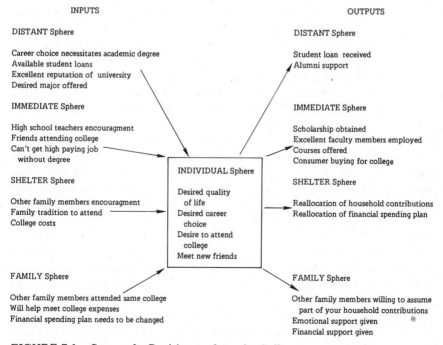

INPUTS

DISTANT Sphere

Career choice necessitates academic degree
Available student loans
Excellent reputation of university
Desired major offered

IMMEDIATE Sphere

High school teachers encouragment
Friends attending college
Can't get high paying job
  without degree

SHELTER Sphere

Other family members encouragment
Family tradition to attend
College costs

FAMILY Sphere

Other family members attended same college
Will help meet college expenses
Financial spending plan needs to be changed

INDIVIDUAL Sphere

Desired quality
  of life
Desired career
  choice
Desire to attend
  college
Meet new friends

OUTPUTS

DISTANT Sphere

Student loan received
Alumni support

IMMEDIATE Sphere

Scholarship obtained
Excellent faculty members employed
Courses offered
Consumer buying for college

SHELTER Sphere

Reallocation of household contributions
Reallocation of financial spending plan

FAMILY Sphere

Other family members willing to assume
  part of your household contributions
Emotional support given
Financial support given

FIGURE 3.1. Scope of a Decision to Attend a College.

quality of life, values, goals, and standards, and future expectations. Ultimately you made the decision and undertook action by enrolling in your university. This decision and the action undertaken then became your output into the sheres of interaction.

As you can see in Figure 3.1 the output of your decision encompasses more than just you and your family. This output was felt in varying degrees in all the levels of the spheres of interaction and subsystems.

Decision making has a specific role in your management. Through effective decision making you are better able to attain your desired quality of life. You do this through recognition of the role decision making plays in effective management. Effective management means you not only recognize the role of decision making but also the extent to which your decisions affect not only you but others.

Classifications of Decision Making

Not all decisions are alike. Nor is every decision made in the same manner. Although some actions you undertake derive their basis from newly made decisions, there are other instances when decision making does not really take place. The latter, according to Deacon and Firebaugh, may involve routine, programmed, impulsive or intuitive action.[1]

When you wake up in the morning and prepare to attend class do you consciously make decisions about such things as which side of your hair to comb first, how to brush your teeth, or which shoe to put on first? Probably not. Although you may have made a conscious decision about what you were going to wear to class, you probably didn't spend any time in making a decision about how to get ready to attend class. Every individual has certain habits or routine behaviors. Although they originated from decisions made at an earlier time in your life, you no longer consciously make these decisions each time you undertake this type of action.

Routine plans or actions serve a useful purpose in your daily life and management. How long would it take you to get up, get ready, and walk to class if you had to make separate decisions for each action you take? You use routine plans or actions as a resource. Since they are applicable each day, you need not use your resources to make new decisions.

In addition to the habitual behaviors or routines you follow, you also have certain specific actions you undertake in a given situation. These are called programmed decisions. Programmed decisions are different from routines. Routine plans or actions are patterns of behavioral actions repeatedly undertaken on a consistent and regular basis. Programmed decisions, on the other hand, utilize your past experience in a similar situation. For instance, you know you are going to have a test. Your method of studying for this test will be done using your knowledge of a similar experience. The degree of success previously achieved will be a determinant in how, when, where, and the length of time you study for this test.

Programmed decisions, like routines, are a resource in your management. When the action undertaken proves to be successful you repeat the same action the next time a similar situation occurs. This successful achievement, measured by the satisfaction you received, determines when and the extent to which you modify the original decision before employing it again in other like situations.

Both routine and programmed decisions serve useful purposes. They act as resources by eliminating the need to make new decisions. They also evaluate managerial action. The success you achieve enables you to by-pass or minimize the use of the decision-making process.

There are, however, times when you undertake action without any real thought process, lacking prior experience as a base, or in the absence of conscious awareness. This action results from either impulse or intuition.[2] In either case, the action taken is not necessarily a negative one.

As you think back over some instances in your life you can probably recall situations where you acted impulsively or upon intuition. Although it is true that some of these might not in the long run have been in your best interests, there are undoubtedly others that were. Many products purchased in the marketplace were obtained through impulsive decisions. There have probably been times when you have acted not on the basis of any knowledge but rather due to an inner sense or feeling you could not explain. Your intuition, in the absence of fact or logic, motivated you. Perhaps you have reviewed your notes just prior to going to class without really knowing why. When the class began, the instructor announced a "pop quiz." This is but one example of intuition. You can probably relate others that have happend to you.

Acting by intuition does not mean making a choice among alternatives. However, daily living does involve decision making.

Diesing defines a *decision* as follows:

> A decision or action is substantially rational when it takes account of the possibilities and limitations of a given situation and recognizes it so as to produce, or increase, or preserve some good.[3]

Diesing's criteria for a decision are (1) "decisions must be an effective response to the situation in that it produces some possible good and (2) the effectiveness must be based on intelligent insight rather than luck."[4]

Using this definition, Diesing developed the five categories of decision making. These categories are technical, economic, social, legal, and political.[5]

Technical Decisions

Technical decisions are "actions undertaken for the sake of a given end."[6] Decisions that fall into this category are goal oriented. The alternatives have some known degree of specificity as do the available resources. These decisions

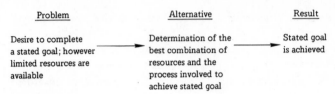

Problem	Alternative	Result
Desire to complete a stated goal; however limited resources are available	Determination of the best combination of resources and the process involved to achieve stated goal	Stated goal is achieved

FIGURE 3.2. *Technical Decision Making. [Adapted from M. K. Keenan, "Models for Decision-Making" (Long Beach, Calif.: California State University, 1969), p. 6.]*

involve weighing the alternatives. This means selecting the alternative that has the highest probability of achieving the desired goal and reducing the degree of risk as much as possible. These are the easiest decisions to make.

An example of a technical decision might be whether to go to class or stay in your room. You know the probability of risk, the instructor may give a quiz, whether or not you can obtain the lecture notes from another class member, and any additional potential risk factors. The decision you make will be based on these known facts.

Nickel, Rice, and Tucker indicate these decisions ". . . may not seem extremely important but set the tone of daily living and can affect the quality or results of more prevasive decisions."[7] They also refer to these decisions as the "how to" ones. Keenan's model of technical decision making is shown in Figure 3.2.

The basic characteristics of a known goal, known alternatives, and known but limited resources are shown in Figure 3.2. The decision, then, involves making a choice which will bring the greatest degree of satisfaction while reducing as much as possible the degree of risk.[8]

Economic Decisions

Economic decisions have two basic components: multiple goals and limited resources. In these decisions, you have a number of goals competing against each other. Each of these goals necessitates allocation of the established resources. Your decision involves determining which goals and what resources Since the attainment of these competing goals necessitate the use of similar or like resources you will have to determine goal priority. Completing this you can allocate resources.

One fallacy that often occurs among students examining decisions is to think these resources can only be monetary. There are many resources other than money. Therefore all resources are involved in these decisions.

Inherent in these decisions are the characteristics of exchange and allocation resources.[9] In order to achieve your goals, resources are either allocated and/or exchanged. Keenan's representation of these decisions is as follows.

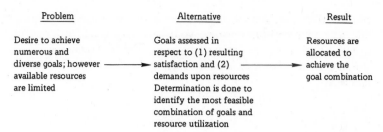

FIGURE 3.3. Economic Decisions. [Adapted from M. K. Keenan, "Models for Decision-Making" (Long Beach, Calif.: Californial State University, 1969), p. 6.]

Assume your multiple goals are to

1. Achieve a high grade on a test to be given tomorrow.
2. Attend a party given at a friend's house this evening.
3. Get the laundry done and go shopping for a birthday present.
4. Clean your room by tomorrow morning.
5. Finish the library research for a term paper due at the end of the week.

Your established but limited resources are time and energy. You must begin by setting priorities for your goals. Following this you allocate your resources among the combination of goals that will bring about the greatest degree of satisfaction while maximizing the resources used.

What resources do you have which might be exchanged for your limited resources of time and energy? Although most college students would not do this, you could use a money resource to pay someone to clean your room and do your laundry. In this instance you are exchanging one resource (money) for another to achieve a goal. Can you think of other resources you might exchange? In making economic decisions you are seeking to allocate and/or exchange your established resources in the most effective manner to bring about the highest degree of satisfaction.

Although these decisions are not the easiest to make, in your daily life you continually make economic decisions. These decisions involve a greater degree of risk than do technical decisions. In the latter decisions you know the alternatives and their respective degrees of risk. This is not necessarily true concerning economic decisions.

Using the economic decision cited earlier what would be the risk factor if your highest priorities were to do the laundry and go shopping for the birthday present? Would the risk factor be the same if your highest priority was to attend the party?

What could you do to reduce the risk factors involved in economic decisions? Gathering factual information is one step you often undertake when the economic decisions involve your monitary resources. Another might be to rely on past experience. Talking with friends, examining the depth of the alternatives, or assessing resources are other ways the risk factor might be reduced.

Social Decisions

In the two previous categories, your decisions involved goals and resources. Although *social decisions* are directed toward goal attainment resulting from the utilization of resources, they occur through interaction between individuals.[10]

You have been involved in many social decisions. When you moved into your dorm room or off-campus housing you and your roommate(s) made several social decisions. Examples of these might well have been: where to place the furniture, which drawers and what part of the closet were to be used by each individual, or determining each person's responsibility for keeping the room clean and neat.

As you made these decisions interaction took place between you and your roommate(s). Your values and role perceptions influenced your interaction. Whether you realized it or not, you had assigned a role not only to yourself but also to your roommate(s). Your roommate(s) also assigned a role to you. These roles and the values of each individual involved in the process affected the decisions made.

Social decisions differ from economic decisions in several ways. In the two previous categories resource allocation and choosing among alternatives were involved in the decision making process. Social decisions mean that interaction is taking place. Thus the values, goals, and standards of each person are involved. The communication taking place also has a bearing upon the process.

In the social decision just cited, you and your roommate(s) undertook the decision making process on the strength of your personal values, goals, and standards. Through communication you interacted. In the process of communication you decoded what was being said to you and the actions taken by your roommate on the basis of your values, goals, and standards. Your roommate(s) did the same thing.

As you can see in Figure 3.3, social decisions may involve conflicting values and role perceptions. Part of the decision making process in social decisions involves recognizing these and determining the cause. Therefore social decisions may never be truly resolved to the ultimate satisfaction of all involved individuals.[11] In the decision concerning your housing, were you totally satisfied with the results? Or did you and your roommate(s) compromise, allowing each person to have his own way part of the time?

Keenan's diagram of social decisions is shown in Figure 3.4.

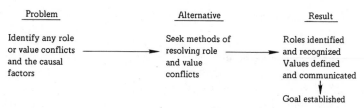

Problem	Alternative	Result
Identify any role or value conflicts and the causal factors	Seek methods of resolving role and value conflicts	Roles identified and recognized Values defined and communicated ↓ Goal established

FIGURE 3.4 *Social Decisions.* [*Adapted from M. K. Keenan, "Models for Decision-Making" (Long Beach, Calif.: California State University, 1969), p. 16.*]

Using a social decision you have made, complete the diagram. What were the value and role conflicts? How were they resolved?

Figure 3.4 makes it apparent in these decisions, too, that there is a risk factor. The risk factor involves values and roles. Since each individual participates in these decisions using his values and on the basis of role perceptions, the risk factor includes value and role conflicts. You may not be aware of the values or role perceptions of the other person. Nor is that individual aware of yours. Both of you are seeking to make a decision when all of the factors involved are not really known. Since incomplete information is available, the risk factor is increased.

Legal Decisions

Within each of your spheres of interaction you have various rules, regulations, and/or policies (*legal decisions*) that pertain to you and your actions within society. These may have been established by law, an authority agency or organization, or by the common consent of a group of people. Regardless of the method of establishment, these rules, regulations, and/or policies derive their basis in the common welfare of the total group. They are the basic structure by which society and the culture function for the common good of all.[12]

When your decisions concerning these rules, regulations, and/or policies are made you are aware of the risks involved and the probability of the consequences should you elect not to observe them. For instance, if you drive 70 miles per hour on a highway you know that it is likely that sooner or later you will get a speeding ticket. You also know that should you get a speeding ticket you will probably have to pay a fine. If you continue to receive speeding tickets, in all probability you may loose your driver's license either temporarily or permanently.

Unlike other categories, you know the risk factors and the probable consequences. It is then a question of what is the degree of risk you are willing to incur. Are you willing to accept the consequences of the risk probability?

Political Decisions

Political decisions are made by a group of individuals whose major purpose is to function as a single unit. Unlike social decisions, the emphasis here is placed upon the procedure of how the decision is made rather than the actual resolution of the problem or situation. Political decisions involve establishing an organizational structure within the group. This organizational structure is then employed to resolve a problem or make a determination.[13]

Suppose your instructor assigned you and five other members of your class to research and make an oral report on any topic you choose. What would the six of you do first? In order to complete this assignment, your group would start by establishing an organizational structure. In so doing you and the other members of your group have been making political decisions. Can you cite other instances where you have been involved in political decisions?

Decision Styles

Within the spheres of interaction you make decisions. These decisions may be technical, economic, social, legal, or political. As you make decisions you will have a tendency to utilize a particular style as you select among the alternatives. Bustrillo's study found decision styles can be divided into the three major classifications of mode, time, and decision rule. Each of these have three subdivisions.[14]

Mode

If mode is your decision style you verbalize throughout your decision-making process. The subdivisions herein are hypothetical, factual, or action-suggestive. Each of these subdivisions can be characterized by key words or phrases.[15]

The individual who uses the hypothetical mode often prefaces sentences in the verbalization process with key words or phrases expressing or denoting the element of doubt or lack of conviction such as "If I do . . ." or "What if this or that happens. . . ." The final choice of alternatives too, is often expressed in doubtful terminology.[16]

Factual mode, on the other hand, uses phrases denoting facts. Throughout the verbalization process facts are stated and continual reference is made. The key phrases include factual statements or indications of fact such as "On the basis of this study (fact). . . ."[17]

The individual who uses the action-suggestive mode is often one who jumps to an immediate solution without considering all of the possible alternatives. The key phrases here include suggestive terms such as "should or would" coupled with action terms such as "do."[18]

Time

The three subdivisions of the time decision style are past, present, and future. The focal point is time. All decisions are made on the basis of this focal point as opposed to any other. Some individuals rely totally on past experience to serve as the basis for decisions. Still others make all decisions on the basis of the future expectations or considerations. The present-oriented individual makes decisions only in terms of the current moment. In each of these time is the focal point or basis upon which decisions are made and action is taken.[19]

Decision Rule

The decision rule style places its emphasis on the method used by the individual to select among alternatives. The three subdivisions are preference ranking, objective elimination, and immediate closure.[20]

Nickell, Rice, and Tucker indicate when using preference ranking, you examine the alternatives available. These alternatives are then ranked according to preference from the most to the least desired. This ranking on the basis of personal preference is not necessarily logical or factual. Rather, it is according to the most desirable, not necessarily the most optimum alternative. Although the most desirable and optimum may be the same, the emphasis is most desired.[21]

The use of objective elimination means each known alternative is analyzed and evaluated. As each is analyzed, some are rejected. This process of evaluation and analysis continues until one alternative remains. The decision results when the elimination and analysis has produced but one remaining alternative.[22]

Although verbalization is an aspect of immediate closure, the major emphasis in this subdivision is to make a decision as rapidly as possible.[23] The individual who uses this decision style is seeking to resolve the problem and/or make a decision rather than to find the most feasible alternative that will lead to potential success.

The Decision-Making Process

Thus far you have examined the categories and kinds of decision making. Earlier in the chapter, you noted there is a difference between just decision making and effective decision making.

Effective decision making occurs when your choice among alternatives is arrived at through a logical, thoughtful process. This means you use the steps in decision making.

John Dewey suggested there are three steps involved in decision making: (1) identify the problem, (2) identify the alternatives, and (3) select the best alternative.[24]

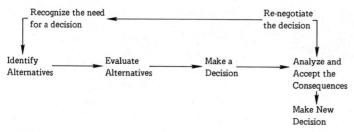

FIGURE 3.5.   The Decision-Making Process.

The decision making process involves:

1. Recognize a decision has to be made.
2. Identify the alternatives.
3. Evaluate the alternatives.
4. Make a decision.
5. Analyze and accept the consequences of your decision.

The process of decision making model is shown in Figure 3.5. Each of these is important in making an effective decision. Effective decision making plays an important role in your management.

Recognize a Decision Has to be Made

Decision making does not take place until you recognize it is necessary. This process of recognition involves becoming aware of the factors that initiate or indicate the need for a decision.

Here you examine the situation or occurrence that has brought about the need for a decision. It is here the categories of decision making become important. Which category is involved in your decision?

To determine this, you must look at the factors creating the need for a decision. Effective decision making means there is more involved than just thinking: "Hey, I've got to make a decision!" It means you need to really explore the factors or the situation. You look beyond the obvious. Effective decision making involves determining what is the specific decision which needs to be made. Unless this is done, you may be trying to make the wrong decision or one based upon incomplete or inaccurate information. In-depth examinations of the problem or situation may mean the difference between just decision making and effective decision making.

Until you consciously recognize a decision must be made, no decision exists. This does not mean you ignore the need for a decision. It means that you are not consciously aware of the need for a decision.

As a sixth-grader, you perhaps knew that following high school graduation you would enroll in a college or university. However, you were not consciously aware of the need to make a decision as to which college or university. You were not ignoring the situation. As graduation became a reality you became consciously aware of the need for a decision.

It has been emphasized that recognizing that a decision has to be made is the first part of the decision-making process. You not only recognize that a decision needs to be made but you also are aware of the factors that have created or brought about this need.

Identify the Alternatives

As you recognize a decision has to be made, you begin to identify the possible alternatives. Effective decision making occurs when you identify as much as humanly possible all of the possible alternatives. Identifying as many alternatives as possible will enable you to select the most effective one. This also enables you to reduce to some extent the risk factor involved in decision making.

Unless you identify possible alternatives you cannot make a logical, thoughtful, and reasonable decision. As you began to select the college or university you would attend, didn't you consider several as possible choices? In so doing, you were identifying your alternatives.

Evaluate the Alternatives

Once you have identified your alternatives, you begin to evaluate each one as to its possible feasibility. This process of evaluation utilizes a criteria you have developed to measure or weigh the alternatives. This criteria allows you to immediately eliminate those alternatives that are not feasible. You use this same criteria to rank in order the remaining possible alternatives.

As you examined the colleges and universities you could attend, what was your criteria? Why did you immediately eliminate some and not others? How did you develop your criteria?

Your criteria for evaluating alternatives is an integral part of the decision-making process. As you assess and weigh each alternative, your values, goals, and standards are sources of input. The criteria you established is greatly affected by these.

Effective decision making involves assessing each alternative in terms of the opportunity costs and benefits. The satisfaction you anticipate each alternative will produce should also be an evaluative criteria.

Any other information such as performance standards, friends, research, and family members can also be used to develop an evaluative criteria. The extensiveness of information you employ as evaluative criteria will reduce the risk factor involved in the final decision.

The purpose of evaluation of alternatives is to assess the costs, benefits, and anticipated satisfaction which would be derived from each alternative.

You should remember that in so doing, your values, goals, and standards are also acting as a source of input. Therefore these will have a bearing upon the evaluative criteria used and the judgments made.

Make a Decision

On the basis of your evaluation you make a choice among your alternatives. The choice you make is your decision. In most instances, the ease or difficulty of arriving at the final decision will depend upon the extent to which the preceding were completed.

How difficult was your final choice for your college career? By the time you made this decision, you had probably eliminated all but a few colleges or universities. Some individuals may have found the decision was an easy one; for others, this might not be true. How do you feel about your decision now? If you reemployed the decision-making process now, do you feel you would have made a different choice?

Analyze and Accept the Consequences of Your Decision

Effective decision making does not terminate when the decision is made. The feedback from your decision should be analyzed. Decision-making is effective only when the feedback, regardless of the degree of success achieved, is used in a constructive manner.

Your decision may produce either positive or negative results. When you employ the decision-making process one of the sources of input is previous decisions you have made in similar situations. Unless you analyze the consequences of your decision you will tend to follow a similar pattern in future decisions. When the decision you make produced a high degree of positive results, this procedure will not be detrimental. However, if the results produced are negative or less than optimum, without using analysis, your input in future situations will not be valid.

Just as your values, goals, and standards are sources of input upon the evaluation of the alternatives, so too are the input sources during analysis of the outcome and acceptance of the consequences of the decision. Your standards are the criteria used to assess the extent to which your decision was successful. Your decision was directed toward the attainment of one or more goals; the extent of forward progress is assessed. The values involved and the reinforcement of these is expressed by how you feel about the outcome.

Combined with the analysis of the decision is the ability to assess and accept the consequences of the decision you have made. As you make future decisions one of your inputs is the success of past decisions. This means you not only assess the outcome of a decision but you also recognize that a decision outcome could produce a positive or negative outcome. In so doing, you assess not only the outcome but also recognize that when a negative one occurs, your decision did not produce a positive outcome.

Some decisions that produce negative outcomes can be reversed. However, this does not or cannot occur unless you are willing to recognize the decision you made was an invalid one. The person who accepts only the positive consequences of decision making will have a tendency to repeat ineffective decisions simply because he or she will not recognize the consequences of his or her negative producing decisions.

Effective management is dependent upon developing and refining the skills necessary to make thoughtful, logical decisions. This will occur when you not only assess the outcome but also accept the consequences of the decision. This knowledge is then used in the future. As stated, failure to accept the consequences of negative outcomes will result in future ineffectual decisions. Through accepting the consequences, whether positive or negative, you are able to more readily progress toward the attainment of your desired quality of life.

Linking of Decisions

Decision making is a continual and on-going process. As one decision is made, another follows, and then still another. Although there are several methods to illustrate how one decision is linked to another, only three will be discussed here. Decisions can be linked together in a single chaining, as a Central-Satellite decision, or to form a decision tree.

Decisions may be linked together in that each decision is related to those that follow by a common bond or pattern. When this occurs, decisions are said to form a single chain. On the other hand, although decisions themselves are not related to each other, they center around a critical or central decision. Plonk calls this linking of decisions a Central-Satellite decision model.[25] Decision making is choosing among alternatives; the decisions made then form a pattern. As the alternatives and the decisions made branch outward, one from another, a decision tree is formed.

Chain Decisions

Although in each case, one decision follows another, Gross, Crandall, and Knoll feel this occurs when (1) one decision leads to another and then another, (2) it is logical for the second decision to follow or come from the first, (3) all decisions are either of equal or increasing importance, and (4) a trend or pattern has been established.[26]

In this instance the decisions you make are all related. They form a single line of decisions as shown in Figure 3.6. The decisions you have made concerning your college studies are an example. Decision 1 was your college major.

D_1 --------- D_2 --------- D_3 ------ D_4 ------ D_5 ------ D_6 -----

FIGURE 3.6. Decision Chaining.

Decision 2 was to enroll in the required courses. Decision 3 involved the order of the courses you would take. Decision 4 was to enroll in a specific section of a specific course. Decision 5 was made when you determined which instructor would be the teacher for those sections. What is decision 6?

The decision chain is formed when one decision brings forth another and still another. All are related to the same topic or situation. This type of linking of decisions is the easiest to understand. You can probably think of many decision chains you have made throughout your life.

Central-Satellite Decisions

In researching aspects of decision making, Plonk found that although one decision leads to another there are times when the ensuing decisions, while related to a central decision, are not related to each other.[27] This study also showed the ensuing decisions resulting from the central decision varied in terms of form, range, and scope. From this research, Plonk established the Central-Satellite Decision model shown in Figure 3.7.

A central decision represents a critical or crucial decision you have or will make. Surrounding this central decision are several bands. The number of bands indicate the range or depth of the decision. Located on each of the bands are satellite decisions which have occurred from the central decision, but are not necessarily related to each other. These satellite decisions form a chain linking the various bands together. This linking between bands demonstrates the scope of decisions within the Central-Satellite decision.

Decision Tree

As you make decisions you are choosing among alternatives. The decision tree, shown in Figure 3.8, represents this form of decision linkage.

When you graduated from high school you had two alternatives. You could go on to college or you could go directly into full-time employment. You chose the alternative of college. This lead to a choice among colleges you could attend. You chose among your alternatives. This process continued. Each decision resulted in a new choice being made among the available alternatives.

The decision tree can be a useful management tool. By charting the original decision you made, the alternatives that were available, and the choices you made among the available alternatives, you can identify your decision-making patterns. You can also use this as a method to review your previous

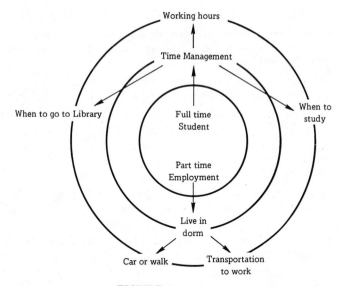

FIGURE 3.7.   Central-Satellite Decision.

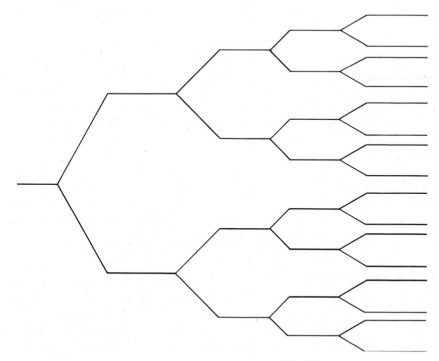

FIGURE 3.8.   Decision Tree.

decisions to determine the point at which a trend or decision pathway you have taken can no longer be reversed.

If you were to chart the major decisions you have made in the last three years you would discover you have developed a pattern. This pattern has enabled you to attain some of your goals while directing your progress toward the attainment of others.

As you have progressed toward your goal attainment you have made decisions. Can you identify a decision that cannot be reversed? Use of the decision tree will help you determine if and at what point prior decisions can no longer be reversed.

Suppose you had decided not to enroll in college. Undoubtedly this decision could be reversed. But suppose you had decided not to go out for the university football team during the entire time you were a college student. However upon graduation you decided to become a pro-football player. Although in theory this decision could be reversed, you would experience a high degree of difficulty in so doing. What decision might you make that could not be reversed? Although there are very few decisions that cannot be reversed, some are much more difficult to reverse than others. The decision tree can aid you in identifying these.

Decisions are linked together. Decision making is a continuous and ongoing activity. The ability to recognize linkage will aid in effective decisions.

Decision Conflict

Some decisions are more difficult to make than others. Some also have a greater degree of perceived risk than others. Not all decisions once made prove to be successful. There are instances when you will be forced to choose between alternatives all of which are viewed as producing positive satisfaction. The reverse may also be true. There may also be times in which you perceive yourself as being in a "no win" situation. None of the alternatives are anticipated as producing satisfaction. Certain decisions can also involve a greater degree of stress and/or conflict than others. As an individual you will be making decisions by yourself. Yet at other times, you will be involved in group decision making. Each will affect your overall decision making.

Forced Choice Decisions

As you undertake more and more of the decisions that will influence and direct your life you will encounter situations where you are forced to make choices between two equally positive producing alternatives or among alternatives where no satisfaction is anticipated regardless of your choice. As you make these decisions, you may experience stress, frustration, and/or conflict. The degree to which you experience these will be to some extent governed by your decision style. However, there are other factors that will enter into this stress and/or conflict.

Conflicts are more prevalent when neither alternative is anticipated to produce a measureable degree of positive satisfaction.[28] When the resulting decision is also considered to have a risk potential of future loss, the conflict is further increased.[29] Additional conflict is incurred if the decision is one which may not be reversible at some later date.[30]

Although you may not be aware of it, you also experience conflict and stress when you are forced to choose among equally satisfaction producing alternatives. Despite the fact that there has been research on negative alternative choices, Janis and Mann cite several studies that report stress and conflict accrues when positive alternatives are present. These authors indicate that the implications to personal lives, the judgmental factors of other individuals, and the aspects of potential loss of self-esteem were conflict producing factors.[31]

Every decision has an inherent risk factor. It is not necessarily true that satisfaction will automatically result when a decision is made anticipating no social disapproval. Unless cognitive awareness is given to internalized standards and values, satisfaction does not necessarily result. In support of this Janis and Mann state ". . . self approval is an essential requirement for being satisfied with a decision. Gaining unitarian and social rewards is not enough; the person has to be able to live with himself."[32]

Forced choice decisions do occur. As you undertake the decision-making process there will be instances where you will be forced to choose among alternatives viewed as producing equally positive satisfaction, or no satisfaction at all. Decision conflict, while an inherent part of the decision-making process, increases when forced choices must be made.

Group Decisions

You have undertaken the decision-making process as a single individual and as a member of a group. Which do you prefer? Are there some decisions you would prefer to make as an individual rather than as a member of a group? Are there some group decisions easier to make than others?

Although more of your decisions originate from individual rather than group action, you have and will continue to take part in group decisions. Your participation in the group decision-making process will vary. As a member of a social organization, within your professional endeavors, or through your civic participation, you will be called upon to take a role in group decision making. Regardless of whether you are making decisions as an individual or as a group member, the process of decision making remains the same. The difference then lies, not in the process, but rather in the manner in which the process is applied and the extent to which each participant in the group views the process.

The decision making of an individual evolves around the values, goals, standards, and roles this individual assumes within the spheres of interaction. Group decisions culminate from the collective action of several individuals each of whom has distinct values, goals, standards, and role perceptions. This is in and of itself a potential conflict producing situation.

Janis and Mann indicate several factors that will affect group decision making. These include leadership, the group's sense of commitment, and the difficulty of the decision to be made.[33] The *Communications Handbook* cites the roles of participants within a group as a mitigating factor in the group process.[34]

The extent and effectiveness of the leadership is a key factor. The absence of leadership often yields inadequately defined and clarified goals, the loss of a sense of commitment among the members, and a poorly established purpose for group action. When these are coupled with a decision which is perceived as being a difficult or controversial one, the group may accomplish little if anything. In addition to this, where possible the group may seek to shift the responsibility to another group.[35]

Groups are composed of individuals. Although each individual enters the setting with specifically held values, goals, standards, and roles, each is expected to assume one or more roles within the group. The extent to which role conflicts may or may not emerge will be governed by the extent to which the roles projected upon individual members harmonize with those each is willing to self-assume. If you do not see yourself as the leader of a group but this role is projected upon you by others, how willing are you to accept this role? Even if you do accept the projected role, are you happy about undertaking the task?

The *Communications Handbook* indicates the following are roles within the group process. The *initiator-contributor* seeks to obtain new ideas or approaches to goals and objectives. The *information-seeker* desires to clarify and validate information. Values are clarified by the *opinion-seeker*. Data and personal experiences are the prime contribution of the information-giver. The coordinator pulls together the ideas and relates one to another. The elaborator uses the ideas and approaches of others to develop meanings and alternatives. The opinion-giver, on the other hand, contributes beliefs or convictions which may not necessarily be relevant nor pertinent to the discussion. Bringing the group discussion back to the main objective is the task of the orientor. Although the energizer seeks to maintain the forward progress of the group action, the elaborator-critic measures the action against the established standards. Inherent within this group is also the procedural technician whose major task is to undertake the routine activities of the group while the recorder takes notes.[36]

Each of these roles is undertaken within a group setting. The extent to which each occurs and is exercised in the setting will be dependent upon how the individual perceives his or her role and the role projected upon the individual by other group members.

An individual may assume one or more of these roles at any given time. The probability of conflict, stress, or dissonance in group decision making will be increased when these roles are self-assumed in a negative rather than a positive manner.

When an unacknowledged or hidden objective is present the probability of stress, conflict, or dissonance is increased.[37] Awareness of this objective may be limited to only a few members or it may be known to the entire membership. It may or may not be consciously acknowledged. A hidden objective will have an effect not only upon the group process but also upon individual participants. Group decision-making is often, at best, a time consuming task. When an incident occurs that produces either directly or indirectly stress, dissonance, or conflict, an emotionally charged atmosphere may also exist.

Throughout your life you will be involved in group as well as individual decision making. The satisfaction accruing from this will be governed by the individual role assumption, role projection, the degree of leadership present, the sense of commitment to the stated goal or objective, and the anticipated degree of risk.

Summary

Decision making is a continuous, on-going process. Each day you make decisions affecting your management. The decisions you make emanate from your values, goals, standards, past experience, and input received from your spheres of interaction.

The difference between just making decisions and effective decision making involves recognizing the categories of decision making, using the decision-making process, and identifying the style of decision making being employed. It also means recognizing the linkage between your decisions and using this knowledge to make future decisions.

Decisions can be classified using Diesing's categories of technical, economic, social, legal, and political.[38] Knowledge of the category of a decision being made will aid in using the steps in the decision-making process.

There are instances where action is undertaken without using the decision-making process. This action may occur from routines, habits, impulse, or intuition. Decisions can also be classified as to being programmed or non-programmed.[39] Each of these classifications and the steps in the decision-making process enable you to make logical, thoughtful decisions, if you use each as a tool in your management.

Recognizing that a decision must be made is the first component in the decision-making process. The second component is to identify the alternatives. Evaluating these alternatives is the third component. Choosing among the alternatives and making a decision represents the fourth. The final component in the decision-making process is to analyze and accept the consequences of the decision.

One decision leads to another which in turn leads to still another. This continual process of making decisions is shown in the linkage that occurs between decisions. Some decisions are related to one another to form a single chain. Others center around a critical or crucial decision. These are called Central-Satellite decisions.[40] Another way to demonstrate the linking of decisions is the decision tree. This method can be used to illustrate the path taken by previous decisions or as a cost-benefit analysis in order to make anticipated decisions.

Every decision has a risk factor. To make rational and effective decisions, you want to reduce this risk factor as much as possible. Reduction of all risk is not feasible. However, using your knowledge of decision making and the decision-making process will increase your ability to reduce this risk factor.

Decision making is a part of your management. It has an important and well-defined role throughout your life. The decisions you make will affect not only you and your future but also others as well. The impact of each decision you make becomes input into your spheres of interaction.

Knowledge of decision making and its role and scope in management are vital. Successful management is dependent upon effective decision making. Effective decision making does not just happen. Like the other skills you possess, it is a learned one. The art of decision making is a valuable tool in management. For it to remain a valuable tool, your knowledge must be continually increased and your skill continually used.

ACTIVITIES

You are trying to decide whether or not you want to have a car on campus. Your parents have indicated you could bring the "old car" back with you. It is a 1970 four-door sedan which looks terrible, drives well, and uses regular leaded gasoline. However, you will only get eight miles to the gallon in city driving. You will have to pay all the costs of having the car with the exception of the car insurance. You have saved slightly over $1,500 toward the purchase of a car when you graduate in the coming year. If you decide to use this money to buy a car now, you can insure it under your parents' policy.

1. Using the decision indicated, complete the following:
   a. Diagram the decision tree.
   b. Identify the classification of the decision to be made.
   c. Indicate the central and satellite decision that might result.

d. Describe the steps in the decision-making process you would follow to make the final choice.

e. Show the scope of your decision.

2. Make a decision based on the information given. On the basis of your decision,

a. Identify the standards you would use.

b. List the values that would influence your decision.

c. Indicate the goal(s) that influenced your decision.

3. Routine decisions have become a part of your daily living. List as many of your routine decisions as you can. Identify the classification of each one. Which classification appears most often? Why?

4. Packing your suitcase is a programmed decision you frequently use. Compare your current program decision with the first time you undertook this action. What modifications and adjustments have you made and why? Identify two other programmed decisions you use.

5. Describe an intuitive and an impulsive decision you have made. What were the outcomes and the feedback of each decision? If you had used the decision-making process would you have made the same decisions? Why or why not?

6. Record all the decisions you make for two days on the chart shown. Identify various information about each decision. As you complete the chart, remember some decisions will have more information than others.

Decision	A	B	C	D	E	F	G

Column A: Record whether the decision was a Programmed one (P), Routine (R), Intuitive (I), or Impulsive (IM).

Column B: The classification of the decision according to Diesing's categories.

Column C: Resources used by the decision.

Column D: Whether the decision was a central (C) or a satellite (S) one.

Column E: Input received prior to making the decision.

Column F: Outcome of the decision.

Column G: Any feedback received from the decision.

7. John has decided to go home for the weekend. Assuming that this is the first in a series of chain decisions, what are the decisions that will follow?

8. Using a decision tree, diagram the major decisions you will make in your senior year and the first year following your graduation. Show the opportunity costs for each alternative.

9. You made a decision to obtain a college degree in order to enter your chosen profession. What were the risk factors involved in this decision?

What are your values that influenced you to make this choice? What are your standards for this decision?

10. As a consumer you make many decisions. Using your last major purchase decision as a reference point,

    a. Identify the input you received.

    b. Describe the feedback of the decision.

    c. The decisions that have resulted from this initial decision.

    d. Analyze your decision-making process and its validity in reference to the feedback you have received.

JEAN AND DAVID

Dave and Jean have been married less than a year. Both are recent college graduates. Jean comes from a large metropolitan city where she lived with her parents. She has no brothers or sisters. Her father has a position as the vice president in a huge corporation. Her mother has never been employed outside the shelter sphere but is quite involved in several voluntary organizations. Money has never been a real problem for Jean until Dave said they had to live on what he makes without any help from her parents.

David is from a small university town. His parents are both university faculty members. He is one of three children and is the middle child. He has worked during college more to obtain extra money than because of financial need.

Since graduation is only a few months away, Dave and Jean are trying to decide which of three alternatives they should undertake in the future. Jean's father has offered to see that Dave gets a job in his corporation, which would probably mean working in the same area and possibly in the same office. It would be a high paying job with the potential for advancement. Dave would like to set up his own business in a small community much like the one he grew up in—possibly even his own hometown. He knows that he won't make a great deal of money for several years until the "business really gets going." He has also been offered a job with a small industrial firm with the potential for growth. If he takes this position he will not earn as much of a starting salary as he would if he goes to work for his father-in-law's firm. However, he probably would advance much faster in this smaller firm.

Jean wants to move back to her hometown where most of her friends will return to as soon as they graduate. She would also like to live closer to her parents. If Dave takes the job with the smaller firm, they will have to move from the state where they now live to the East Coast and probably won't be able to come home more than three times a year.

Dave likes the challenge of starting a new business but is aware of the long hours of work and the financial hardships which might occur. He wonders if he has the right to impose these on Jean. Then, too, if he started his own business, she might have to help until he can afford to hire someone to work in the office.

Discussion Questions

1. Diagram a decision tree for the decision Dave and Jean are trying to make.
2. What are the inputs being received in this decision? How are Jean's and Dave's values influencing the decision?

3. Select one of the three alternatives as the central decision and then identify the satellite decisions that would occur from this central one.

4. What are the risk factors for each alternative? From the decision tree drawn, indicate the opportunity costs for each alternative.

5. Assume that you are either Dave or Jean; you want to use the steps in the decision-making process to resolve the problem. How would you use them and what logic would you employ to convince the other that your decision was the logical one?

GLOSSARY

Central-Satellite Decisions A decision linkage pattern established by Plonk. It graphically represents the form, range, and scope of decisions resulting from a central or critical decision.

Chain Decisions The linkage pattern of a series of decisions that logically follow one after another.

Cost-benefit Ratio An analytical method to assess the costs and benefits of a decision.

Decision Making An action in which a choice is made between two or more alternatives.

Decision Rule A decision style by which the selection among alternatives is done through (a) preference ranking, (b) objective elimination, or (c) immediate closure.

Decision Style The specific method such as mode, time, or decision rule used by an individual to choose among alternatives in making a decision.

Decision Tree A graphic representation of the pattern a series of decisions made and the alternatives which are available for each decision. This is used to demonstrate previous decision patterns, or to identify future decisions, or to establish the opportunity costs of alternatives, or to isolate the point at which a decision cannot be reversed.

Economic Decision One of the classifications developed by Diesing in which the choice being made involves multiple goals and limited resources.

Immediate Closure A form of decision rule in which the emphasis is on verbalization of alternatives until an alternative is found which will resolve the problem. The alternative is the first and not necessarily the best one.

Impulsive Decision A decision that is made without conscious thought or consideration nor on any recognized logical basis.

Intuitive Decision A decision made in the absence of fact or logic but based upon an inner sense or feeling of being a correct one.

Legal Decision One of the classifications developed by Diesing in which the choice among established rules, regulations, and/or policies is made and where the probability of risk and resulting consequences are known.

Mode A decision style that uses verbalization of the decision-making process to resolve the problem or situation.

Objective Elimination A form of decision rule in which the alternatives are analyzed, evaluated, and eliminated until only one remains.

Opportunity Costs The opportunities that the individual would not be able to obtain if the alternative is not chosen.

Political Decision One of the classifications developed by Diesing in which a group of individuals are participating in the determination of the procedures and policies to be employed to resolve a problem or situation.

Preference Ranking A form of decision rule in which alternatives are ranked according to personal preference rather than upon logic or feasibility.

Programmed Decision A decision made on the basis of previous decisions, similar situations, or events.

Risk Factor The measurable degree of risk produced by an event, situation, demand, fact, or occurrence.

Routine Decision A predetermined choice of behavioral patterns used on a consistent and repeated basis without conscious thought.

Social Decision One of the classifications developed by Diesing in which decisions involve the interaction between individuals in the decision-making process to achieve a goal or resolve a situation.

Steps in Decision Making A process used to make an effective decision. These involve (a) recognizing that a decision must be made, (b) identifying the alternatives, (c) evaluating the alternatives, (d) making a decision, and (e) analyzing and accepting the consequence of the decision.

Technical Decision One of the classifications developed by Diesing in which a choice is made among known alternatives and known degrees of risk to attain a specified goal.

Time A decision style which uses time: either past, present, or future, as a basic reference point to determine the choice among alternatives.

REFERENCES

1. Ruth E. Deacon and Francille M. Firebaugh *Home Management Context and Concepts* (Boston: Houghton Mifflin Company, 1975), pp. 118–119.
2. Ibid.

3. Paul Diesing, *Reason in Society: Five Types of Decisions and Their Social Conditions* (Urbana: University of Illinois Press, 1962), p. 3.
4. Ibid.
5. Ibid.
6. Ibid. p. 9.
7. Paulena Nickell, Ann Smith Rice, and Suzanne P. Tucker, *Management in Family Living,* (New York: John Wiley & Sons, Inc., 1976), p. 95.
8. Diesing. op. cit. p. 9.
9. Ibid.
10. Ibid. pp. 97–98.
11. Ibid.
12. Ibid. pp. 124–128.
13. Ibid. pp. 169–171.
14. Nena Bustrillo, "Decision-making Styles of Selected Mexican Homemakers" as quoted in Irma H. Gross, Elizabeth Walbert Crandall, and Marjorie M. Knoll, *Management for Modern Families,* 3rd ed. (New York: Appleton-Century-Crofts, 1973), pp. 231–232.
15. Nickell, Rice, and Tucker, op. cit. p. 97.
16. Ibid.
17. Ibid.
18. Ibid.
19. Ibid.
20. Ibid.
21. Ibid.
22. Ibid.
23. Ibid.
24. John Dewey, *How We Think* (Boston: D. C. Heath & Company, 1910), pp. 68–78.
25. Martha A. Plonk, "Exploring Interrelationships in a Central-Satellite Decision Complex," *Journal of Home Economics* (December 1968), 789–792.
26. Irma H. Gross, Elizabeth Walbert Crandall, and Marjorie M. Knoll, *Management for Modern Families,* 3rd ed. (New York: Appleton-Century-Crofts, 1973), pp. 224–225.
27. Ibid.
28. Irving L. Janis and Leon Mann, *Decision Making A Psychological Analysis of Conflict, Choice, and Committment* (New York: The Free Press, 1977), p. 48.
29. Ibid. p. 46.
30. Ibid.
31. Ibid. pp. 416–419.
32. Ibid. p. 9.
33. Ibid. pp. 107–116.
34. American Association of Agricultural Editors, *Communications Handbook,* 3rd ed. (Danville, Ill.: The Interstate Printers and Publishers, Inc., 1976), p. 10.
35. Janis and Mann, op. cit., p. 107.
36. American Association of Agricultural Editors, op. cit., p. 10.

37. Janis and Mann, op. cit., p. 109.
38. Deising, op. cit., p. 3.
39. Deacon and Firebaugh, op. cit., pp. 118–119.
40. Gross, Crandall, and Knoll, op. cit., pp. 224–225.

CHAPTER FOUR

The Management Process

Thus far you have examined the concepts of values, goals, standards, and decision making as well as how management takes place in the spheres of interaction. You are probably wondering how each of these relate to your total management.

To attain your desired quality of life you must achieve the goals you have set. These goals whether they are short-range, intermediate, or long-range involve the management process. You might already be achieving your goals. After all, you and others do achieve your goals and in a sense do manage; the question is how well are you and others managing? Are you really managing or merely "coping"?

There is a vast difference between those individuals who are effectively managing and those who are only "coping." "Coping" individuals are working just to maintain their present status quo. The individual who manages achieves a great deal more.

Your knowledge and the meaningful use of the management process will increase the probability of attaining your desired quality of life. To achieve your desired quality of life you set priority rank goals. These priorities and your goals have come from the decisions you have made based on your value structure. Effective management uses the management process as a tool to achieve those components that you have identified as your desired quality of life. The person who drives down the highway of life without a map has no real direction; the individual who does not effectively manage also lacks a basic direction.

Through the management process you can purposefully and actively seek those goals that will enable you to attain your desired quality of life. The use of the management process also aids you to maximize the use of your resources. This method of using your resources and the achievement of your goals will yield a higher degree of positive satisfaction.

Through effective management you are doing more than merely "coping" with your daily life. You are purposely establishing the direction and forward progress you are seeking. The outcome of the management process enhances your sense of well-being, affords the opportunity to assess your roles, and increases the probability of achieving a higher degree of positive satisfaction.

The Management Process

As you begin to explore the management process you might well ask what do I manage? Is management concerned only with me or does it involve others? Will mine and the lives of others become so business-like that we function as a corporation rather than as individuals and a family unit?

Why you manage is actually coupled with the question of what will you manage? You, like every other individual, have limited means and unlimited wants. In other words you want more than you are able to attain or achieve. You have a limited degree of resources available for your use at any given time. Management will enable you not only to more effectively allocate these resources but also to maximize their use. In this manner you can attain more of those wants than before. Your management may involve only you or it may involve others. How many times have you been responsible for the achievement of a mutually desired goal? Thus the question is not have you managed, but how well have you managed?

As you manage is there a danger that you and those around you will begin to function impersonally as a corporation rather than in the context of a human unit? In all honesty yes, there is this possibility, if you let the management process manage you rather than you managing it. However if you use the management process as a tool, this will not occur. It is a tool that will bring many rewards to your life rather than a process to be feared. Management is a learned skill; it involves planning, implementation, and evaluative feedback.

The first phase in the management process is *planning.* Planning involves establishing the sequence and organization. It means a direction is established, the sequence and the organization are established, and a plan emerges which will lead to achieving the goal you have set.

The second phase in the management process is *implementation.* Here you are actually putting the plan into action. As this section takes place you are controlling, checking, and adjusting the plan.

Evaluative feedback, the final phase, is important. As you evaluate the feedback, you identify those parts of the plan which were good and which ones should be changed or modified if the plan is used again.

Planning

The success of this first step is vital to the management process. Deacon and Firebaugh state the following: "Since management cannot occur unless there is a plan of some nature—written or unwritten, general or specific— planning is a necessary function for guiding actions in meeting the demands of the family."[1] Thus planning is essential to management.

What is planning? Are there different kinds of plans? What is specifically involved in planning? Who plans and why? Are there any constraints on planning?

The need to develop a plan is derived from a felt need to resolve a problem, achieve a specific goal, or to satisfy a demand. Regardless of which one is actually taking place, this is the input you are receiving. Your need is to develop and implement a plan that will produce an acceptable outcome. The degree of satisfaction you attain will be dependent upon the completeness of the plan.

Although the demand, goal, event, or problem is the initial input that triggers the necessity for a plan, your values, goals, and standards are also inputs.

These will continually provide input throughout the management process as decisions are made, communication will occur, and the other concepts of management will be employed.

The plan you develop will emerge after you have identified and clarified the demand, goal, problem, or event. From this you will determine the sequence of actions or events needed to achieve the desired outcome. These actions or events will then be placed in an order so that the outcome or events flow smoothly from one to the next until the demand or event is met, the goal is attained, or the problem is resolved. Figure 4.1 shows the planning process.

In order for a valid plan to emerge you must begin by identifying and clarifying the demand, event, problem, or goal. The inputs during this include your values, standards, and any communication you have received. Coupled with these is the input of other goals you have.

As you identify the demand, event, or problem, you are seeking to determine not only the specifics but also the origin. The successful completion of the management process is dependent upon this. In order to do this, you must take the time to identify and clarify the exact nature of the demand that has created the need for a plan to be developed. Even though you have undertaken all of the component parts of the management process, when your procedures are based on only partial knowledge of the demand, the outcome produces questionable or limited satisfaction.

As you identify and clarify the demand initiating the need for a plan your values and standards become sources of input. Both of these function in many ways. Your values help you to determine priorities. Your standards serve as enablers encouraging you to progress to meet the demand. At the same time, they establish the degree of success you desired to obtain.

The other goals you have also serve as input. The demand you are experiencing may be compatible or competing with other goals. Or completion of this goal may be necessary to achieve other goals.

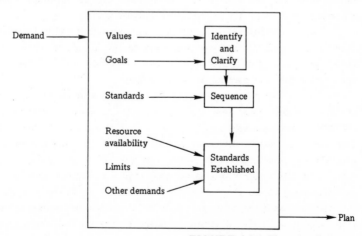

FIGURE 4.1. Planning Process.

Still another source of input is the communication you have received. This communication is decoded and becomes input. This may involve a time frame indicating a deadline for completion. It may indicate the involvement of other individuals; or it may provide additional information.

The inputs of each of these will be enablers as you determine the specificity of the demand that necessitates the emergence of a plan. This specificity is vital. It not only identifies the exact nature of the demand but also helps you to determine the nature and type of the plan you need. As you develop the plan, you need to know the duration and scope of the demand. A demand of short duration necessitates a far different approach than one which will continue for a lengthy period.

The type and extent of the plan you develop will be based upon the input you receive from your values, standards, and communication, as well as your other goals. The identification and clarification of the demand will determine the type of plan and the sequencing and ordering within the framework of the plan.

Types of Planning

The concept of planning can be assessed from different aspects: use and level, or general and specific. These are important to the management process. Knowing which of these aspects are involved will increase your probability of success.

Use

Some plans are devised with the anticipation they will not be used or repeated at any time in the future. Single-use plans are developed in this instance. Other plans are developed with the anticipation they will be repeatedly used when the need arises. These are called repeat-use plans.[2]

Each one of these is important to management. Although basically developed in the same manner, each serves different functions. Single-use plans may center around major events such as planning the fiftieth wedding anniversary celebration for your parents or grandparents.

Since these plans are usually quite detailed in scope, they involve major events or goals. Your values and standards are a major source of input. The priority you attach to attainment will be determined by your value structure. The standards you establish for a successful outcome will also input here. Since you have no prior experience to serve as a guide in developing this plan, it will tend to be more elaborate and detailed than a repeat-use plan. Because of this, you will tend to do more extensive sequencing to insure you will meet your standards of a successful outcome. When the single-use plan involves other individuals, you must decode the communication being received and also incorporate this into the planning.

What single-use plans have you developed? How extensive were they? What were the inputs which affected the development of this plan?

Repeat-use plans may also be referred to as standing plans.[3] They are a valuable tool in management. Repeat-use plans are developed in the anticipation that similar situations, goals, or demands will occur. When they do these plans can be used again to meet the demands. One repeat-use plan you have developed and will continue to use throughout your college career involves moving from your home to your college residence in the fall and reversing this procedure at the end of the academic year.

Repeat-use plans are another valuable management tool; they can be used or modified as the need arises. Throughout your life you will experience demands. In many instances a new demand will be similar to one you have previously experienced. When this occurs, you can utilize a repeat-use plan to meet the new demand. In so doing, the expenditures of your time and energy resources are less than with single-use plans. Repeat-use plans have the foundation of previous experience to build upon. In these instances you are modifying a previous plan rather than developing a completely new one. Therefore your time and energy resource use is decreased.

Repeat-use plans should not be confused with routines and habits you have established over the years. Repeat-use plans are continually modified and reestablished in accordance with the current demand. Habits and routines are not revised. Think about some of the habits and routines you have developed. Have these been revised?

Repeat-use plans tend to center around daily activities and established patterns of work. You have several repeat-use plans. For example, what pattern do you follow to get to your first class in the morning? How do you study for a test? These are repeat-use plans.

These repeat-use plans are useful management tools. However, their continued use may represent a potential management hazard. Repeat-use plans were designed to be modified and revised depending upon the current demand to achieve an identified goal. If this revision and/or modification does not take place, the real value of the repeat-use plan is lost.

General or Specific Planning

A plan may also be a general or a specific one. Plans that involve long-range goals are often rather general. Those directed toward the attainment of an immediate demand are much more specific.

Think about your plans for employment after graduation. At this point, how specific are those plans? Perhaps you have identified a geographical area in which you hope to be employed and the type of career you eventually intend to pursue. However, for the most part, these plans for your life are rather vague. A general plan has been developed but it does not have a great deal of specificity.

On the other hand, there are plans with a high degree of specificity. Your desired outcome is more clearly defined and clarified. The details of the plan have been developed. Your course of action has been established. Unlike general plans, this plan has been carefully considered.

General plans may or may not require continual and on-going consideration and attention. Specific plans do. In order to follow your general plan, you periodically check to ensure you are continuing to follow the indicated course of action. This is not true with specific plans.

This category of planning, too, serves a useful function in management. General planning provides you with an overall direction in meeting long-range demands. Specific planning, on the other hand, is used to resolve the short-range and immediate demands.

Levels

All planning does not occur at the same level. Burk found planning can be divided into the levels of master planning, operational planning, and day-to-day planning.[4] You use each of these throughout your management.

Master planning can be viewed as the planning that occurs as objectives and goals are established and policies are created.[5] Although at first glance, master planning may appear to be synonomous with general planning, such is not the case. General planning occurs as you move in an identified direction to meet a specific demand. Master planning is used to identify the goals and objectives of your desired quality of life (your life plan) or the direction you intend for your life to take in the future.

You have a master plan for your life. In addition to this, you have operational plans. Operational plans may occur within the shelter sphere as well as those developed for individual use.

You have general plans which is the master plan you have developed for your life. In this instance your goals and objectives, although somewhat vague, have been determined. As this plan has evolved you have also identified the goals you will need to achieve in order to progress.

In order to progress, you use operational planning. Operation plans may be developed to encompass individual action or the actions of several individuals. In either case, they emerge as a result of a specific demand or desired goal. This planning generally involves actions that reoccur on a frequent and regular basis. The demand may originate as a felt need by a single individual or to achieve an overall objective or goal for a collective group. The weekly time schedule you develop to meet the demands placed upon you by your college courses is one form of operational planning. You may also use operational planning to meet the demands of employment or household operation.

Day-to-day planning involves those continuously and repetitious actions you undertake. Many times you don't think about the day-to-day planning you actually do. This planning uses repeat-use plans. Do you really plan the procedure you follow when getting up in the morning? In most cases, you do not. You might have when you first arrived on the college campus, until you had established a reliable day-to-day plan. Day-to-day planning enables you to use your time and energy for other efforts rather than in planning your daily activities.

Just as you have different levels of plans, you also will continue to do both single-use and repeat-use plans. At the same time, you have some general and some specific plans. Each of these aspects of planning are important to your management.

Planning includes developing a sequence of actions or behaviors designed to meet the demand. In order to accomplish this, you identify and clarify the demand. The plan is developed to meet this demand.

Sequencing

As a phase of the planning component of the management process sequencing involves identifying the tasks, actions, or behaviors necessary to meet the demand. Later, these must be placed in a logical order. As you identify the tasks, actions, or behaviors you should also assess the length of time needed to complete each. This information will be necessary to establish the order of the plan. Sequencing also involves identifying the logical pattern or order in which the action or behavior should take place.

Sequencing, therefore, involves identifying the actions or behaviors necessary to meet the demand. As these are identified, the length of time needed for each will be determined. Sources of input here will be your values, past experiences, communication, other goals and demands as well as input being received from other spheres of interaction.

Ordering

Although at first glance, ordering may appear to be synonymous with sequencing, it is not. As you undertook sequencing, you were identifying the actions and behaviors. The procedure of ordering commences when sequencing terminates.

Using sequencing information, you will determine which actions or behaviors can be clustered together to be undertaken simultaneously and which must occur separately. This phase also includes assessing the specific resources and the amount of each resource needed to produce the desired outcome.

Your standards are a source of input in this phase. As you establish the logical order you will also determine the standards for the anticipated actions and behaviors. During the implementation component, these standards will be used to measure the forward progress of the plan.

Although sequencing may have identified where, when, and to what extent other individuals may be involved in the plan, it is imperative that this be taken into account as you undertake ordering. The inclusion of others is an important factor to be considered. The ordering you determine for yourself will vary from the one which involves others. You may or may not be fully conversant with their skills and capabilities. When others are involved you will need to provide for a continuous and on-going flow of communication. You may also need to incorporate other aspects such as supervision, training periods, or orientation sessions.

During sequencing you identified the needed resources and the anticipated length of time necessary to achieve the outcome. Ordering involves establishing not only the logical order for completion but also making certain the needed resources are available when they are required and in sufficient quantity to meet the standards you have established. As you undertake this, you may well encounter actions or behaviors which place a drain upon a few resources. During the process of ordering you can anticipate this and make any possible adjustments.

You have examined how planning involves sequencing and ordering. Inputs into this component part of the management process originate from within and outside the individual sphere. As you undertake these, you are clarifying the actions and behaviors involved, identifying and allocating the needed resources, establishing a logical ordering, and if so, assigning actions and responsibilities to others. Both sequencing and ordering are vital to the planning component if the plan is to produce the desired outcome and the anticipated satisfaction. This must be completed before implementation occurs if success is to be obtained.

Enablers and Constraints in Planning

Have you found some plans are easier to develop than others? Have you noticed some individuals seem to have more difficulty in planning than others? If you implemented the plans developed by someone else have you encountered some excellent and some inadequate plans? After all, isn't planning just that—planning?

As you have seen, planning has different levels and uses. When you plan, you should be aware of the factors that may encourage or inhibit the process. Elements which encourage planning are called enablers. Constraints are factors which inhibit or restrict planning.

It would be much easier if a list of enablers and constraints could be developed. Then all you would do is avoid the constraints and use the enablers. Unfortunately this is not possible. There are times when some factors are enablers while at other times they can be constraints.

The planning will not take place until you recognize the necessity to develop a plan. This occurs when you become aware of a demand being placed upon you. Thus the process of recognition is an enabler.

There are numerous enablers which aid in planning. One of the most important is your motivation. Your motivation is much different when attainment of the plan has a high degree of importance than when it does not. The extent to which you personally are involved is another motivational enabler.

Still other enablers are your talents, abilities, and skills. Each time you undertake the planning component you increase your skills and abilities. These coupled with your talents, previous experience, and your other management skills also become enablers.

Constraints in the planning component would be the absence of one or more of these enablers. Motivation may be expressed in positive or negative terms. When it is positive it is an enabler. However, negative motivation would be a constraint. Numerous categories of planning enablers and constraints have been proposed by various authors. For the purposes of clarity only the broad aspect of plan involvement will be discussed herein.

Plan involvement refers to the aspects of complexity, type, duration, and number of people involved in the plan. Each of these can be either an enabler or a constraint.

A simple plan incorporating a limited number of actions or behaviors could be relatively easy to develop. In this instance, the simplicity of the plan is an enabler. As an increase in actions or behaviors is required to complete the plan, the complexity of the plan also increases. This complexity may be a constraint or an enabler. Can you cite instances where either of these has occurred in your planning?

Whether your plan is a general or a specific one may be an enabler or a constraint. The level and use of the plan may also be either a constraint or an enabler. A simple specific plan could be an enabler. So, too, could a broad general plan. The opposite might also be true.

Master plans may act as enablers for operational planning. Operational plans may serve as enablers for day-to-day planning. The reverse could also occur. Can you think of instances where one level of planning could be a constraint upon another?

Since repeat-use plans are continually revised and modified to meet the current demand, they are valuable enablers. Single-use plans are intended to be used only once. In these instances you do not have the benefit of previous experience to serve as a guide. Thus the development of a single-use plan could be a constraint. Like the levels of planning, the opposite could also occur. Can you think of instances where repeat-use plans were a constraint, or where a single use plan was an enabler?

The duration or length of the plan may also be a constraint or an enabler. Assume you have just been told semester examinations will be given two weeks early. Would this be an enabler or a constraint for you?

Other enablers or constraints might be the involvement of people. As you think back to instances where this has occurred, what enablers were present? What constraints existed? Are there ways that some of the constraints could have become enablers?

Within the planning component, there are both enablers and constraints. As you undertake the planning component of the management process you need to be cognizant not only of their existence but also their effect upon your planning. This awareness could enhance your potential degree of success. Unless you are aware of their existence, your planning is based on insufficient data. If you do not make adequate provision for potential constraints, you are developing a plan using inadequate data.

Implementation

Implementation is the second component in the management process. It is here your plan is put into action. This involves the phases of controlling the action, checking the progress, and adjusting the plan where and when necessary.

As shown in Figure 4.2, the emphasis of this component is the forward movement of the plan to meet the demand. In order to do this, action is taking place. At the same time, the two other phases of implementation are also occurring. There are instances when all three phases may be taking place simultaneously. At other times, only one or two are involved. Each of these phases, however, is vital to the implementation component of the management process.

Controlling the Action

During implementation, three different phases may be taking place almost simultaneously. "Controlling" is the actual "doing" of the previously established ordering of actions or behaviors. Resources previously allocated during planning are now used. The forward progress of the plan takes place. As actions or behaviors are undertaken, standards are being observed. Decisions previously made during planning are implemented. Your major responsibility is the "doing" of the designated action. Since no decisions are required during this phase, your activity is directed to the completion of actions or behaviors.

When the plan incorporates action assigned to other individuals they may be independently pursuing these, each of which is necessary to the total plan.

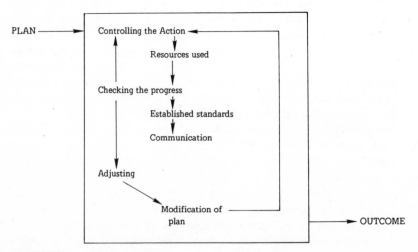

FIGURE 4.2.   Implementation.

However, they may or may not be involved at the same time nor working together. Since this is the work phase, the emphasis is placed upon completion of
assignments regardless of who is actually assigned to complete the action.

Checking the Progress

Deacon and Firebaugh refer to checking the progress as the examination of the
action.[6] They further indicate there are two distinct types of checking: planned
and unplanned.[7] Throughout this phase of implementation, your responsibility
lies in checking the progress of the action taking place against the established
plan. Hahn refers to this phase as measuring performance of the action against
the plan.[8]

The checking you do will be to determine if the action taking place is
being done in accordance with the previously established plan. That is, to
ascertain that tasks are being completed in the designated order, standards are
being met, resources previously allocated are being used, and the time frame
is being observed.

The checking phase of implementation serves the function of providing
you with information. Through checking you will be able to identify where and
if any changes in the plan are needed, possible deviations from the plan, and the
extent of the progress being made at any point.

The process of checking can be done objectively and subjectively. One
objective measure is the standards you previously established. Are these being
met? As you check these standards, you may find the original standards were
too high, too low, or just correct. If the first two instances occur, you need to
make adjustments.

Still another objective measure is the time frame you established. Is it
being met? Are there changes to be made or considered? Worker productivity
may also be an objective measure. Are the individuals who were assigned various
tasks completing them in the manner and rate you anticipated? If not, why not?

Subjective measures are also used in the checking phase. These measures
often involve your senses and/or feelings and attitudes. Although no identifiable
measure can be placed upon these they are, nonetheless, a part of checking.
Examples of subjective checking might be a feeling of uneasiness about a particular scheduling. If other persons are involved, there might be a sense that an
individual does not completely understand the assigned task. Communication
may indicate that an uncertainty or insufficient skills or knowledge exists.
You should remember subjective checking is measured in terms of your values
and decoding of communication. As such its validity is highly questionable
if this is the only method of checking. However, when used with objective
measures it serves as an additional checking method.

When others are involved in implementation, your role needs to be clearly
defined. Is your role supervisory, as a worker, or as a co-worker? This is a vital
part of implementation and particularly so during checking. As noted throughout this text, role perceptions are a factor in management. Nowhere is this more

apparent than in the checking phase of implementation when other individuals are involved.

It is difficult indeed for one person to undertake and pursue a plan developed by another individual. This difficulty is increased when the individual doing the action is not aware of the assigned roles or role perceptions. If the communication between the planner and the worker is minimal, the difficulty is further increased.

Involvement of other individuals in the plan means you must define and observe your role during implementation. You must also make certain communication lines have been established and are maintained throughout implementation. Once your role has been established, you must observe it throughout. Inconsistent role performance will impede the forward progress of the action. Throughout implementation, you will also need to continually check the existing lines of communication. A breakdown in communication could result in insufficient action being taken by one or more of the individuals involved in the action.

Adjusting the Plan

The data obtained during checking is utilized in the adjusting phase of implementation. This phase may not occur during the initial stage of implementation. However, it should not be left until all or the major portion of the action has taken place. Just as checking is done throughout the implementation phase, adjusting, too, should occur when data from checking denotes developing patterns or trends indicating the necessity for an adjustment. Indications of the necessity for adjustments could originate from numerous sources. These may point to one or more potential alterations such as changing a time frame, reexamination of standards, reallocating resources, or reassigning responsibilities and/or people. To ascertain the necessity for change, analyze the informational data obtained from the checking. Your analysis should be directed toward identifying factors indicating the need for alteration.

Identifying the need for adjustment should incorporate assessing both the indicators and causes. You need to look beyond the obvious surface indicators. When a worker is not completing the assigned action, were the standards set too high? Did you assume the worker had more skills than those which actually existed? Or does a communication gap exist? In each of these instances, the corrective action taken would be quite different. Isolation of the causal factor is imperative before corrective action is done.

The ability to adjust an existing plan requires a certain degree of flexibility. You must not only be able to recognize the need for adjustments but also have the flexibility to make the changes. You have probably met someone who developed and implemented a plan. However, when the indicators clearly demonstrated the plan would not succeed, she or he continued to follow the original plan despite evidence to the contrary.

Adjusting necessitates ability to recognize the need for a change and identify the factors indicating change. It also means accepting these factors as change agents. You must be receptive to the elements of change and be willing to alter the plan when necessary. This requires flexibility. When all of these abilities are present, the adjustment phase of implementation can be a viable tool.

Enablers and Constraints in Implementation

Enablers and constraints occur not only in planning but also in the implementation component of the management process. Enablers and constraints in planning are those factors that encourage or inhibit planning. Certain inherent factors tend to encourage or inhibit implementation as well. It is also true that any single factor or combination of factors could be either an enabler or a constraint.

During controlling, three different types of enablers or constraints exist. One deals with the management skills possessed by you and/or others who are undertaking the action or behavior. The second involves the actual plan itself while the third centers around where the action or implementation is taking place.

The extent and use of existing management skills can be either an enabler or a constraint. Your knowledge and use of work simplification techniques can enable you to complete the assigned task in the prescribed time allotted. Or as was cited earlier, when an individual who does not possess the high degree of skills and abilities needed for a specific task undertakes the task, a constraint may be present.

When other individuals are involved, your communications may be either a constraint or an enabler. If it is to be an enabler, this communication should extend far beyond task assignment and should be established early in the management process. The communication to each person should include: the complete plan; individual task assignment within the total plan; the standard criteria established; the criteria for the anticipated outcome; the frequency and types of assessment measures; role perceptions of the planner, worker, and supervisor; established lines of communication; and additional information to assist in the forward progress of implementation.

Your plan can also be an enabler. The degree and depth of sequencing you have done in the planning step will affect whether it is in reality an enabler or a constraint. Those enablers and constraints put in during the planning component will have an affect upon the implementation.

Where and under what circumstances the action or behavior takes place can also be an enabler or a constraint. Combined with these two are the additional aspects of the work surface, equipment, materials, supplies, and work areas. These include the materials, supplies, tools, and the space needed to complete the action. The absence or presence of these determines whether they are enablers or constraints. If you have insufficient space, a work surface that is too high or low, or inadequate equipment, a constraint would exist.

As action is initiated and progress is made, the checking phase is instituted. Potential enablers and constraints are also present. During the planning component you designated several enablers such as sequence of tasks, task assignment, and the standard criteria. Each of these are objective measures. As enablers they provide information, indicate progress, and identify performance. Their absence or inadequacy would be a constraint on this phase. Through checking these against actual progress being made you can identify if or where deviations are occurring. In this sense they are enablers. The absence of this assessment or the misinterpretation of indicators of needed change would be an additional constraint.

The adjusting phase, like the other two, also has both enablers and constraints. In the process of checking you received information. As you receive information you need to identify which sources are valid indicators of a need for change. When a plan deviation occurs, what is creating it? Is it insufficient skills, poor task assignment, improper sequencing, lack of motivation, or are there other possible causes? Isolation of the causation factor is vital before you can determine if, when, or where to make any adjustments. Accurate assessment is an enabler. The corrective action you take may be either an enabler or constraint. Inappropriate or insufficient corrective action would be a constraint. Other enablers and/or constraints would involve the number of new decisions you make, when you make them, your willingness to undertake new decisions, and how effectively you employ the decision-making process.

It must be apparent the enablers and constraints that exist within the implementation step involve the planning component, the analysis of information being received, the action taking place, and any adjustments made. It should also be apparent that an increase in the number of individuals taking part in the action may also represent enablers or constraints.

Your initial communication and the lines of communication you have established are enablers. Insufficient or inadequate communication can become a severe constraint. Communication encompasses more than just task assignment. If it is to be a valid enabler, it must be continuous and on-going throughout the entire management process.

As was indicated earlier, other individuals involved in implementation must be aware not only of their respective roles but of your role as well. If these individuals are to actively undertake the action assigned to them, they must be knowledgeable of the plan, their role, and the criteria being used to measure performance and progress.

Knowledge of roles and tasks does not terminate when the individual undertakes the assignment. You, too, must be knowledgeable and assume your identified role. Just as the plan and each individual can be an enabler, so too, are you. Knowledge, acceptance, and assumption of the role you have assigned and communicated to others is a vital enabler. Constraints occur when you assign yourself a role, communicate this to others, and then you modify or fail to assume this role. You have communicated your role as being a supervisor. However if during implementation you actively assume the worker role and not the supervisor role, you have switched roles. In so doing you become a constraint.

The degree of success you achieve during implementation is dependent upon your recognition of enablers and constraints. You should use enablers to the fullest extent while minimizing constraints as much as possible. Regardless of whether implementation is done by you alone or with a number of individuals, enablers and constraints must be recognized. The lack of awareness or use of an enabler may result in it becoming a constraint. In many cases a constraint can become an enabler if you are aware of the probable effect and make the necessary adjustments. The plan is yours. Its success will depend upon the degree to which you recognize and use enablers while minimizing existing constraints.

Evaluative Feedback

An inherent and integral part of the management process is evaluative feedback. All too often in the glow of achieving your goal, this step is lightly passed over or inadequately completed. The individual who does this has lost much of the value of this component. The result could be inadequate or poor management in the future.

When limited solely to an analysis of the outcome, much of the value of evaluative feedback is also lost. This is not intended to discount the importance of the outcome but rather to denote that evaluative feedback encompasses more than just the outcome produced from the management process.

But just what is evaluative feedback and how can it help in your management? Evaluative feedback, as shown in Figure 4.3, is the assessment and/or

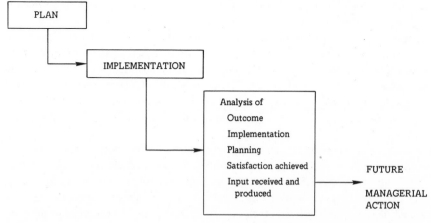

FIGURE 4.3. Evaluation Feedback.

analysis of the outcome, each component and phase of the management process, and of your management skills.

Although evaluative feedback may center around the outcome, it has many other functions. In addition to assessing and/or analyzing the outcome, evaluative feedback is a source of information that can be used in the future. Assessment and/or analysis should be viewed in both positive and constructive connotations. You should assess the total management process. During checking you employed evaluative devices in order to obtain information and to measure the forward progress of the plan. Although this was evaluative in nature, a more thorough analysis should be done. This includes assessing the changes you made during the adjustment phase of implementation, the analysis of the initial plan, and any changes made. In other words, evaluative feedback involves going back over all of the phases of the management process, seeking to ascertain positive results and areas of possible improvement.

As you manage throughout your life, you will tend to use more repeat-use than single-use plans. As was examined earlier, repeat-use plans are continually modified and revised to fit the current situation. Evaluative feedback can be a valuable enabler. In the absence of adequately conducted evaluative feedback you may be modifying and revising repeat-use plans on the basis of insufficient evidence.

As evaluative feedback occurs, the information concerning your management skills will become apparent. This information can then be used to point to areas where you have a high degree of competency as well as areas where you might need to improve skills. Therefore this can be used to continually reinforce and improve your skills in planning, implementing, communicating, supervising, checking, and adjusting.

Your plan and its implementation were done in anticipation of a specific outcome, one that would yield an anticipated degree of satisfaction. In other words, the outcome would not only produce satisfaction, but it would occur in a specified degree. Evaluative feedback enables you to measure the degree of satisfaction you achieved against the satisfaction you expected. The satisfaction that resulted may have been what you anticipated or it may have been more or less than what you expected. Deacon and Firebaugh express any differences you encountered between anticipated and obtained satisfaction as being either positive or negative.[9] When the satisfaction you receive is greater than what you anticipated, it is said to be positive. Negative feedback occurs when the satisfaction is less than what was expected. When the satisfaction yielded is either positive or negative you need to determine the causal factors which produced this outcome.

Evaluative feedback can and does serve many functions in your management. Since it is useful in all aspects of management, failure to complete this component may negate the value of the management process. In order to reap the benefits of evaluative feedback, care should be taken to ensure all aspects are given as much attention as the other components of the management process.

Summary

The management process is a tool used to achieve your goals. Through its use you are better able to attain your desired quality of life. Resources must be allocated and used in daily life. Through the management process you can identify the demands being placed upon these resources. This knowledge then is used for effective allocation and use of resources. Effective management results.

There are three components in the management process. These are planning, implementation, and evaluative feedback. Planning involves developing a sequence of actions or behaviors within an overall organizational structure. There are different levels and types of plans. Implementation involves putting the plan into action. As progress takes place through implementation, checking the forward movement of the plan and making adjustments where needed occurs. Checking includes ascertaining where and to what extent progress is being made while making certain that communication lines remain open. Adjusting takes place when the information obtained from checking indicates deviations, patterns, or trends are developing which necessitate changing the plan. Corrective action is taken on the basis of this information. Evaluative feedback is concerned with assessing not only the final outcome of the plan but also the phases of all of the components. This includes the initial plan, the checking phase, any adjustments made, and any corrective action. Evaluative feedback is an important part of the management process since it will become part of your past experience to be drawn upon as future use of the management process occurs.

Throughout the management process enablers and constraints are considered. Enablers are used to enhance the plan. Constraints are recognized and minimized as much as possible.

Effective management recognizes the validity of the management process. Through its use you are able to better attain your desired quality of life, use your resources more effectively, and give direction to your life. Effective use of the management process means the difference between "coping" to maintain the status quo and achieving your lifetime plan.

ACTIVITIES

1. Identify the repeat-use plans you rely upon frequently and two different single-use plans you have developed. Analyze one of the repeat-use plans and one single-use plan in terms of your management skills in using the management process.
2. Select one of your repeat-use plans and complete the following:
   a. List the sequencing that takes place.

b. Identify the standards for each task involved.

c. State the evaluative feedback that occurs.

d. Discuss the modifications you will make when this plan is used again.

3. Select two single-use plans you have developed and complete the following:

a. Identify the function, situation, or event for which the plan was developed.

b. Indicate why you developed a single use plan rather than modify a repeat-use plan.

c. Discuss the scope of each plan and list the sequencing that took place.

d. State the outcome for each plan and the evaluative feedback.

4. You have developed a master plan for your lifetime. You also have general and specific goals for the future. Each of these have either general or specific plans that you have developed. Starting with your master plan, then your general, and finally your specific plans

a. Identify the goals or objectives of each plan and indicate the order in which each plan occurs.

b. State the sequencing of each plan.

c. Indicate the anticipated outcome for each plan.

d. Record the enablers and constraints you anticipate for each plan.

5. In question 5, you have developed a sequencing of plans for your lifetime. How and when would each plan be implemented? For each of the plans, indicate how you would

a. Control the action.

b. Check the progress.

c. Make adjustments.

d. Identify indicators showing the need for corrective action.

6. Refer to your master plan and answer the following:

a. What values have influenced the development of the master plan?

b. What standards have you established which indicate progress?

c. What do you anticipate will be the input of attainment upon your spheres of interaction?

d. What input do you anticipate receiving from the spheres of interaction as various parts of the master plan are implemented?

7. Select one goal you have recently achieved. Clarify your goal, state your plan, and indicate how you implemented the plan. Describe the evaluative feedback you received. Complete the following:

a. Identify the resources used and the effect of this utilization upon other aspects of your management.

b. Analyze the effectiveness of your management.

c. State the enablers and constraints.

d. Indicate the adjustments you would make prior to using the plan again.

e. Assess your management skills and the satisfaction you achieved.

f. Discuss how and to what extent the attainment of this goal has become input upon your spheres of interaction.

MARIE AND LARRY

Marie and Larry are co-chairpersons for the dorm Spring Dance which is six weeks away. Their committee is composed of two members from each of the seven floors of a co-ed dorm for a total of fourteen people.

Although the committee has met at least once every two weeks for the last three months, nothing seems to get done. Larry is always griping about how they seem to spend at least two hours on every committee meeting but there are still so many things to be decided and to be done. Marie is quick to point out that this just isn't true. They have picked the theme of the dance, contracted the band, and most of the table decorations are planned.

Larry and Marie are constantly arguing about what should be done at each meeting. Marie's idea is to have separate meetings for each item that needs to be accomplished. Her idea is that each meeting should be devoted to the accomplishment of a single task. If they do this then everything will be finished by the time the dance starts.

Larry wants to have a committee meeting this week and assign each floor one of the remaining tasks. Each task is to be completed by a certain date well in advance of the dance. Marie is opposed to this. She feels everyone should be involved in each task and all work should be done by the total group. Besides, she feels it's more fun to work as a group and more gets done this way.

Larry is upset about not only how many meetings have been held but also because less than half of the committee attended the last meeting and the one before it. Marie wants to have another committee meeting tonight and every night until everything is done so Larry will quit griping.

Discussion Questions

1. Why are Larry and Marie constantly fighting about the Spring Dance and the progress of the committee?
2. Identify the type of planning that is being done, the task standards, and possible task assignments. Why does Larry want to assign tasks to floors and Marie does not?
3. Determine all of the tasks to be accomplished and their sequencing. Now develop a plan to accomplish these tasks.
4. What are the resources, enablers, and constraints that are present? What is the evaluative feedback Larry and Marie are receiving?
5. If you were a member of this committee, what would you do and how would you feel about serving on the committee? If you were asked to serve on the committee next year with Larry as the chairperson, would you do so? Why or why not? If Marie were the chairperson, why or why not?

GLOSSARY

Adjusting A phase of implementation in which information and data obtained from checking forms the basis for alteration of the plan in order to achieve the desired goal.

Checking A phase of implementation involving both planned and unplanned evaluation of the forward progress of the plan, and to ascertain the degree to which standards are being achieved.

Constraint A causal factor that restricts or impedes the action, event, situation, or occurrence.

Controlling A phase of implementation in which the action of the plan is completed by the individual or under the supervision of the individual.

Enabler A resource, event, situation, mechanism, human capability, or fact that affects the attainment of a desired goal or objective.

Evaluative Feedback The third component in the management process in which the assessment of preceeding components and phases, the outcome produced, and the management skills used is conducted by the individual.

General Plan A broad long-range plan lacking specificity that is directed toward the attainment of general goals and which does not require continual and on-going attention.

Implementation A component in the management process in which the plan is put into action. The three phases of implementation are (a) controlling the action, (b) checking the progress, and (c) adjusting the plan.

Management Process The development of a plan to provide purposeful action to achieve a desired goal. The three components of the management process are (a) planning, (b) implementation, and (c) evaluative feedback.

Master Plan A broad plan developed to achieve objectives, goals, and policies to attain your desired quality of life.

Negative Feedback Occurs when the satisfaction of the outcome is less than what was anticipated.

Operational Plan A plan involving the operations undertaken on a regular and frequent basis by an individual or family unit.

Planning The first component in the management process in which the sequence or series of actions or behaviors are developed to achieve a goal, resolve a problem, or meet a demand. This component involves making decisions, sequencing activities, allocating resources, and organizing the flow of action.

Positive Feedback Occurs when the satisfaction achieved from the outcome is greater than what was anticipated.

Repeat-use Plan A plan developed in the anticipation it will be modified and frequently used in similar situations, for similar demands or events, or to resolve like problems. It is also called a standing plan.

Sequencing A phase of the planning component of the management process in which all tasks necessary to achieve the goal are placed in a logical order, the standards for each task are established, and task assignments are made.

Single-Use Plan A plan developed for a specific function, event, or activity with the anticipation it will not be used again.

Specific Plan A carefully developed plan having specificity that requires continual and on-going attention in order to achieve the stated goal.

Task Assignment The designation of a specific individual to complete a certain task.

Task Ordering The establishment of the logical progression by which tasks will be completed.

Task Standard The objective criterion established for the completion of a specific task.

REFERENCES

1. Ruth E. Deacon and Francille M. Firebaugh, *Home Management Context and Concepts* (Boston: Houghton Mifflin Company, 1975), p. 167.
2. Irma H. Gross, Elizabeth Walbert Crandall, and Marjorie M. Knoll, *Management for Modern Families,* 3rd ed. (New York: Appleton-Century-Crofts, 1973), pp. 298–299.
3. Ibid.
4. Marguerite C. Burk, "Food Economic Behavior in Systems Terms," *Journal of Home Economics* (May 1979), 321.
5. Ibid.
6. Deacon and Firebaugh, op. cit., p. 204.
7. Ibid., p. 206.
8. Julia Mae Scheiver Hahn, *Families Control of the Allocation of Financial Resources for the College Education of Their Children* as cited by Gross, Crandall, and Knoll, op. cit., p. 318.
9. Deacon and Firebaugh, op. cit., p. 233.

CHAPTER FIVE

Resources

As you develop and implement different plans, what resources do you use? What do you immediately think of when you hear the term *resources?* Is it the growing concern about the increasing consumption of our natural resources? Repeatedly the mass media is being used to urge citizens to curtail their consumption of these resources. The federal government has recognized the increasing scarcity of natural resources and is trying to identify possible substitutes. Nations, states, communities, businesses, industries, and people have resources. Each one draws upon their respective resources to achieve goals, objectives, and meet demands.

What are your resources? How do you use them? Why should you be concerned about your resources? Are some more readily available than others? Can they be classified?

The term *resources* has been referred to many times throughout this textbook. Mention has been made of their use and allocation as well as their availability. Just how do you determine their limits? Does everyone have the same resources? Or do some have more than others?

The term *resources* can be viewed in several different contexts. The retail merchant may well list his or her resources as being the store inventory, sales personnel, building structures, financial status, and consumers. The manufacturer might also include such things as the raw materials and production equipment. When this term is used herein, *resources* refers to those tangible and intangible components you use to achieve your goals, objectives, and to meet demands. Resources vary for individuals, communities, states, and nations. Each has different ones. The degree to which each occurs and each one's availability also differs.

Role and Scope of Resources

When your goal is to write a term paper, how do you go about achieving this goal? What resources do you use? If you made a list of your resources on the basis of the definition just given, you would probably include the books, periodicals, and pamphlets in your campus library, your time, perhaps your course instructor, paper, and pens. But would these be your only resources? What about your writing skills, other courses you have completed, your educational attainment to date, people and agencies within the community, classmates, and your typewriter? Were you really aware you used all of these resources to complete a term paper? Can you think of other resources you might also have used?

113

Each time you identify a goal, develop and implement a plan, attain a desired outcome, or meet a demand, you are using resources. In fact, as you read this textbook, you are using resources. Throughout our daily lives, resources are used on a continual basis. The question then is not whether you use resources, but how they are allocated.

You have many resources. If you are like most people you are not aware of all of your resources. Consequently, you probably do not use them. Nor do you probably use to the fullest extent those you do recognize.

Resources have a definite role in your management. They are the enablers you use to achieve your goals, objectives, and meet demands. Since resources are enablers, it is important each is used in the most effective manner. To do this, you need to recognize all of your resources, not just those that are most apparent. This recognition enables you to also identify the limits of each. Once you have done this, the decision-making process is used to allocate these resources to bring about the highest degree of satisfaction.

In using resources there is an "opportunity cost" factor. As you use a resource to accomplish a task, complete a goal, or meet a demand, you have decreased its availability for future use. The difference between "coping" and managing lies in recognizing the "opportunity costs" of using resources. This knowledge is used to make more effective choices.

Some resources exist to a larger amount than others. Each has a relative degree of importance to you. Some are more readily replaced than others. If you use a resource in its entirety to accomplish a desired task, goal, or meet a demand, it will not be available for other goals or demands. The "opportunity cost" of a resource will be dependent upon its importance to you, the amount consumed, and when or if it can be readily replaced.

Assume for a moment one of your resources has little if any importance to you. Would you be more willing to completely use this one? In all probability, you would. How reluctant are you to spend all of your money? If you know you will receive more tomorrow are you more likely to spend the money you have today? As resources are allocated and used the "opportunity cost" factor should be considered.

One of your resources is time. How have you used this resource today? Did your use yield a high degree of satisfaction? What were the opportunity costs involved in your consumption of time? Does your time resource have various degrees of importance on different days of the week? How would you rate your use of time resource this past week?

Resources are continually used. As you plan, you make decisions to allocate your resources. Throughout implementation you use resources. The decisions you make and the resources you use affect other resources and future decisions. Resources have a definite role in your management. As you recognize, allocate, and use more of your resources, your management takes on new dimensions. You progress from just "coping" with daily life to becoming its manager.

Classification of Resources

Why are resources classified? What function does classification serve in management? Resources can be classified according to their source of origin or their use within the spheres of interaction. Through the examination of these classifications you are better able to identify your resources, the availability of each, and probable ways each could be allocated. The study of resource classification in reality, is an enabler for your management.

Although there are a number of methods of classifying resources, only two will be used herein. Deacon and Firebaugh use the classification of human and material.[1] Gross, Crandall, and Knoll use two classifications: human and nonhuman and economic and noneconomic.[2] The classification of human and nonhuman, in most cases, is almost synonymous with human and material. The latter term will be used herein for matters of clarity.

Human and Material Resources

Human and material resources is a method of classifying by point of origin. Deacon and Firebaugh define material resources as those tangibles which belong to you; are available for your use; but are not physically or mentally a part of your being.[3] They further define human resources as your less tangible personal characteristics and attributes.[4]

Using these definitions, your human resources are those which originate internally and exist because of the person you have become. Any other resources available for your use are classified as being material ones.

This method of classification divides resources into two identifiable groups. In this classification, it is often much easier to isolate material rather than human resources. Material resources are, for the most part, tangible in form and can readily be determined. These resources consist of your personal and family possessions such as cars, home, and financial status. This broad definition also encompasses those resources available to you within your community, state, and nation such as agencies, people, recreational facilities, and parks.

Less easily identified are your human resources. These comprise such tangibles as your educational attainment, hobbies, interests, personality, skills, abilities, and all other aspects of your individuality.

This method of classification affords you the opportunity to put into two groupings those resources available for your use. It is the simplest method of classification. Using it you can readily identify those resources which originate internally and those which do so externally. This method of classification often aids in identifying additional resources which might not have been previously considered. For instance, have you ever thought of your city parks and recreational facilities as potential resources?

Economic and Noneconomic Resources

In the classification proposed by Gross, Crandall, and Knoll, resources are separated according to their utilization.[5] These authors define economic resources as having the characteristics of being scarce, transferable, measurable, and usable for production purposes.[6] Noneconomic resources are defined as those which are not involved in services, production, human capital, tangible or material goods.[7]

The major distinction of the two lies in their utilization. Noneconomic resources involve your nonproductive consumption and personal characteristics such as your beliefs, religion, loyalty, and pride.[8] Your productive resources such as land, labor, capital, household operation, and other forms of production constitute your economic elements.

The emphasis here is whether the resource is being used in a consumptive manner or a productive one while in the previous classification, resources were categorized by their point of origin. As such, the present method of classification places emphasis upon your value hierarchy. You might classify a specific resource as noneconomic while another person might consider the same resource as being economic.

Identifying resources in this manner allows you to not only ascertain the specific resource but at the same time assess its potential use in the management process. Using this method of classification, you begin to determine potential utilization. This process is important in that not only do you categorize but you also consider how resources might be used within the management process.

Use of Resources

Throughout the management process, resources are used as enablers. In the planning component you allocated resources as you established the sequencing. You also allocate resources for various actions. During implementation resources are used. Still other resources are called upon for evaluative feedback. In each instance, the resources are human or material, economic or noneconomic.

The success of the management process depends upon your recognition, allocation, and use of resources. In order to effectively do this, you need to begin by understanding how resources can be allocated and used.

Resource allocation depends upon determining how resources are used and the existing limitations of each. There are times when either substituting one resource for another or using one to serve a specific purpose can increase the availability or enhance another one.

Each potential resource you contemplate using should be examined in terms of its availability and quality. Gross, Crandall, and Knoll use the terms *quantitative* and *qualitative* to express these aspects. *Quantitative* is used to express the supply or availability of the resource.[9] This measure refers to the limitations of the resource. Time is a limited resource in that there are only 24 hours in each day. Your energy can also be measured in terms of its limitations.

Qualitative refers to the quality of the resource or its usefulness to you.[10] You may have a resource but it is of poor quality. Others may be available but have little if any real usefulness. On the other hand, you may have resources which have a high degree of usefulness but are of poor quality. For instance, an individual may possess a typewriter but not have good typing skills.

In allocating resources you need to determine the qualitative and quantitative measures of each. If you have readily available resources but they are of a poor or low quality, extensively allocating their use may be questionable. On the other hand, allocating a highly limited resource means it will not be available for another use.

Assume you have complete accessibility to a car whenever you need it. However, this car is very difficult to start. It can only be driven on sunny days and never when it rains or the humidity is above 50 percent. The outside temperature must be at least 78 degrees Fahrenheit or the car will not continue to run. How would you rate this car as a quantitative and qualitative resource?

Once the qualitative and quantitative aspects of a resource has been determined, your allocation should be concerned with the possible uses of these resources within the management process. Resources, according to Deacon and Firebaugh, can be used in managerial activities for purposes of exchanging, consuming, protecting, transferring, producing, or saving-investing.[11]

How you allocate resources can have both an immediate and long-range effect upon your management. The intended function of resource use should be a factor in your allocation.

Exchanging

Sometimes you exchange one resource for another. In this instance the value of the resource has not been altered—only its form. You exchange money resources for consumer products in the marketplace. When you purchased your textbooks at the beginning of the term you exchanged resources. In this instance an exchange of two material resources has taken place. You may also exchange human resources, such as time and energy, for a material resource such as a salary, goods, or a service. Economic and noneconomic resources can be exchanged. Each time you use your productive skills instead of making a purchase in the marketplace, you are exchanging an economic resource for a noneconomic one.

Resources can also be exchanged within the spheres of interaction. You and another person may exchange resources. Two individuals who agree to exchange task assignments is but one of many examples of resource exchange within the spheres of interaction.

The exchange of resources can enhance your management. You might exchange one of your abundant resources for a limited one, or you might exchange one of your resources having a high quality for a poor quality one. An example of this might be when you exchange the high quality resource of being a good typist with another individual for one of your low quality resources.

Consuming

There are instances where in order to meet a demand the supply of a resource may be partially or completely consumed. Some of your resources are consumed on a regular basis. Time, is an example of a consumed resource. When you consume a resource you are reducing the amount and/or its availability for its future. Your decision to consume a resource will depend upon how easily and quickly it can be replaced, your willingness to consume it, and the satisfaction you anticipate from its consumption.

Three resources often consumed are time, energy, and money. Each day your time and energy resources are replaced. When you are regularly employed, your money resource is replaced at the end of each pay period. Since these resources are relatively easy to replace, you may be more willing to consume them than others which are not or have a limited supply. You are more willing to consume time, knowing that tomorrow will yield another twenty-four hours, than you might be if your time resource was available in varying amounts.

Closely related to the anticipated satisfaction is the function the resource is intended to accomplish. When you use your money resource to purchase a ticket to a campus activity, you anticipate enjoying the activity. In this instance the function of your money resource was entertainment. Would you anticipate the same satisfaction if the money resource being consumed was to purchase a textbook? When you consume your time and energy resources to study for a test, do research for a term paper, or read the textbook, what is the intended function? What satisfaction do you anticipate receiving?

You are more willing to consume readily available or easily replaced resources. Suppose you had only one ball point pen for the entire academic year. You cannot replace it until then. Would you be willing to loan it to another person? Would you be more careful about when, how, and where you used it? Although this particular situation is not likely to happen, there are instances when a resource is limited or cannot be readily replaced.

As you use resources in the management process some will be partly or completely consumed. The extent of consumption is an important factor. The consumption of a resource reduces or eliminates its availability for other consumption. Earlier a reference was made to "opportunity cost" factors. When a resource is partly or completely consumed you have minimized or eliminated the opportunity to allocate and use it in a different manner. Although the consumption of a resource will produce satisfaction, this must be weighed against the satisfaction which might be produced if a different use of the resource occurred. In the management process, resources must be consumed to some extent to produce the desired outcome which yields satisfaction.

Protecting

Sometimes resources are used for protective purposes. In this instance resources are used to reduce the risk factors to other resources, to yourself, or to other individuals. You wear a winter coat to protect yourself from the weather. You purchase insurance as a protection for health, car, or loss of income or life.

When resources are used this way, consideration is given to the risk factor. The loss or absence of the resource you are protecting represents a high risk factor. Therefore you use one or more of your resources to minimize the risk factor. Your value hierarchy is used in determining which resources to protect.

Transferring

The use of transferring involves a one-way transaction.[12] Transferring occurs when one of your resources is given to another person or agency.

This resource use takes place probably more often than you realize. When you paid your tuition and fees, you transferred part of your money resource to the university. Other examples of this transference occurs when you pay taxes, give a gift, or make a contribution to an agency or organization.

The transfer of your resources may appear to be a one-way process; yet it is not always true. You transfer your money resource when paying taxes but you receive community services in return. When you give a gift you anticipate one will be given to you at a later date. Although this transference of some of your resources depletes their immediate existence, you anticipate either the reversal of this transfer at some future date or the receipt of other resources in return.

The transference of resources should not be confused with exchanging. When resources are exchanged, no fluctuation in value takes place. The exchange can also be reversed. Your exchange of money for a car can be reversed. The car can be sold and your money resource reinstituted.

Resources once transferred cannot be reversed. Money resources are transferred to pay taxes. Although this transfer yields other resources in the form of community services, once made you cannot reverse the transfer. You cannot decide not to use the community services and have your tax dollar returned. Nor do you have any guarantee that whoever received your gift will return one of a similar amount.

There are instances where the time factor of when the transfer occurs becomes a factor in determining the extent of the expenditure of the resource. In most instances, when you transfer your money resource in payment of your taxes it will affect the dollar cost. If you fail to pay your taxes on the specified date, you will be required to spend additional funds as a late payment penalty. In other instances you may receive a rebate for early payment.

The transfer of resources may be mandatory or voluntary. Resources may voluntarily be transferred to increase another person's resources; bring pleasure to another individual; demonstrate respect, appreciation, or affection; observe special holidays and/or events; or in anticipation of receiving a return of the resources at a later date. Mandatory transfers are those over which you exercise little or no control such as paying taxes.

Producing

There are times when one resource is used to produce a different resource. You may use your skills, time, and energy resources in household production. Building your stereo from separate components is one example. Producing a new resource through the use of an existing resource is not synonymous with either transferring or exchanging resources. In this instance, the resource did not exist until you produced it.

Currently, you are producing the resource of a college degree in your chosen field. As you produce your college degree, it in turn will produce your employment resource. The production of new resources is a continuous and on-going process. Each time this occurs your supply of available resources is increased. As this increase in resources occurs you have more resources to draw upon, thus affording you more choices and opportunities as you allocate and use resources. Throughout your life you will use existing resources to produce new ones.

Saving-Investing

Sometimes you can save or invest your resources for future rather than current use. A savings account is a common example of the saving-investing of a resource.

An individual or a family may "save" days in order to take a prolonged vacation. The outgrown wardrobe of an older child may be "saved" for a younger one. When you keep your textbooks after completing a course, you are "saving" a resource.

You may also invest your resources. You are now doing this by investing your resources of time, energy, intelligence, skills, abilities, and money in your future career. Although it is true you are producing a new resource, the investment of these resources in yourself will be used in the future when you enter your professional career.

The saving-investing of resources means you are delaying their use to a future date. The satisfaction you anticipate receiving at a later date is greater than the satisfaction you would receive from immediate use.

There is a difference between producing a resource and saving-investing one. During producing a new resource is created. When resources are saved-invested, the outcome may yield an increase in the resource or possibly a new one. However, the emphasis is upon the delayed use not on the creation of a new resource.

This use of resources allows you to draw upon them when necessary or desired. Resources may be saved-invested because they are not currently needed, their delayed use will yield a greater satisfaction, postponement of their use will yield an increase in either supply or quality, or their use at a later date is more important than immediate use.

Resource Allocation and Use

How you allocate and use your resources, in some cases, is not based solely upon your own desires. There are instances where you have little or limited choices concerning resource use. There are others where you have great latitude. Effective management necessitates recognition of both occurrences. Effective management also means you use your resources in the most productive manner to bring about the greatest degree of satisfaction.

The decisions you make concerning your resource use are vitally important ones. As you make these decisions you should consider not only which resources are to be involved but also the extent and the way in which each will be used. The "opportunity costs," replacement capabilities, the current and future demands, and the classification of resources are all pertinent determinants in the utilization of resources.

Management of Resources

As an individual you make decisions concerning your resources. If you make the decision to continuously consume them, they are used as the need arises. If this occurs, undoubtedly you may encounter a situation where a resource is needed but not available. In this case, your management has not been adequate.

Managing your resources means more than just using them. It means you take the time to assess the qualitative and quantitative aspects of each. It also means you analyze the best use to which each should be put to bring about the highest degree of satisfaction. Would greater satisfaction be achieved by transferring, consuming, producing, protecting, saving-investing, or exchanging the resource?

As you begin to allocate resources, possible uses of each are determined. Managing resources encompasses both their allocation and use. It means taking the time to look ahead to future demands as well as the present ones. It means making sure that if and when resources are needed they are available and in the quantity and quality which will bring satisfaction.

Everyone is familiar with the demands placed upon their money resources. But what about the demands on your other resources such as time, energy, skills, talents, and abilities? Unfortunately many individuals do not adequately consider the demands placed upon their own abundant resources. They assume these will always be present to draw upon when needed and will be in sufficient supply. Consider for a moment your resources which presently are in abundant supply and of high quality. What would you do if these were suddenly no longer available for use? What resources could you use in their place? If you had to substitute resources, what changes would occur in your management process?

Management of resources involves ascertaining the best possible use of each resource and then allocating the necessary quantities to accomplish the task, resolve the situation, or to meet the demand being placed upon you. In order to do this, you need to be aware of your resources, possible uses, and existing as well as future demands.

Allocating and using resources also means you should consider the "opportunity costs" involved. When a resource is used, what opportunities are no longer open? What has it cost you in terms of meeting other demands?

Everyone has unlimited wants and limited means to achieve them. Resource allocation and use involve setting priorities for your wants, then allocating and using resources to attain those having a high priority. Management of your resources will help you to achieve a greater number of these wants. As you attain more of your wants, you also achieve a higher degree of satisfaction.

You are aware that management of your money resource means you are better able to attain more of your economic wants while maintaining a stable financial status. The same is true concerning the management of other resources.

As you manage your resources you need to be cognizant of the fact that in some instances your allocation and use is not derived solely from your own choices. There are instances where you have little or limited control over resource expenditures. The society in which you live exercises some control over resource management. The input received from your spheres of interaction may be a constraint upon your resources. What are the constraints placed upon your money resource by input from the spheres of interaction? This input might occur as taxes you are required to pay, purchases you are expected to make, or activities you are required to attend as a result of your organizational membership.

Another constraint upon resource use occurs from implied expectations of the roles you assume within each of the spheres. The input of role expectations can have an effect upon resource use. To what extent does your role as a college student direct your resource allocation and use? As a son or daughter do inputs received from the family sphere place any constraints upon your resource use?

Although these constraints do occur, the degree of freedom of choice in resource allocation and use varies. In some instances you may have more choices as to where, when, and how resources are allocated. In other instances, you may have very little freedom of choice. Income taxes are paid on or before April 15 of each year. In this matter you have very little freedom of choice. As you allocate and use your time resource, you also have some constraints which limit your freedom of choice. These constraints might originate from course requirements, course instructor, college calendars, or test dates. To manage your resources, you must be aware of the limitations or constraints which exist as well as the other aspects of their allocation and use of resources.

The major purpose of resource management is to allocate them in a manner which will produce the greatest amount of satisfaction while minimizing the amount of each one used. In order to achieve this, you need to be conversant with the extent of all resources, constraints upon your choices, manner in which resources can be used, "opportunity cost" which might be involved, and the availability and quality of each resource.

In the management process you make decisions to allocate resources in the planning component. As you implement the plan, these resources are used to produce the desired outcome to yield an anticipated degree of satisfaction. The choices you make as you allocate resources throughout the planning component will have a direct influence upon the progress made during implementation. The satisfaction you obtain from your desired outcome will be dependent upon not only the allocation but also the use of these resources. Allocating insufficient or inadequate resources in the planning component becomes a constraint during implementation. The constraint experienced in implementation necessitates corrective action. If the resource needed for correction action is no longer available or exists to an insufficient degree, your implementation may either be severely hampered or terminated. In either instance, the outcome and anticipated satisfaction are affected.

Can you think of an instance when this has happened? The equipment you used when you were employed last summer was a resource. Did you make a decision to allocate part of this resource to someone else for the day and then discover you, too, needed it? Have you ever allocated and used your time and energy resources only to discover they were needed for another purpose? How did either of these affect your management, the outcome, and anticipated satisfaction?

Resources are vital to the management process. As such the choices made concerning their allocation and utilization affect the satisfaction you receive from use of the management process. The decisions concerning resource management mean the difference between "coping" and effective management as demands are made, input is received, and action is undertaken.

Summary

Resources are an important part of your management. Everyone uses their resources. The manner in which resources are allocated and used means the difference between "coping" and managing. The management of resources involves knowing the quantitative and qualitative aspects, the classification of resources, the possible uses, and the aspects of allocation.

Resource management begins by identifying all of your resources. Combined with this is recognizing the quality and supply of each. This knowledge is important to meet the continual demands being placed upon your resources.

In addition to this, resources should be classified. Resource classification enables you to determine the extent and possible uses. By classifying resources as to human or material you are indicating their source of origin. The further classification of economic and noneconomic provides information as to their possible utilization.

Through resource classification, you can determine the best possible combination of resources to achieve a goal, resolve a problem, or meet a demand. These same classifications are drawn upon to ascertain how you would best benefit from exchanging, transferring, consuming, protecting, producing, or saving-investing of each resource.

Decisions are made and resources are used throughout the management process. It is the difference between merely surviving and achieving your desired quality of life.

ACTIVITIES

1. What are your five most valuable resources? Classify each resource as
   a. Material or human.
   b. Economic or noneconomic.
   c. Quantitative or qualitative
2. Three of your resources are intelligence, motor skills, and youth. Indicate how each of these resources might be used for
   a. Protecting other resources.
   b. Exchanging with another resource.
   c. Consuming purposes.
   d. Producing another resource.
3. Develop a plan to study for class. Identify all of the resources you would use to complete this plan. Classify each resource as to whether it is material or human. Does this plan use more of one classification than another? Why?
4. Assume your time and energy resources were reduced to one half of their current availability. What would you do? What are your opportunity costs? Could you still achieve your goals by using other resources? If so, what resources would you use? What opportunity costs would be involved? What effects would this have on your management?
5. What are the inputs you receive from the political and cultural subsystems affecting your resource allocation? Identify three specific inputs you have received and describe how each has affected your resource allocation and your management?
6. What are the inputs your resource allocation produces in the political and cultural subsystems? Identify three specific inputs you have had on these subsystems and describe how these inputs have affected management within these subsystems.
7. Suppose money resources no longer existed in your community. What would be the impact of the absence of this resource upon you and your spheres of interaction? How would this absence affect management within other spheres and subsystems other than yours? Could other resources be substituted? Why or why not?

CINDY

Cindy is a sophomore in college. She is very talented and an excellent student although she never seems to be able to get an A in any of her courses. Whenever there is a party being planned, Cindy is always the first to be asked because she makes everyone else feel good and have a good time. She is quite attractive and seems to always be glad to see and talk with her friends.

Cindy has a problem. She can never get anywhere on time. Nor is she able to get anything done on time. She always has an excuse: her clock stopped, she forgot the time, or something came up. Her parents bought her a good watch and alarm clock but she still doesn't seem to be able to get anywhere on time. The same is true of any project she is assigned. Her teachers and friends are continually hearing: someone borrowed her typewriter, she didn't have any carbon paper and the stores were closed, or she had to stop her work to help a friend with his project.

Needless to say, Cindy does everything at the last minute. As a thoroughly unorganized person, she often is found the night before something is due working all night long in an attempt to get her work done on time. In most cases, she doesn't get it done. This inability to get her projects in on time is the major cause of her lowered grades.

Cindy's room, her belongings, and her lifestyle reflect the same pattern. Her room is a continual clutter of her belongings. Her closet contains only the clothes which have just come from the cleaners while the rest can be found on the floor, chair, or desk. What isn't on one of these is probably falling out of a drawer.

Cindy doesn't have a roommate which is probably a good thing. Not so much because of the constant clutter but due to the constant stream of people who drop by to chat or to tell Cindy their problems. It seems as though someone is always there. Cindy "doesn't have the heart to tell anyone she is busy and can't talk to them right now", so she doesn't. She is never too busy to go somewhere or do something with friends. In addition to this, Cindy is always willing to loan whatever she has to someone. This includes her clothes, personal belongings, and money from her ample allowance. She never seems to know who has borrowed what and doesn't really care. "After all, they are my friends!"

Discussion Questions

1. What are Cindy's resources? Use one of the methods of classification to group them. Which are abundant and which are limited?
2. What are Cindy's values? How are these values affecting her resource allocation?

3. Cindy has a term paper due in one week. Naturally she has not picked the topic nor started work on it. Develop a plan for her to accomplish this task.
4. What is Cindy's real problem? What has created this problem? If she were asking you for help, what would you suggest to her and why? Do you honestly feel she would follow your suggestions? Why or why not?

GLOSSARY

Allocation   The process of assigning or determining the amount of an item or component to be devoted to a specific activity or endeavor.

Consuming Resource   A process in which a resource may be partly or completely used thus reducing its future availability.

Economic Resource   A measurable, transferrable scarce resource used for productive purposes.

Exchanging Resources   A process in which one resource is substituted for another without affecting the measurable value of either.

Human Resource   A method of classifying resources that can be used to achieve goals or outcomes, meet demands, or serve as enablers or constraints upon management according to the personal characteristics and capabilities inherent within the person.

Material Resource   A method of classifying resources having tangible and intangible components which extend beyond human capabilities and characteristics used to achieve goals or outcomes, meet demands, or serve as enablers or constraints upon management.

Noneconomic Resource   Those resources not used for productive purposes but which are a part of the individual's personal beliefs and behaviors.

Producing Resources   A process in which one or more resources are utilized in creating a new resource.

Protecting Resources   A process in which one resource is used to reduce the probability of loss of another resource.

Qualitative Resource   A measure of the degree of usefulness of a resource.

Quantitative Resource   A measure of the supply, availability or limitations of a resource.

Resource   A tangible or intangible component used to achieve goals or outcomes, to meet demands, or which serve as enablers or constraints on management.

Saving-Investing Resources   A process in which the utilization of one or more resources is deferred for a future use.

Transferring Resources   A process in which the control and use of a resource is given to another individual, agency, or institution.

REFERENCES

1. Ruth E. Deacon and Francille M. Firebaugh, *Home Management Context and Content* (Boston: Houghton Mifflin Company, 1975), p. 158.
2. Irma H. Gross, Elizabeth Walbert Crandall, and Marjorie M. Knoll, *Management for Modern Families*, 3rd. ed. (New York: Appleton-Century-Crofts, 1973), p. 156.
3. Deacon and Firebaugh, op. cit., p. 158.
4. Ibid., p. 159.
5. Gross, Crandall, and Knoll, op. cit., p. 157.
6. Ibid., p. 158.
7. Ibid.
8. Ibid.
9. Ibid., pp. 154–155.
10. Ibid.
11. Deacon and Firebaugh, op. cit., p. 225.
12. Ibid., p. 228.

CHAPTER SIX

Communication Resource

Have you ever been in a conversation where you felt the person you were talking to really wasn't listening? Why did you feel this way? What was the other person doing while you were talking? Have you experienced a time when you and a classmate compared ideas about a class assignment only to find each of you had a different connotation of what was expected? Have there been times when you have communicated to another person yet neither of you spoke a single word? Has there been a time when you thought you had said one thing but the other person reacted in a totally different manner than what you expected?

In the span of one day, how many different ways have you experienced some form of communication? In this same time period, how many different ways have you communicated with others? Is your communication different depending upon who is present? Just how important is communication to your daily life. How does communication affect your management?

What is meant by the term *communication?* Are there different forms or ways to communicate? Why do some individuals communicate more clearly than others?

As an individual you continually communicate with others. This communication takes place in many different ways. Throughout your waking hours you are continually receiving some form of communication. You decode the communication you receive. On the basis of this communication and your decoding, you make decisions and undertake managerial action. This action then becomes a source of communication to others.

Communication, per se, has been an integral part of your life since the day you were born. As an infant your parents communicated their love and affection. You, too, communicated to them your wants and needs. From this time onward, you have been developing the skills and capabilities to communicate with others.

The process of communication is, at best, a difficult one. Yet it is a part of you and your daily life. Although there have been times when your communication has been misunderstood or when you have misinterpreted the communication you have received, could you imagine your life without any communication taking place?

Today's technology enables individuals to communicate in a variety of ways throughout the world. You are able to see and/or hear not only what is happening on the earth but in outer space as well. Within a matter of minutes, messages and pictorial images can be transmitted to all parts of the world.

Although you may not have thought of communication in quite this manner, the process of communication is a learned skill. As such it is a resource which is allocated and used in the management process. Effective communication can be a valuable resource and as such is an enabler within the management system. Conversely the inability to effectively communicate can be a constraint upon management. Since you communicate each day in diverse ways, the process of effective communication is an important part of the management process.

Communication Process

How would you define the term *communication?* Why do people communicate with each other or to objects? What is the purpose of communication? Define what the term *communication* means to you?

What did you include in your definition? Did you define it as conveying a message, thought, or ideas to someone? Or is it a process by which a message is sent and received? Did you define it as a process through which behavior is changed, modified, or altered? Is it a process whereby the use of language, signs, gestures, body movement, voice inflection, and facial expressions are used to convey personal feelings, attitudes, thoughts, ideas, or needs to another person? Communication may involve one or all of these. It is a process whereby a sender using a specific format conveys a message to a receiver.

Thus, in order for communication to take place, four different components are needed. Communication requires a sender, a message, a specific format to convey the message, and a receiver. The sender identifies the message to be communicated. The message is then coded and sent using a specific format to the receiver who decoded the message. The process of communication is shown in Figure 6.1.

As the sender, you have to decide the message you wish to convey and the format that will be used. Each of these are vital to the success of the communication process. These decisions are influenced not only by you but also by the message to be sent and the receiver.

Assume the message you wish to convey is your support for a particular political candidate. What format would you use to convey this message to your roommate? How would you convey this same message to your parents, a political organization, government, or to a friend who resides several hundred miles away from you? Would you select the same format for each? Why or why not? If you choose to use the same format in each instance, would each receiver decode your message in the same manner? Why or why not?

Sender ────► Message ────► Message sent ────► Receiver
               Coded   decoded the
                                              message

FIGURE 6.1. *Communication Process.*

Each day as you communicate you are conveying your feelings, attitudes, thoughts, ideas, and roles. Although the process of communication may appear from Figure 6.1 to be a relatively simple action, this is not necessarily true.

The ability to communicate is one of your resources. How effectively you use this resource depends not only upon your ability to communicate but also upon an understanding of the factors affecting the communication process. Although the sender, message being sent, and the format chosen are all important factors in the communication process, there are also other factors that influence the process.

As the initiator of a message you have a certain degree of control concerning the communication process. You originate the message and determine the format to be used. However, once the message has been sent, you have a limited degree of control concerning how and in what manner it is decoded. Your communication may also be hampered by the environment in which the message is sent. In addition there may be communication barriers.

Effective communication necessitates an awareness of the components which comprise the process. Each will be discussed separately.

Sender

Communication is initiated by the sender. The effectiveness of communication depends upon the capability of the sender to first determine if a message should be communicated and second, to code the message in a format that will convey to the receiver the intended message.

Of all of the people you know, can you identify one person who effectively communicates almost all of the time? Is there someone else you know who just can't seem to get a message across no matter how hard he or she tries? Although both of these people share a common language, one is an effective communicator and the other is not. What has created the differences?

You have many communication skills. Your ability to write, speak, and think are basic skills. The knowledge you have obtained from your educational endeavors, past experiences, your management skills, values, personality, and the sum total of the talents, and abilities you possess also comprise your communication skills. Each of these has a direct bearing upon the effectiveness of your communication. As the sender of a message, you draw upon each of these as you originate your message and select a specific format to convey this to others.

The process of communication is initiated by the sender. What you determine should be sent will be influenced by your values, goals, and standards. The manner in which you code the message will depend upon your knowledge and abilities. How you code the message will be affected by your knowledge of the receiver as well as what you assume is your role during the communication process. As you code the message you anticipate a specific response accruing from your message by the receiver. Thus as you initiate the communication process you have identified the message to be sent, your role in the process, the format of the message, and the anticipated response. To achieve this you have used resources. How effective you are as a sender within the communication process will be governed by the validity of the decisions you have made and the resources you have used.

Message

The purpose of communication is to transmit a message from the sender to the receiver. The process of communication may be to convey an idea, attitude, feeling or suggestion; change, alter, or modify the attitude or behavior of others; initiate an exchange of ideas; give directions or information; stimulate discussion; respond to a question; or gain further information. In each of these instances, the message being sent has a specific purpose or function. As the sender you determine not only the specific message you wish to convey but also the purpose or function.

Just as values, goals, and standards are influential in the determination of the message to be sent, so too, are they influential in the message coding. For instance, how many times have you communicated to someone that you have to get busy or you won't have your term projects done on time? This communication gives clear evidence of your values, goals, and standards.

As you code the message, basically you are determining the best possible manner in which to convey the message to the receiver. Although you may not be totally aware of it, decisions are being made. These decisions may involve determining whether to use pictures or sketches rather than words, identifying the methodology in which to send the message, and establishing the anticipated response of the receiver.

The decisions you make will be influenced by your knowledge of the receiver as well as your communication skills. Who the receiver is and the receiver's skills and abilities will affect your coding of the message.

Message Format

Closely aligned to the message coding is the format to be used. Although these decisions are simultaneously done as the message is being coded, this component has been separated for purposes of clarification. The choice of a format for your message relies upon your knowledge of the receiver as well as your values, goals, standards, and communication skills. Still another factor is the availability of formats to be used. A message can be sent verbally, nonverbally, or by combining the two.

The choice of the format will be determined by the receiver. Suppose you wish to convey the message of a billing error on your charge account. What format would you use? How would you convey the message to someone asking directions to a building on your campus? Would you use the same format to convey your message in both instances?

There may also be instances where your choice of format is limited. For instance, this textbook is a communication format. Your course instructor is able to choose from a variety of formats as you learn about management. The same is not true for the person writing a textbook.

The selection of the format to be used in the communication process is important. Your message, decoded by the receiver, therefore should utilize a format which as clearly and effectively as possible conveys the message you intend to be received.

Decoding the Message

The message you sent will be decoded by the receiver. The selection of the format and the coding must be analyzed and decoded by the receiver. This may be objectively or subjectively done depending upon the format and the coding you have used. If you have selected a nonverbal format, the receiver must decode your message on the basis of his or her knowledge of you as well as his or her interpretation of your nonverbal communication. When a written format is used, the receiver considers both the word meanings and the phrasing within the message. In a verbal format, however, the word meanings, phrasing, and vocal aspects are used to decode the message.

Use of the Communication Process

The communication process is continually used by individuals, families, business, industry, and government. As an individual you communicate in a variety of ways and in various situations. You use communication to plan, solve problems, analyze, encourage thinking, exchange ideas and thoughts, convey feelings, and obtain information. This takes place within all of the spheres of interaction and throughout all of the roles you assume. You are both a sender and a receiver. You communicate to other individuals, groups, agencies, and organizations. As a receiver, messages are sent to you from other individuals, agencies, organizations and the media.[1] Although there is still much to be learned, the process of communication involves human interactions which is used to attain the desired quality of life.[2]

The ability to communicate is a learned skill. This is a skill you have been developing for many years and one which will become even more important in the future as you attain your professional goals. Of the twenty-four hours in each day, how many are there that do not involve the flow of communication? In reality there are only a few in which you do not assume either the role of a sender or a receiver.

As was previously mentioned, your communication skills are one of your resources. Since you are continually involved in the communication process, this resource is a vital one. In order to increase your skills, you need to be aware of the manner in which communication occurs, the types of communication, the factors that encourage or impede communication, and the managerial use of communication.

As indicated earlier the communication process involves a sender, a receiver, and a message. In some instances the process terminates when a message is received; in others it does not.

In the first instance one-way communication has taken place. As you listen to the radio or watch television, you are involved in one-way communication. Reading this textbook is also an example of one-way communication. This one-way communication process limits the sender's capability to secure a response or immediate evaluative feedback.[3]

The interaction that takes place in meetings, discussions, social activities, and between individuals represents two-way communication. As the sender you have immediate evaluative feedback through the receiver's response. This response enables you to evaluate any response you receive and to clarify your message.[4]

Although two-way communication affords you an immediate response for evaluative feedback, one-way communication does not necessarily eliminate the possibility of evaluative feedback. You listen to the radio and don't like the music. What do you do? You turn to another station and perhaps you even write a letter of complaint. In each case evaluative feedback has occurred but the impact of your evaluative feedback will not be immediately felt by the radio station. There are also instances in one-way communication where no evaluative feedback ever occurs at least from the receiver's standpoint.

Communication is a resource used in management to serve many different purposes. The qualitative aspect of this resource will be dependent upon your communication skills.

Types of Communication

You want to communicate a message to another person. How could you convey this message? As the originator of the message you might choose to convey the message verbally, nonverbally, or to combine the two.

Nonverbal communication encompasses a written or pictorial communication format as well as physical expressions and/or movements. It may or may not be accompanied by verbal communication. In discussing nonverbal communication, Flannery, Hillman, McGee, and Rivers state that nonverbal communication includes ". . . facial gestures, body shapes and appearance, personal space, territoriality, vocal qualities, and even aspects of physical environments such as furniture and color."[5] Through nonverbal communication you attach an importance to your verbal communication, signify an emotion, and indicate the function of the message.[6] Thus nonverbal communication is a vital part of the communication process.

Which type of communication do you do most often—verbal or nonverbal? It is indeed difficult to separate the verbal from the nonverbal. Combined with your verbal communication of a message, nonverbal communication is also taking place in most instances. The reverse may not be true. There are other instances where nonverbal can be substituted for verbal communication.

Nonverbal communication plays a major role in the communication process. Therefore it should be more closely analyzed as to its effect upon the total process. When you are involved in the communication process how do you decode a message you have received? Are you aware of the extent to which your verbal communication is affected by your nonverbal?

Flannery, Hillman, McGee, and Rivers indicate how nonverbal communication is used to decode meanings and messages as well as the creditability of the sender. You measure the creditability of the sender by the length and duration of eye contact. Hand gestures are used to indicate the importance of the message. Facial gestures are a source of evaluative feedback. In addition to these, body appearance, clothing, cosmetics, and hair are also nonverbal criteria. The body appearance mirrors the individual's self-image and characteristics. Clothing reflects the individual identification with a specific group. Cosmetics identify the individual's desired image while the hair style will tend to stereotype the person with a group identification.[7]

Along with these are the nonverbal aspects of your vocal qualities. Their studies indicate the volume of your voice will determine the receiver's measurement of you. For instance a loud voice conveys an importance while a soft voice denotes weakness or uncertainty. The absence of a variation in pitch is viewed as dull and boring. Silence may indicate emotion. The rate at which you speak will also be an evaluative measure of your creditability. Voice quality is also important. If you are "breathy" you may be viewed as being weak. Enunciating words and vowels denotes importance or emphasis. A highly pitched voice is seen as signifying a person who is insecure while a low-pitched voice is considered to be an unemotional one.[8]

The territorial and personal space of the sender and receiver are also creditability measures. Territorial space often indicates status. Corporations and agencies indicate the importance of an individual by the location and size of the person's office or work area. In addition to these each individual has a personal space. This is the space that surrounds each individual. It has an effect upon the communication process. When an individual's personal space is invaded one or more reactions may occur. If the "invader" is not a friend or someone you don't know you tend to resent this invasion and indicate your displeasure by moving. However, if the "invader" is a friend, it denotes intimacy.[9]

The absence or presence of personal space has an effect upon the communication process in other ways. For instance, suppose you were one of five students sitting in a classroom designed for 200 students. How do you feel? Do you experience a difficult time in concentrating on the lecture being given? But what if there were 300 students in this classroom? How would you feel now? In one instance, you had too much personal space whereas in the other there was not enough. Increased personal space tends to reduce communication. The same is also true when personal space is severely limited.

In order to effectively communicate, you must be aware of not only the message you are sending but also the manner in which your message is being decoded. Although your message may be a verbal one, the receiver is decoding it using both the verbal and the nonverbal aspects. Unless you are conversant with the nonverbal communication taking place, your verbal message may be decoded quite differently than you intend. As you walk down the halls have you asked someone, "How are you?" Did the person respond, "Fine." Yet as you look at this person, you can obviously see that he or she is ill. In this case the nonverbal communication you received was contradictory to the verbal. Which one has the most validity for you—the verbal indication of feeling "fine" or the nonverbal appearance of the person? In most cases, the latter is true. In instances where verbal and nonverbal communication are in opposition to each other, individuals tend to rely more on the nonverbal rather than the verbal aspects. The rationale is that nonverbal communication is harder to fake than verbal. Nonverbal communication enhances or minimizes the creditability of verbal communication. It is obvious that effective communication involves the knowledge and skilled use of each.

Barriers to Communication

Although contradictory nonverbal communication may impede communication, there are other barriers that inhibit, deter, or restrict the communication process. These barriers may accrue from the spheres of interaction, the sender, or the receiver.

Within the spheres of interaction there may be barriers over which you may or may not have any control. Your communication may be restricted by pragmatic noise.[10] The loud volume of a stereo in the next room or the voices of several people walking down the hall may carry into your room. When it does, this distraction interferes with the message you are sending or receiving. Whether you are the sender or receiver, you experience difficulty in concentrating. In some instances you are able to exercise control over pragmatic noise while in others you are not.

The sender's coding of the message can also be a communication barrier. This barrier may be the verbal coding or it may accrue from a combination of verbal and nonverbal coding. In either case, it impedes the receiver's decoding. A mother coded the following message to her daughter: "Barbara, I want this room cleaned with pride." How did you decode this message? Did you decode the word "pride" as being a standard or a commercial product? In this case, the daughter decoded the message as a standard while the mother's coding was a commerical product.

There are other instances where the coding of messages can be a communication barrier. Words that sound alike when verbally communicated can have entirely different meanings. The phrasing of words within a sentence can produce entirely different connotations. Within each age, group, agency, organization, and/or discipline there exist highly specialized words. In coding messages a communication barrier may occur if the receiver does not have a relevant frame of reference. A grandmother who is told her dress is "tough" may not have the slightest idea whether her grandchild is complimenting or criticizing her mode of attire.

According to Nickell, Rice, and Tucker, 45 to 75 per cent of communication time is spent in decoding messages.[11] As messages are decoded the receiver's values, goals, and standards are involved. Closely aligned to these are the receiver's interpretation of the message code. Still another is the relationship which exists between the sender and the receiver.[12]

Have you experienced a situation in which what you thought you communicated was positive support for someone's idea but the receiver decoded it as a criticism? Was this caused by a contradiction between verbal and nonverbal communication or was there perhaps a different causal factor?

As messages are received you decode them in reference to your values, goals, standards, roles, and your spheres of interaction. You may "turn off" the communication you receive because it is not relevant to your frame of reference, you do not consider it important, or when the message is unrealistic or threatening. In each of these your values, goals, standards, and role perceptions are involved in the decoding.

You decode the message being sent to you. If during this you perceive the message as not being relevant, you take no further part in the communication process. Suppose you are with a group of students who are receiving basic instruction in how to operate a specific machine. You have used this particular machine many times and are quite conversant with its operation. Do you listen and continue to receive the message? Or perhaps do you instead "tune out" the message being sent?

You and a friend have been asked to give directions to a specific building on the campus. Although both of you know the location of the building, your friend responds to the request. How closely do you listen to the message being sent? In all probability you listen but not as specifically as the other receiver. Your needs are not the same. Therefore the information is not important to you.

Another communication barrier created by your values, goals, standards, and roles may result when the message being received is decoded as a threat. This may also occur when the message implies expectations which you decode as being unrealistic. As you decode messages your values, goals, standards, and roles are drawn upon.[13] These are an integral part of you and as such are involved in the assessing of the implication of any message being received. To cite Koehler, Anatol, and Applbaum: "Values, attitudes, beliefs, and needs are the key components in a receiver's cognitive system."[14] As such they are the factors by which you measure the validity of the message being received.

As you decode messages you also assess their implications upon your managerial procedures. You will tend to screen out messages that imply unrealistic expectations or threats to your self-image.[15]

The creditability of the sender may also be a communication barrier. When the sender is perceived to have a high degree of creditability, the effectiveness of the communication process is enhanced. The reverse is also true. When the creditability of the sender is low, the receiver tends to discount the message. Thus although the communication process continues, the decoding of the message is influenced by the sender's creditability. The receiver may minimize the importance of the message, reduce, or even eliminate the decoding process. The lack of sender creditability may accrue from the misuse of words or phrases, contradictory nonverbal communication, or other evaluative criteria established by the receiver.

Communication barriers can restrict, impede, or inhibit the process of communication. Some of these can be controlled; others can not. Although you may be able to exercise control over the pragmatic noise in your shelter sphere, you have little if any control over the traffic noise of the immediate sphere. Awareness of your values, goals, standards, and roles will assist in the coding and decoding of messages. Knowledge of the receiver's values, goals, standards, and roles will enhance your communication skills. Recognition and understanding the measures that can be taken to counteract communication barriers will result in more effective communication.

Group Communication

Thus far you have been concerned with individual communication. Although much of your communication is individualistic, you also take part in group communication. These groups may be constituted by your family unit, organizations, agencies, institutions, or employment-related. In each case, although the specific topics will vary, group communication has a specific function or purpose: to resolve a problem, develop a plan, identify policies and procedures, interact in a social setting, or stimulate an exchange of ideas.

Group communication involves individuals communicating to each other in a group setting environment. It therefore has characteristics similar to individual communication yet it also has distinctive ones that set it apart. Each individual within the group sends and receives messages. These messages are coded and decoded in respect to values, goals, standards, and roles. The individual has assumed roles outside the group setting, yet each also has an assumed and/or projected role within the group. This will be influential in the coding and decoding of messages.

Just as with individual communication there are aspects of group communication that encourage group participation. There are also communication barriers. Although fundamentally the process of communication is the same for both individuals and groups, differences still remain.

The Individual Within the Group

Only when individuals participate in group interaction does group communication take place. Consequently, it necessitates the participation of the individuals who comprise the total membership. Unless or until all participate, group communication does not occur. What does take place is the domination of the group by one or two persons.

Individual participation is dependent upon how the person views his or her role within the group and the relationship of himself or herself to the total membership. Inherent in this is the self-concept of the individual.

The *Communications Handbook* lists eight "blocks" that may deter the individual's participation in group communication. Each of these involve the individual's self-perception in relationship to the membership of the group. These are fear, insecurity, lack of knowledge about the group, lack of time, lack of skill, vested interests, group values, and group demands.[16] The individual who experiences one or several of these may utilize two different methods of dealing with the situation. One is to withdraw from group interaction. In other words to choose not to participate or to assume the spectator role. The other is to utilize one of several adjustment methods. These methods include aggression, compensation, rationalization, identification, idealism, projection, displacement, conversion, or regression.[17]

Thus an individual's participation is dependent upon his or her role in relationship to the other members of the group. This perception is based upon: the extent to which the projected role is known and accepted, the recognition given to the projected role by other members, and the potential rewards anticipated to accrue from role acceptance.[18]

Group Communication

Communication barriers similar to those experienced in individual communication may also be present in group communication. Pragmatic noise may accrue as a barrier. Inaccurate coding or decoding by the sender and receiver is still another barrier. Each individual also brings values, goals, standards, and roles to a group communication setting.

Moreover, there are other barriers. In his discussion of group behavior, Eisenberg indicates effective group behavior accrues from the presence of a good leader, knowledge of the group's customs, and the group's proxemics.[19] Separately or collectively the reverse or failure to consider these can produce communication barriers.

In addition to these, within the group an individual may assume a role that becomes a barrier to communication. Frequently the purpose of this role assumption is to satisfy a special need or interest. This role may take one of several formats. The *Communication Handbook* cites these roles. The *aggressor* is one who belittles or deflates the contributions of others. The *blocker* is one who is resistant and often tries to reopen discarded issues. The *recognition-seeker* is a boaster who actively seeks to gain attention. *The playboy*, on the other hand, seeks to disassociate from the group through distracting and somewhat childish behavior. The *dominator* seeks to manipulate the group using a variety of behaviors whereas the *special interest pleader* has a vested interest hidden behind pleas made for special interest groups.[20] The presence of any of these roles within the group can and does act as a communication barrier.

Summary

Communication is an on-going and continual process. As such it is a resource you draw upon in many different ways as you undertake your daily management. Effective communication can and does increase your resource reservoir; you are able to maximize the allocation and utilization of other resources.

The components of the communication process are the sender, the message coding, the message format, and the receiver who decodes the message received. Each of these are vital to the communication process.

As you send and receive messages there are factors that influence the process. Knowledge of these factors is vital to the communication process. Communication between individuals is enhanced when the sender is aware of and utilizes the knowledge of the values, goals, standards, and roles of both the sender and receiver. Communication is also increased when awareness of the process and its implications to the overall daily managerial actions are recognized and accepted.

The process of communication can be restricted, impeded, or hampered. These barriers can accrue from the spheres of interaction, message coding, the values, goals, standards, and roles, or the decoding of the message. You may or may not be able to exercise control over one or more of these barriers.

Communication takes place between individuals and society. This communication may be one or two way. It may also be an individual or group setting.

Group communication encompasses the interaction of individuals in a group setting. The extent of interaction will be determined by the roles each participant assumes. The success of group communication depends upon the leader, knowledge and acceptance of individual roles, and roles each person assumes within the group. Group, like individual communication, share similar barriers.

Through communication you can maximize the allocation and use of your resources as well as increase your resource reservoir. Effective communication affords you the opportunity to interact in social and group settings within your professional position and with family members. As this interaction takes place, it affects your management. Communication is a valuable resource. Effective communication is a learned skill. As both a resource and a skill, you will continue to draw upon it throughout your life as you utilize the management system.

ACTIVITIES

In class

1.
  I'm going to class
  Do you want to go to the library?
  Hamburger, fries, and coffee, please
  I've got to study for a test tomorrow.
  Come on, we're already late now!

These are five phrases or statements you might hear. How could you send each of these messages to your roommate using only nonverbal communication (without writing)? Could you convey these statements for a ten-year-old child using the same nonverbal techniques? Why or why not? Using these statements, develop at least five different nonverbal techniques you could utilize to convey these messages without writing.

2. Individuals are continually communicating to each other and to society. Most people are not aware of the extent to which these take place. In your campus library, select one person who is not a personal friend to observe for a 15-minute period. During this time record this individual's nonverbal communication. This should include those identified in Chapter 6. From your recorded data, draw conclusions concerning this person's attitude about the time spent in the library. Indicate why the nonverbal communication exhibited enabled you to arrive at these conclusions.

3. Television programs use both verbal and nonverbal communication to develop and sustain a characterization in the story. Select a television program in which you are unfamiliar with the story and the characters. Pick one of the major characters to intently observe. During the first ten minutes of the program, sit with your back to the television set. Listen to the verbal communication. On the basis of only verbal communication, what is the extent of your knowledge of the character? Now watch the remaining part of the program observing both the verbal and nonverbal communication. Does the actor's use of nonverbal communication increase your knowledge of the character? If so, in what way?

4. To ascertain the impact of communication upon your daily life, record for a period of one hour all the messages you receive, the messages you send, the format of both kinds of messages, and whether the message was sent verbally, nonverbally, or a combination of both. Were you aware of the extent to which you sent and received communication? Which were you most often: the sender or the receiver? Which occurred most often: verbal, nonverbal, or combined verbal and nonverbal?

5. In the last two weeks you have been a participant in group communication. From those instances, select two different group settings such as a meeting and a social activity. What was your role in each one? Describe the extent of your participation in each. Were there differences in your roles and participation in each setting? Can you recall any communication barriers? If so what were they? What were the causal factors? Could these causal factors be minimized or eliminated? Why or why not? Analyze your participation in each of these group communication instances by answering the questions just listed.

THE CHRISTMAS PARTY

The dorm social committee is composed of Ned, Sarah, Judy, Jake, Rod, and Janice. Their job is to plan the major social events for their dorm. The current event they are working on is the Christmas party.

At the first meeting Ned was elected the chairperson. Since then they have had at least one meeting a week. Jake is usually late for every meeting but then so is Sarah. Rod and Janice haven't missed a meeting yet and are considered the "workers" of the group.

When the meeting finally gets started the first order of business is to review the work accomplished since the last meeting. Judy usually insists that every detail be completely covered in depth. Jake often makes remarks to whomever is sitting beside him such as "Do we have to go over this again?" Rod and Janice, who have done most of the actual work thus far, elaborate on each detail repeatedly until Judy's questions are answered. Sarah usually stares out the window or draws pictures on her notes while this is taking place. Ned resents Judy's questions but tries to go along with her to have "peace in the group."

The Christmas party is two weeks away. Ned has called a meeting to finalize the remaining plans. He is surprised to find both Jake and Sarah have arrived early. As usual they go over all of the details because Judy keeps asking questions and wanting more detail. Although it seems as if they will never get through Judy's questions they finally do. Jake now wants to know what he is supposed to do during the party although these details have been discussed numerous times in several other meetings. He also wants to know if the students in another dorm can attend as guests if they buy tickets. This, too, has been discussed and voted down.

Sarah assumes her usual role of sitting in the meeting but saying very little. When asked what time she can help with the decorations, she says she doesn't have any time and besides this was to be done by students who had volunteered to help with the party.

As the long meeting finally draws to a close, Ned learns that although Rod and Janice will be there to help put up the decorations neither is planning to attend the party. The remaining members of the group try to talk them into changing their minds, yet neither will. As the group leaves the room, Sarah announces that if neither Rod or Janice have to attend the party, she won't either.

Discussion Questions

1. Identify the roles each person is assuming in this group setting. Select one member of the group and describe the nonverbal communication you would anticipate this person to exhibit.

2. Do you feel there are any communication barriers present? If so, what barriers existed? What are the causal factors? Could one or more of these barriers be eliminated or minimized? If so, how?

3. On the basis of your answers, what changes would you make if you had been the chairperson of this group? Why would you have made them? What do you anticipate would have been the reactions of this group if you had been the chairperson and instituted your indicated changes? Why?

4. Both Rod and Janice have indicated they are not attending the party. What do you assume are their reasons? Upon what do you base your assumptions? Identify the values and goals of Rod and Janice and compare them with the values and goals of Jake and Sarah.

5. Each person brought to this group communication setting individual values, goals, standards, and roles. What are the values, goals, standards, and roles of Ned? Why did he accept the chairperson's job? What is Judy's role perception? Contrast her role perception with the role perception held of her by Jake and Janice?

GLOSSARY

Code A procedure in which the sender organizes the methodology to be used to convey a message to a receiver.

Communication The flow of interaction among individuals within society.

Communication Barrier A factor that inhibits, impedes, or restricts the communication process.

Communication Process The procedure by which a sender conveys a message to a receiver.

Decode A phase of the communication process in which the receiver analyzes the verbal or nonverbal message conveyed by the sender.

Group Communication The flow of interaction among several individuals which takes place in a group setting.

Message A component part of the communication process that involves the information being conveyed from one individual to another.

Message Format The specific method by which the message is conveyed from the sender to the receiver.

Nonverbal A method other than the spoken sound by which messages are conveyed from the sender to the receiver.

Receiver   The individual to whom the message is directed.

Sender   The originator of the communication process who codes the message to be sent to the receiver.

Verbal   A procedure in which a message is sent using spoken sounds.

REFERENCES

1. Agricultural College Editors, *Communications Handbook,* 3rd. ed., American Association of Agricultural College Editors (Danville, Ill.: The Interstate Printers and Publishers, Inc., 1976), p. 3.
2. Paulena Nickell, Ann Smith Rice, and Suzanne P. Tucker, *Management in Family Living,* 5th ed. (New York: John Wiley and Sons, Inc., 1976), p. 195.
3. Ibid., pp. 199–200.
4. Ibid.
5. Gerald V. Flannery, Ralph E. Hillman, Jerry C. McGee, and William L. Rivers, "Communication and Society" in James John Jelinek (ed.), *Improving the Human Condition. A Curricular Response to Critical Realities,* ASCD 1978 Yearbook (Washington, D.C.: Association for Supervision and Curriculum Development, 1978), p. 55.
6. Ibid., pp. 56–57.
7. Ibid., pp. 57–59.
8. Ibid., p. 57.
9. Ibid., p. 62.
10. Ruth E. Deacon and Francille M. Firebaugh, *Home Management Context and Concepts* (Boston: Houghton Mifflin Company, 1975), p. 129.
11. Nickell, Rice and Tucker, op. cit., p. 199.
12. Ibid.
13. Ibid., pp. 200–201.
14. Terry W. Koehler, Karl W. E. Anatol, and Ronald L. Applbaum, *Public Communication Behavioral Perspectives* (New York: Macmillan Publishing Company, Inc., 1978), p. 47.
15. Nickell, Rice and Tucker, op. cit., p. 199.
16. *Communications Handbook,* op. cit., pp. 6–7.
17. Ibid., p. 7.
18. Ibid., pp. 8–9.
19. Abné M. Eisenberg, *Understanding Communication in Business and the Professions* (New York: Macmillan Publishing Company, Inc., 1978), pp. 191–196.
20. *Communications Handbook,* op. cit., p. 10.

CHAPTER SEVEN

Time and Energy Resources

You have established a goal or there is a demand placed upon you. To achieve this goal or meet the demand, you use the management process. Using the management process involves the allocation and use of your resources. Although the achievement of a goal or the resolution of the demand might involve the allocation and use of several resources, your most frequently used resources are time and energy. In fact, it is difficult to identify a goal or a demand that does not require the use of one or both of these resources.

Resource allocation and use within the management process often incorporate one or both in combination with other resources. The extent to which each is allocated and used varies depending upon the goal sought or the demand being experienced. Thus the use of your other resources is often dependent upon the availability of the primary resources of time and energy.

Although they are allocated and used collectively they are, nonetheless, separate and distinct resources. As such, when allocation and use take place, each should be considered as separate from the other. Despite the fact they are both vital to the successful achievement of goals and meeting demands, each has distinct characteristics. The scarcity or availability of each is an important factor in the management process. A knowledge of their individual characteristics is vital to your management.

Time as a Resource

Time is a resource common to all individuals. It is a quantitative resource in that it can be measured. However, the quantity you have available on any given day is limited to twenty-four hours. Although it can be measured, it cannot be seen. It is therefore, an intangible resource.

Your time resource has other characteristics. Its exact classification varies among authors. Gross, Crandall, and Knoll classify it as a human resource.[1] Using the definition given in Chapter 6, its point of origin classifies it as a material resource. When seeking to classify it as being either economic or noneconomic, its use would be the final determinant. In most instances, it would be classified as being economic.

This resource has boundaries that limit its availability. It is readily replaced each day without any expenditure of thought or effort on your part. This often results in its assumed availability. Because you receive a new supply each day, you may not allocate and use this resource as carefully as you do others.

147

Unfortunately this misleading assumption has a direct effect upon the total management taking place. Do you really manage your time resource as carefully and as closely as you do your money resource? Do you manage your time resource only when you need to accomplish a number of tasks in a limited period of time? Or do you manage your time resource each day regardless of the demands being placed upon it?

How much control do you really have over your time resource? This is one resource which is difficult to save-invest. Once time has passed you cannot bring it back in a quantitative sense. You cannot return to a former time to make changes. Nor can you control the given amount of time you have available at one instance. Your only control over its passage lies in how you allocate and use the time available to you on any one day.

Time is a focal point around which other resources are allocated and used. This factor means it should be managed as closely and as carefully as any other resource.

Time Orientation and Perceptions

As a focal point in the allocation and use of other resources, time is often an enabler in your total management. As such it has a definite influence upon your daily life. Your time resource serves as an enabler in two different ways. In some instances it is an enabler as other resources are allocated and used. You allocate and use your time resource to make planning decisions. However, there are other instances when your time resource is allocated and used as a separate and distinct resource.

Thus you allocate and use your time resource in many different ways. Although you may not be aware of it, your time resource serves many different management functions. You are time-oriented and have a time perception. These are valuable assets to your management.

Time Orientation

You probably are not aware of the extent of your time orientation, or possibly cognizant of how this orientation can be used throughout management. Just what is meant by time orientation? How can it be used in effective management?

Your time orientation occurs in several ways. You use time as a reference point. Your past time reference points indicate events and happenings which have or will occur in your life. Future events and goal attainment are time reference points. Think about some conversations you have heard which use time as a reference point such as, "Tomorrow I'll do . . . ." or "On our vacation last year, we went to . . . ." Future-oriented people plan their time usage in the context of happenings, events, and demands still to come. Thus managerial action is undertaken solely in the context of the future with little or no thought given to previous events or occurrences.

Another reference point is physical time orientation. Your body indicates when you are hungry, tired, or need rest. If you forget to eat, after a certain length of time, your body reminds you in a variety of ways. The same is true when you go without sleep for a long period.

Decision making is often influenced by your time orientation. Some individuals have a past time orientation, others are present-oriented, or future-oriented. Your time orientation past, present, or future, will be a source of input for decision making and ultimately your management. The past-oriented person manages totally in the context of the past. The past is revered. Goals are set by previous happenings. The present-oriented person manages totally in the context of the present moment with little thought to the future or the past. As such, managerial activities may be impulsively done with little or no regard to what the future will bring.

At the same time, you measure progress in achieving your lifetime master plan by the events and occurrences which have happened. You also use these past experiences as reference points. How often have you in talking with your friends, discussed memories of different events such as the first few weeks on your college campus?

Routines and habits also provide you with a time orientation. Aren't there certain tasks you do on specific days of the week? Do you sleep later on weekends than you do during the week without realizing it?

Your time orientation is not solely internal. Your spheres of interaction are also a source of time orientation. Your membership in organizations, and your class schedule are but two examples of time orientation derived from the input received through your spheres of interaction. How many other inputs give you a time orientation?

In decision making you employ the knowledge gained from past experiences through evaluative feedback to make new decisions. As a reference point, these experiences enable you to pin-point happenings in your life. At the same time, future time reference points give direction to your life pathway. Thus these time reference points link the past and future together to give continuity and meaning—to provide you with a sense of security. You know where you have been and where you intend to go.

You, like every other individual, are either past-, present-, or future-oriented. This orientation may be an enabler or a constraint. An individual who is totally past-oriented looks backward rather than ahead. The managerial action taking place is based entirely on the past. Extreme instances of this may result in an individual who cannot adjust to the continual technological changes taking place in society. You may have met someone like this. How does this individual react to changes taking place? The end result may be an individual who is frustrated and unable to successfully function in an advanced society.

The human body in order to function properly needs food, rest, and exercise. Physical time orientation serves as a reminder of these needs. Throughout your life you have established patterns that have evolved into these physical time orientations. When do you eat lunch? What happens when you have a class scheduled for this time? How long does it take for your body to adjust to the new schedule? How does your body tell you when food, rest, or exercise is needed?

Routines and habits also aid in time management. Their repetitive aspects help you to better plan your use of time. Your knowledge of the length of time needed to accomplish certain, routine tasks enables you to use the remaining time in a productive manner.

The input from your spheres of interaction may also be an enabler or a constraint. When you are aware of responsibilities in the shelter sphere, you plan the remaining time accordingly. Knowledge of the economic subsystem enablers and constraints can also affect time utilization. Purchases in the marketplace are usually restricted to certain hours of the day. This affects the allocation of time in the management process.

Knowledge of your time orientation can be a valuable enabler in your management process. Each of these enablers helps you in determining the allocation and use of your time and other resources.

Time Perceptions

How does time orientation differ from your time perceptions? Time orientation involves the relationship of events, locations, persons, objects, and happenings to you and your life. You adapt these to your environment. Time perception, on the other hand, involves an awareness brought about by your senses. These stimulate you to take action through a sensory stimuli.

On weekdays have you ever found yourself awakening slightly before the alarm goes off? Are there instances when time seems to pass slower or faster than you had anticipated? Do you sense the time of day without looking at the clock? These represent time perceptions. Think about how many different ways you are aware of time without looking at the clock.

Time perceptions can also be valuable tools in the management process. When you walk into a retail store and see a certain display it may trigger a stimulus forcing you to remember an event or a specific need. For instance, a display of gloves is a stimulus reminding you that winter is coming.

Have you ever had an instructor whose lecture consistently ended at the close of the class period yet this instructor could not actually see the clock? Have you ever sensed that a task you were undertaking was consuming more time than you anticipated? Both these instances of time perception produced a sensory stimulus.

Although you may not be aware of it, your time perceptions are enablers as you undertake managerial action. For instance how much time is used as you arise, dress, and walk to your first class? These time perceptions enable you to allocate your mental resources of thought to pursue other unrelated endeavors. When you sensed the task you were undertaking consumed more time than anticipated, you responded by taking corrective action, and adjusted your plan.

As with time orientation, these perceptions can aid you in your allocation and use of your time resource. A teacher who has taught for several years automatically knows the length of time needed to teach a certain unit. You also are aware of the length of time required for certain tasks. These time perceptions are valuable tools in management.

Time an Enabling Resource

As a resource, time can be used in several ways. It is combined with other resources to achieve a desired goal or meet a demand. As you assess your time usage, you waste, use, or manage it. Within the management process you make decisions concerning its use. It may be allocated for transferring, exchanging, producing, protecting, saving-investing, or consuming.

The management of your time resources not only affects its utilization but in many instances the use of other resources as well. Every person has the same quantity of this resource. How you use this resource will determine the degree of success you have in achieving your goals and demands. The effectiveness of your use of time will determine the extent to which you attain your desired quality of life.

Using time effectively calls upon your knowledge of the quantitative and qualitative aspects of any other resources combined with your time resource. In addition to this, it also necessitates examining available rsources and determining which combination of resources will bring about the greatest degree of satisfaction while minimizing the use of each. It means examining time resources along with all the others. As you do this, you must also weigh the opportunity costs involved with each resource.

Effective time management involves the following:

1. Recognizing the demands placed upon your time.
2. Ascertaining the goals which necessitate the use of your time resources.
3. Identifying and setting priorities for these demands and goals.
4. Determining which resources to combine with your time resource to enable you to meet demands and achieve goals.

    5. Recognizing those demands which cannot be altered or changed.
    6. Identifying any constraints upon both your time and other resources.
    7. Developing a plan to allocate and use your time resources.

Effective resource management (as indicated in Chapter 6), is directed toward maximizing the use of resources to yield the highest possible degree of satisfaction. Although the availability of your time resource is replenished each day, its allocation and use should be as carefully monitored as any other resource. To do so, the demands being placed upon you and the input you are receiving should be carefully assessed prior to allocation. The essence of time management lies in allocating this resource as effectively as possible.

Since this resource is used concurrently with other resources, it is all too easy to place more emphasis upon effective allocation of another resource which may not be as easily replaced or as readily available. Should you fall into this pattern in allocating resources, you are reducing the options open to you in your overall management.

Time is a resource you should manage as effectively and efficiently as you do any other resource. You will find that as you increase the management of your time resource the allocation and use of other additional resources are often altered, and in many instances, increased. The decisions you make as to whether your time resource should be used for transferring, exchanging, producing, protecting, saving-investing, or consuming are just as vital to your management as those made concerning any other resource.

Planning the Use of Time Resources

A time schedule is a plan you develop and use in order to effectively manage this valuable resource. Time can be used, wasted, or managed. The choice is yours. Unfortunately the words *time schedule* often bring forth negative connotations. Some misconceptions concerning time schedules can be listed.

    1. They are rigid and inflexible.
    2. If used, you live by the clock.
    3. They are used only by efficiency experts.
    4. When used, the humanizing aspects of life are gone.
    5. If used, a time schedule runs your life giving you very little choice or freedom.
    6. Every minute must be accounted for during the entire day.

This list represents only a few of the common misconceptions of a time schedule. What came to mind when you saw the words: *time schedule?* Under certain circumstances, any or all of the misconceptions can happen. Again the choice is yours. Time schedules developed and used in the intended manner can be a valuable tool in management. The misconceptions then become fallacies.

Your time resource is a fixed one. A time schedule is merely an organized plan developed to aid in using this resource more effectively. When it is used in this manner, it is a management tool. Whether it is a tool or a constraint depends upon your attitudes, planning, and your use. Time scheduling when approached as a disagreeable chore, loses its value. A rigidly detailed one leaves little, if any, room for flexibility. The individual who develops such a schedule and meticulously follows it is misusing this tool.

Three different approaches can be used to develop a time schedule. The first is to record your use of this resource in a time log for a two-week period. This method is based on the assumption that the two weeks selected represent your normal activities and time pattern usage. Using the time log as a reference, analyze how you used your resource. Your plan for the coming week is developed on the basis of your analysis.

The second way is to develop the plan for the coming week without considering previous time usage. You start by recording all known time demands such as classes, meetings, and so forth. These represent all of your time demands over which you have little, if any, control. Following this, allocate the remaining time according to priorities. These might include time for laundry, studying, library assignments, and social activities. The remaining time is allocated to lesser priorities.

The third method is a combination of the two. Although this method initially may consume more of your time resource, it will produce the most reliable time schedule. In recording how you actually do use this resource, your patterns of time usage emerge. Here is where your time orientation and perceptions are shown. This time log will also demonstrate the value you place on this resource in relation to others.

After recording time usage, one student discovered that his activities evolved around half-hour time blocks. If a task was completed before the half hour, he waited until the next half hour to being a new one. Another student discovered his value of friendship was greatly affecting his time usage. He was amazed to discover he averaged six hours per day talking with his friends. When he added this to the five hours per day he was spending in classes, he could readily see why he was having to stay up so late at night to complete his course work and meet other time demands.

Start to develop your time schedule using your analysis of the two previous weeks. From your analysis, determine your time use patterns. What are the longest and shortest blocks of time? What are your most common time blocks? These may be either hour or half-hour blocks. Using this as a basis, develop a time chart similar to the one shown in Figure 7.1. These time blocks should start and end with your normal "waking hours."

Once your chart is complete, fill in the blocks for all of your known time

TIME	MONDAY	TUESDAY	WEDNESDAY	THURSDAY	FRIDAY	SATURDAY	SUNDAY

FIGURE 7.1. Individual Time Chart.

demands such as classes, meetings, and work. Referring back to your time log for the past two weeks, block in the time spent in regular routine activities such as getting ready for class, doing laundry, or washing your car. From the analysis of your time log, write in any regularly occurring time patterns such as TV programs you watch on a regular basis, specific study times, or meetings with friends. Most of these form a regular pattern and therefore should be included in the time schedule.

Take a look at your time schedule. Did you realize how much of your time is used on such a predetermined basis? The next items to be completed on the chart are your time demands for the coming week. Do you have any tests scheduled? If so, you may need to allocate additional study time. Include this and any other known time demands on the chart.

The remaining time blocks can now be allocated for your other wants such as leisure and social activities, special projects, privacy, and such. In this final phase of developing the time schedule, you should be cautioned: do not plan every single minute. Remember, interruptions do occur. Some flexibility should be provided in the time schedule.

You now have developed a time schedule for the coming week. Implement it. Undoubtedly you will find as the week progresses, changes will need to be made. You may encounter unforseen demands which will necessitate alteration of your plan. Your time schedule should have enough flexibility to enable you to meet these demands and interruptions. When this occurs, make a note on the time schedule as to what change was made and why.

Once the initial plan has been developed, it should be refined and modified in the coming weeks until you have established a basic time schedule which is workable. Once this has been done, you will have a valuable management tool. You will find you maximize the use of your time resource. In all probability you will be able to accomplish more of your goals than before, and allocate your other resources in a more productive manner.

However, you should remember that repeat-use plans to be effective must be continually modified. A time schedule is a repeat-use plan; therefore, it should be modified for each week to reflect the anticipated demands.

As you use your time schedule you may discover you are more conscious of this resource. As such, you will begin to seek additional ways to use it more effectively. When your class is dismissed ten minutes early, how do you use this "found" time. If you find you completed a task in less time than you anticipated, what do you do? There are probably many instances when you have "found" time. These minutes can be wasted or used productively. How could you productively use five "found" minutes? Or ten? Or fifteen? These "found" minutes might be used to address an envelope, water plants, make a telephone call, or to accomplish many other tasks requiring only a short period of time. Using time productively means becoming aware of your time and constructively using not only the hours but also the minutes.

Time is a valuable resource. Because it is a limited one, its allocation and use are just as important to your management as any other resource.

Using Time Effectively

Business and industry have long been concerned with the use of time resources. In the 1920s Gilbreth and Emerson worked with business and industry.[1] The work of these two men was to have far reaching effects not only upon business and industry but also upon the household. They demonstrated the importance of using time resources in a productive manner. Their work initiated a concern that has continued to the present day. Much research has been devoted to the importance and use of time resources. Jackson and Hayden indicate the scarcest national resource is the time of business's "competent managers."[2]

The importance of time utilization and the individual employee has lead many corporations and industries to adopt the *flextime plan*. When this plan is adopted, the employee determines his or her specific hours of work. The employee must work the normal required hours each day. However, each individual can decide the time of arrival, departure, the length of the lunch hour, and time absent from work for appointments. For instance, one employee may arrive at 7 A.M. but the employee at the next desk may not arrive until 9 A.M. This plan allows the employee to alter the length of the work day to meet obligations and time demands such as medical appointments, civic meetings, and family responsibilities.[3] Corporations and industries are finding a decrease in overtime pay, declining absenteeism, increases in employee moral, greater employee commitment and loyalty, increasing worker productivity, and reductions in sick leave when this plan is adopted.[4]

The adoption of the flextime plan by some corporations and industries is but one example of the increasing emphasis being placed upon time utilization. If large corporations are emphasizing the importance of time as a valuable resource, shouldn't you?

Energy as a Resource

Your energy resource shares many characteristics in common with your time resource. You have a fixed amount available for allocation and use each day. Like time, its replacement necessitates little, if any exertion from you. It, too, is combined with other resources in its allocation and use. Unlike time, quantitative aspects of this resource varies with individuals. Some have more than others. Your supply of this resource may also vary somewhat. Some days you may have more energy than others. This variation in quantity also occurs not only from day to day but also within the day. Are there certain times of the day when you have more energy than others? Your energy resource is important to your management. Knowledge of its availability and potential utilization are vital. This resource, too, is combined with other resources within the management process.

How much energy do you have when you forget to eat? Does the amount of sleep you have determine the amount of available energy? When you work extra hard for long periods of time without a break, does this affect the energy you have for other tasks? Do you find you have less energy when you are doing boring, dull tasks?

Each of these are important factors in determining the quantity of your energy resource. Time is a material resource. Energy is classified as a human resource. As such its availability is governed not only by how you allocate and use it but also by your diet, hours of sleep, rest periods, and your attitudes. As you explore your energy resource you will find there are other aspects which also affect it.

Identifying Energy Resources

As a resource, energy is intangible. Evidences of its existence can be demonstrated by the tasks you accomplish, the activities you undertake, and the speed at which you complete tasks. Your actions and outcomes of energy use are evident to others. As an individual you are aware of the extent which you have used your energy.

Human energy research has been directed toward ascertaining the amount of energy expended while various tasks are being accomplished. The initial studies done by Langworthy and Barott in the 1920s used a calorimeter.[5] Although much of the research concerning energy expenditures for task completion was done in the 1950s, the results are still valid today. Current research is concerned with the factors of stress and fatigue.

The major emphasis concerning your energy resource is maximizing its utilization. As was pointed out earlier, your energy resource occurs in limited amounts. Your management, therefore, should be directed toward maximizing as much as possible the use of this valuable resource to ensure that you have enough energy remaining to meet your other demands. This necessitates becoming aware of your physical energy patterns, your physical actions, and the effect of your attitudes upon this resource. Each of these play an important role in energy utilization. Each time you physically move a part of your body or use your mental capabilities in the thought process you are consuming energy. Thus allocation and use should be directed toward conservation rather than consumption. In order to do so, you need to be aware of your energy levels and the factors that affect them.

Factors Affecting Energy Consumption

Initial energy research was directed primarily at two major objectives. First, to determine the amount of energy expended in the performance of specific tasks. This was accomplished by determining the amount of energy consumed by various portions of the human body. Second, to use this knowledge to determine the best possible way to perform tasks. Energy conservation was accomplished in two ways. The first was to minimize the number of motions used to complete a task. The second was to use, wherever possible, the portions of the body which required the least expenditure of energy.

Gilbreth and Emerson were the forerunners of many "efficiency experts" employed by business and industry. They observed and recorded the motions used by workers in production tasks. These findings were then used to develop worker routines and mechanical apparatus which would reduce body movement. This reduction increased worker productivity.

These early studies were to have an impact not only upon business and industry but also upon the home. The principles and concepts devised for business and industry by Gilbreth and Emerson were adapted for the family and shelter spheres by Mrs. Lilian Gilbreth. Although the equipment and materials used in your home have changed since then, several of the techniques developed are still valid and used today.[6]

As the knowledge of energy conservation increased, this research began to point to other factors affecting energy consumption, such as fatigue, physical impairment, and stress. It was found each of these had an effect upon the consumption of energy resources. These studies, begun in the 1930s, have continued to date.[7]

Physical Impairment

The inability to use certain portions of the human body has an effect upon both the time and energy needed to complete a task. Have you ever been on crutches, had your arm in a cast, or been physically impaired in any other way? Or have you observed someone who was physically impaired?

The extent and nature of a physical impairment will determine how much additional time and energy will be required for task completion. To the physically impaired person, task completion may necessitate not only more time and energy but also special equipment. It may also mean having to retrain muscles, learning to use different muscles, learning to complete tasks using different portions of the body, or developing new skills and techniques. It does not mean that the physically impaired person can no longer undertake task accomplishment. It does mean the physically impaired person can independently, through the use of work simplification techniques, perform task accomplishment. It also means these tasks, in order to be accomplished, will require more energy to complete.[8]

Fatigue

Although the initial research concerning energy consumption viewed fatigue in the context of physical exertion, further research began to examine the concept of fatigue more closely. As these studies continued, it became apparent that fatigue can have many causes other than physical exertion. Studies soon found environmental factors, human factors, and task factors were directly related to the reduction of work performance.[9]

Physical Fatigue

The causal factor of physical fatigue is the actual expenditure of physical effort to complete a task. The specific amount of energy expended can be measured and assessed. Physical fatigue results from physical activity. As you perform operational tasks you use energy.

Although task complexity and the duration of the task are important, when an individual's capabilities do not exceed the demands being placed upon them, fatigue does not occur to the same extent as it does when the individual seeks to perform a task which is beyond physical capabilities.[10] Age and physical fitness have been found to be fatigue related factors.[11] Still another factor which will produce physical fatigue is a nutritional deficiency.[12]

In addition, environmental factors can produce physical fatigue. These would include: aspects of temperature, humidity, clothing, and noise.[13] Fatigue inducing environmental factors are also created when deviation from normal conditions occurs.[14]

Although environmental factors in and of themselves are fatigue inducing factors, far greater factors are the human and task-associated ones. Human factors include: age, sex, fitness, nutrition, body build, physical and mental capabilities, and emotional stability.[15] Task-associated factors include: the complexity, duration, skills, and the physical and mental exertion needed.[16]

Mental Fatigue

Mental fatigue occurs as energy is used in intellectual activities involving the thought process. Haven't you found yourself extremely tired after spending several hours studying or doing research? When this occurs you are experiencing mental fatigue.

Mental activities require the use of your energy just as does the physical actions required to wash a car. Although authorities differ in equating physical and mental activities, both draw upon your energy resource. The full extent of this causal factor is still under study.

Boredom, Frustration, and Stress

The causal factor in boredom, frustration, and stress is quite different from either physical or mental fatigue factors. Yet in each case, energy consumption takes place. Have you ever found yourself extremely tired after just sitting through a long, dull lecture? Why did you feel tired?

Boredom can be caused by different factors. Wyatt and Langdon found boredom occurred more often among workers who continually repeated the same actions with no anticipation of change in the future.[17] Bullen, in studying office personnel, found the continual repetitive nature of a single task produced boredom. This, in turn, yielded day-dreaming and a reduction in work performance. Boredom was further increased if the individual completing the task did not understand either the importance or the relationship of this specific task to the entire production process.[18]

Fatigue caused by boredom can be reduced by frequent work interruptions.[19] It can also be reduced by altering the physical environment. The office workers in Bullen's study responded to variations in music tempos and in the physical setting where work and rest periods occurred.[20]

As you think about different tasks, perhaps one of the reasons you disliked a certain task was because it was boring. Perhaps another reason you disliked a certain task was frustration. Have you ever been frustrated about an assigned project? Why were you frustrated?

Frustration can stem from a variety of factors. Steidl found the difficulty, complexity, and the intensity of tasks were factors in whether a homemaker liked or disliked a task.[21] Gross, Crandall, and Knoll report frustration is also induced when (a) the task being undertaken is one which is unfamiliar, (b) when external feelings or concerns are projected into the task, (c) the individual is unable to accomplish the task, or (d) the nature of the task is such that it must constantly be repeated.[22]

Your frustration in seeking to complete an assigned project may have resulted from the lack of communication. In other words, you may not have specifically known what was expected of you. The person making the assignment did not effectively communicate the necessary information for you to complete the task.

Have you ever tried to accomplish a task and continually been interrupted? Disruptions that break the work rate are an effective method of reducing boredom but can also produce frustration if they are unplanned and occur repeatedly.

In seeking to alleviate frustration you need to isolate the causal factor. When frustration occurs it is all too easy to isolate the symptom as the causal factor. For instance, was your frustration with an assigned project your inability to locate information in the library? Or perhaps was the causal factor quite different. Frustration can be controlled only when the real causal factor is determined and remedial steps are taken.[23]

Stress is still another causal factor inducing fatigue. The occurrence of stress may stem from the task being undertaken or from human factors.[24] Bullen's study of factory workers found the pressure to meet a specified work quota induced stress. Other stress inducing factors were inadequate or improperly functioning equipment, poorly lighted or inadequate working conditions, noise, vibrations, lack of sufficient materials, and the attitude and actions conveyed by supervisors.[25]

Stress along with boredom and frustration increases energy consumption. When you have to complete a task under a great deal of pressure how well do you perform? How tired are you when the job is done? Although the task you are undertaking may not be an extremely difficult one, the aspects of boredom, frustration, and stress are viable ones in determining your energy consumption. When any or all of these occur, any task, regardless of its complexity, will place a heavier drain on your energy resources. Maximizing your energy utilization necessitates not only reducing the amount of energy needed to complete a task but also recognizing the extent to which other factors affect its use.

Interlinking of Time and Energy Resources

Your time and energy are separate resources. Each has individual characteristics. They also share much in common. During the management process each is allocated and used. Although they are separate resources, their allocation and use are related. The performance of almost every task, attaining of goals, or meeting a demand necessitates the allocation and use of time and energy to some degree. Can you think of any task, goal, or demand which would not involve utilization of both?

Despite the close association of these two resources, some common misconceptions occur. How often have you thought of your time resource as having limitations but not your energy? When you allocate time do you also consciously allocate your energy resource too? How often have you thought or referred to your time resource but not your energy?

These resources, although separate and distinct, are linked closely together. The allocation and use of one, for the most part, is dependent upon the other. Yet when individuals plan they tend to think only in terms of allocating and using time. Effective management necessitates the allocation and use of each as separate resources. It also necessitates developing an awareness of the linkage which occurs between the two.

Your time log can be a valuable aid in determining your use of both time and energy. As you look at this log begin to ask yourself some questions. During what portions of the day can you really accomplish quite a large amount of work? Aren't there also times when you are able to accomplish very little?

During the day you have high, moderate, and low productive times. These time spans represent your work production curve, that is, your capacity for productive efforts throughout the day. When placed in a graphic charting format (Figure 7.2) you can see your available energy levels throughout the day. This chart also demonstrates the interlinkage of time and energy resources. Awareness and use of your work production curve is a valuable management tool.

The typical work curve starts upward at the time you awaken until it peaks at a set level. This level is then maintained for a prolonged period of time. It gradually begins to drop and then rises again. The second peak level is generally not as high as the first and will not be maintained as long as the first. Following this second rise, the energy level will begin a decline and continue to do so until you go to sleep.

Think about yourself and your productive capabilities. What times of the day are you most and least productive? Developing your work production curve

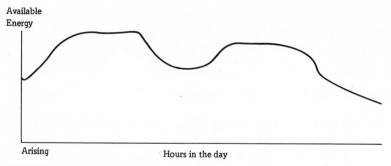

FIGURE 7.2. *Work Production Curve.*

can be a tool in the management of your resources. Knowing when your energy resource is more readily available enables you to use more wisely your time and energy resources.

Although the linkage of time and energy resources is graphically shown in the work production curve both of these resources have limitations. Careful allocation of both is necessary if you are to manage effectively. Your work production curve is an enabler. Tasks that require a high degree of concentration and/or excessive energy should be scheduled during the peak levels of your work curve. Conversely those tasks and activities that do not require extensive concentration or activity should be scheduled during lower peaks.

As you plan your time schedule use your knowledge of your work curve. Highly technical reading assignments should be scheduled during peak levels of the work production curve. This also applies, whenever possible, to the scheduling of your courses. Courses with complicated procedures or that are highly technical should be scheduled during high energy peaks.

Just as your resources of time and energy are linked together, so are your work production curve and your time schedule. The enabling value of each is dependent upon the degree to which each correlates with the other. As you combine the allocation and use of other resources with your time and energy, you may find you are conserving not only these two but other resources as well.

Summary

Time and energy are valuable resources. Although each occurs as a separate resource, their allocation and use are linked closely together. Maximizing the use of both is of prime importance in effective management. The allocation and use of these resources necessitates developing an awareness of their individual characteristics, the tools which can be employed for their allocation and use, and the factors which affect their availability.

Both of these resources have limitations. Time is a material resource while energy is a human one. The decisions made concerning each of these resources is based upon the values attached to each. Both are enabling resources within the management process.

Time scheduling and work production curves are two tools that can be used for effective management. A time schedule should be developed to enable you to meet the demands placed upon you. As it is developed consideration should be given to the work production curve. This should be used in task scheduling to meet demands. When correlation between these tools takes place, more effective allocation and use of both resources is achieved.

The allocation and utilization of other resources is often closely allied to time and energy resources. Effective allocation of these often enables you to minimize expenditures of others as well. Because the correlation between resource utilization is allied with time and energy, these two resources play a vital role in your daily management.

ACTIVITIES

1. What are your time orientations? Identify all the different ways you are aware of the time of the day and the day of the week without looking at either a clock or a calendar. How are these different time orientations important to your management?
2. Draw what you feel is a graphic representation of your work production curve. Compare this to the time and energy demands you have during a weekday. Assume you could schedule your classes during the most optimum time for your work curve, what would be your class schedule and why?
3. Select three different experiences you have had that were either frustrating, boring, or produced stress. Analyze the symptoms and the causal factors in each instance.
4. Keep a log of how you use your time resources for two weeks. Be as specific as possible. Do not record in time blocks of less than 15 minutes. Analyze your use of time. Are there instances where your use of time has not been productive? What has created these? What could you do to remedy the situation in the future?
5. Develop a time schedule for the coming week. Once it is completed, use this management tool for the week. Note on the time schedule each time you change the use of your time resource and the factor that created the change. Analyze your use of time after you have used this tool for a week.
6. Record your use of energy resources for each day for one week. Analyze how you have used your energy resources. Compare how you used your energy resource with your work production curve. What changes would you make to more efficiently use your energy resources in the future?

7. Analyze your time log in regard to your work curve. How closely do they correlate? Where are the differences? How is your time use affected by your energy utilization?

8. Select one of the early forerunners of conservation of time and energy resources. Read an article written by one of these individuals. How many of their ideas, techniques, and studies are still valid today? Can you identify modifications of their original techniques which are currently used?

TIME LOG

A.M.

7:00 Alarm rang. Reached over and pushed the "snooze" button. Fifteen more minutes before I have to get up.

7:15 Alarm rings again. Pushed the five-minute "snooze" button.

7:20 Alarm rings. Sit on edge of bed and push back curtains. Raining again!

7:25 Walk down hall to shower. Come back to room.

7:50 Hunt notebook for class. Can't find it. Grabbed roommate's and started to class. Had to go back to get jacket. Forgot it was raining.

7:55 Sloshed to class. Remembered Sue borrowed notebook to copy notes.

8:05 Late to class again. Class cancelled. Dr. S has flu. Must remember to call Sue about notebook.

8:06 Started to slosh back to dorm with roommate's notebook. Met Jack who was going to library. Have paper due next week. Might as well go with him.

8:15 Got to library. Looked up several references. Tried to read but forgot glasses.

9:30 Went back to dorm to get glasses. Roommate mad because I took notebook. Left note telling me to leave it when I get back.

9:45 Telephone call from Sue. Told me to meet her before the next class. Hunt glasses.

9:55 Finally found glasses under the bed. Went to class in the rain.

10:00 Chem Lab! Sloshed all the way. Forgot to bring lab notes. Dr. J. gave me lecture about it before giving me new copy. Told me he didn't like people to continually come late to class. Remembered I left lab coat in Jake's car. Borrowed Sam's from his locker; he won't care. Got notebook from Sue.

12:00 Back to the dorm for lunch. The food was Ugh! Would have eaten at Union but didn't have any money.

12:45 No class until 3. Decided to study for test tomorrow. Met Pam and talked to her.

P.M.

1:00 Got to my room. Phone ringing. Can't find keys. Roommate in class. Phone stopped ringing. Guess whoever it was will call back. Remembered left keys in jacket in chem lab. locker.

1:10 Walked to chem lab to get jacket. Good thing I did. It started to rain just as I got in the building. As long as I am here and it's raining, might as well finish chem lab didn't get done this morning. Dr. J. Surprised to see me and with my lab notes, too. Didn't tell him why.

2:15 Looked out window. Stopped raining.

2:30 Finished lab. Stopped for a coke before going to class. Found 30¢ in jacket pocket.

3:00 Class.

4:00 Back to my room. Found note from roommate: "Where is notebook?" Also supposed to call Jim. Called Jim. He wants to know how long meeting tonight will last. Forgot about it.

4:15 Sat down to write up agenda for meeting. Sue called. Wants to know if she can borrow notebook again. Told her to call someone else.

4:30 Mom called because I haven't written. Told her I was busy. Wants to know if I am coming home this weekend. Told her I might. Aunt Sarah got on extension to say "hello" and then went on and on about her operation. When she finally got off this subject she spent another ten minutes telling me how hard it is to believe I am in college. Mom wants to know if I need anything. What a question! She is sending $20.00 in the mail. Am not to tell Dad. Mom worried if I am getting enough to eat. Promised to call about this weekend.

5:20 Roommate came in. Raining again. Decided to eat here. Don't want to get soaked again. Meatloaf again tonight! Doesn't the cook know how to fix anything else?

6:20 Started for the meeting. Forgot notes and had to go back up to the room. Remembered my glasses so picked them up, too. Met Sue in the hall and let her have my notebook if she gets it back by 9 tonight. Promised she would.

6:35 Finally got to the meeting. Jim made a crack about how I would probably be late for my own funeral. Funny man!

8:30 Meeting over. Was going back to the dorm but decided to stop at Harry's. I'll have a quick beer and then go back to study for a test.

9:30 Started to leave. Got stopped by Pam and Jack. Had another beer with them.

10:30 Got back to the dorm. Started to the elevator but met Jake. We talked about going home this weekend. Can ride with him but he is leaving at noon. Would have to miss my 3 P.M. class. Told him I probably would if I don't have a test. Dr. B won't care—if there isn't a test. I hope!

11:00 Study time. Looked for notebook. Can't find it. Called Sue. She still had it because she knew I wouldn't be back at 9. Should be finished and right over with it.

11:15 Called Sue again. Said she was just leaving. Decided to order a pizza while I wait for Sue. Roommate will pay this time. Will buy the next time after Mom's money gets here.

12:00 Sue and the pizza got here at the same time. Sue thanked me for the loan of the notes. Stayed to help us eat the pizza. Tasted good but could have been hotter.

12:30 Roommate went to bed. Sue left. Time to study.

A.M.

1:30 Have read half of my notes. Wonder if I should read the book, too? Started to read text but got confused. Decided to stick with my notes.

2:30 Woke up. Guess I must have "dozed" off. Back to the notes.

3:00 Can't stay awake. Will go to bed and get up early. Set alarm for 6 A.M. Went to bed.

Discussion Questions

1. Analyze the student time log as presented. How would you rate this student's use of time and energy resources? What would you suggest this student do to make better use of time and energy resources?
2. Identify this student's values. How are these values affecting time and energy resources? Put this student's values in a priority ranking as they are demonstrated in this log.
3. How would you characterize this student? Would a time schedule help this student? What do you feel would happen if this student developed a time schedule?
4. What would happen if this student's roommate were a completely organized individual? What do you anticipate would occur between these two individuals?
5. Develop a time schedule for this student that you feel would be usable and still reflect the student's priority values.

GLOSSARY

Boredom Occurs when the individual uses energy for actions that are repetitive, have no measurable reward, or are viewed as not producing satisfaction.

Fatigue Occurs when energy levels are reduced due to physical action, mental exertion, boredom, frustration, or stress.

Flextime Plan A plan developed that allows employees to determine specific working hours within a given work day.

Frustration Occurs when energy is consumed in endeavors which are unfamiliar, or the individual feels unable to accomplish the designated task, or external feelings are projected into task completion, or communication skills inadequately convey expectations and directions.

Mental Fatigue Occurs when energy is used in intellectual activities involving the thought process.

Physical Fatigue Occurs when physical actions result in the reduction of energy resources.

Physical Impairment The inability of one or more portions of the human body to function in the normal manner.

Physical Time Orientation The patterns established by the human body such as eating, sleeping, and resting.

Stress Occurs when the individual completing task assignment feels pressured, functions in an inadequate environmental situation, lacks sufficient or operable materials and equipment, or has damaging communication with supervisor(s).

Time Log A written record detailing the expenditures of time for specific activities, functions, or endeavors.

Time Orientation Using past, present, or future time as a reference point to establish the relationship of events, happenings, people, locations, or circumstances.

Time Perception The stimulation of action by a time-related sensory stimulus.

Time Schedule A management tool involving a plan developed to allocate time spans to specific tasks, endeavors, activities, or physical needs.

Work Production Curve A graphic representation of the energy levels of an individual for any given day.

REFERENCES

1. Irma H. Gross, Elizabeth Walbert Crandall, and Marjorie M. Knoll, *Management for Modern Families,* 3rd ed. (New York: Appleton-Century-Crofts, 1973), p. 156.
2. Ibid., p. 671.
3. John H. Jackson and Roger L. Hayden, "Rationing the Scarcest Resource: A Manager's Time," *Personal Journal* (October 1974), 752.
4. Barry Stien, Allan Cohen, and Herman Gadon, "Flextime Work When You Want To," *Psychology Today* (June 1976), 40.
5. Ibid.
6. Gross, Crandall, and Knoll, op. cit., p. 383.
7. Ibid.
8. Ibid.
9. Elizabeth Eckhardt May, Neva R. Waggoner, and Eleanor Boettke Hotte, *Independent Living for Handicapped and the Elderly* (Boston: Houghton Mifflin Company, 1974), p. 19.
10. Ernst Simonson, ed., *Physiology of Work Capacity and Fatigue* (Springfield, Ill.: Charles C Thomas Publisher, 1971), p. 325.
11. Ibid., pp. 325–326.
12. Ibid., p. 406.
13. Ibid., p. 328.

14. Ibid., p. 325.
15. Ibid.
16. Ibid.
17. Gross, Crandall, and Knoll, op. cit., p. 387.
18. Adelaide K. Bullen, *New Answers to the Fatigue Problem* (Gainesville: University of Florida Press, 1956), pp. 31–35.
19. Simonson, op. cit., p. 350.
20. Bullen, op. cit., pp. 29–35.
21. Rose E. Steidl, "Affective Dimensions of High and Low Cognitive Home-making Tasks," *Home Economics Research Journal* (December 1975), 121–137.
22. Gross, Crandall, and Knoll, op. cit., pp. 388–389.
23. Ibid., p. 393.
24. Simonson, op. cit., p. 326.
25. Bullen, op. cit., pp. 59–85.

CHAPTER EIGHT

Time and Energy Management

Business and industry have, over many years, been concerned with the aspects of increasing worker productivity. This concern has continually motivated corporations to search for the most efficient and effective ways to produce goods and services while expending the least amount of available resources. This search is motivated by two factors: (1) to produce goods and services at a price which the consumer is willing to pay and (2) to increase corporate profits. Thus each corporation, whether large or small, is constantly concerned with worker productivity.

Business and industry are aware of their resource limitations and their profit margins. You probably do not view your shelter sphere in the context of a business nor in terms of profit margins, yet worker productivity is an important aspect of household operation. Although in most cases, the term *profit margin* is associated with money and corporations, this same concept also applies to the shelter sphere.

Regardless of the location or size of your shelter sphere, your stage in the life cycle, or your occupational endeavor, you have operational tasks that must be completed. These operational tasks necessitate the use of your resources. You, like business and industry, should be concerned with worker productivity as you undertake and accomplish these operational tasks. You and your shelter sphere have resource limitations. As you accomplish your goals to attain your desired quality of life, you must allocate resources. The degree to which you attain your goals and ultimately your desired quality of life are often influenced by the effectiveness of worker productivity in your shelter sphere.

Your time and energy resources represent two of your most valuable commodities. Time schedules and work production curves are two tools you can use to increase the "profit margin" within the shelter sphere. These tools when combined with a knowledge of worker production aspects increase your management capabilities.

Worker Productivity in Management

Why should you be concerned with worker productivity? Just what is involved in determining worker productivity? How does it apply to you? How can it help in management?

As you have seen from Chapter 7, time and energy are valuable but limited resources. The tools of a time schedule and knowledge of your work production curve are enablers. Sole use of either or both will not totally minimize the use of these resources. However, when these tools are combined with a knowledge of

171

work simplification and the factors affecting energy availability and consumption, worker productivity is increased.

Increasing worker productivity involves developing an awareness of your physical capabilities, learning to use body movements in a productive manner, and the arrangement of work surface areas and equipment. The result is used to schedule tasks on the basis of your work production curve. This applies not only to you as an individual but also to those you are supervising or working with. As you seek to increase your worker productivity, you need to become cognizant of the factors that affect not only your productive efforts but those of others.

All too often the term *worker productivity* denotes a concerted emphasis on the physical motions of the human body. This is a misconception. Although it is true that worker productivity does involve physical action, it also includes an examination of the work space, the scheduling of tasks, the maximum and minimum amount of task completion time, the capabilities of each individual involved in the action, the communication taking place, as well as many other factors.

A high degree of worker productivity is achieved when you incorporate each of these into a total managerial process. To ascertain the implications of each, they should be experienced separately. Although the primary intent is to reduce the expenditure of resources, it does not necessarily mean that the fastest, quickest way to complete a task is the most efficient or effective.

Work Simplification

What is meant by the term *work simplification?* Where did the term originate? How is it used? Why is work simplification important to management? How do you use it in the management process?

The primary purpose of work simplification is to develop techniques that will reduce the allocation and minimize the use of your resources. The goal is to produce the highest degree of satisfaction with the least expenditure of resources while yielding the most desirable outcome. Research on this topic began in industrial firms before the turn of the century. Noted names in this field of study include Harrison Emerson and Frank Gilbreth.[1] They were the forerunners of the efficiency experts in business and industry.

The first research into work simplification was devoted primarily to the study of movements, work space and surface, and the flow of materials and supplies. As society's technology increased, scientific testing equipment was devised and used to measure the specific amounts of energy consumed for various tasks. These studies and the refinement of work simplification have continued to the present time.

The initial application of the principles of industrial work simplification to the household was done by Lillian Gilbreth who worked closely with her husband, Frank. Following his death, she and Christine Frederick continued this work.[2] These two women were the forerunners of work simplification for the home. Christine Frederick's first publication was written in 1911.[3] Her techniques have been refined and modified in accordance with advancing technological changes taking place in equipment, household furnishings, and home-use products.

Today's shelter sphere bears little resemblance to that of Lillian Gilbreth and Christine Frederick. Managerial activities within the shelter sphere have changed too. Equipment has been developed to perform many of the tasks that were previously done manually. The vacuum cleaner used for carpet care is but one example. Technology has also produced materials and supplies to reduce some of the physical effort needed. Despite the advances made, work simplification is still a necessity, and the need for its use has not diminished.

The length of the work week of the employed person has been continually reduced over the years.[4] This has yielded an increased emphasis on leisure-time activities.[5] Although the work week of the employed individual has been reduced, the demands upon time resources has increased.[6] Family members are participating more in activities outside the shelter sphere. Parents are finding the time gained from reduced work hours is often devoted to other demands such as transporting children to out-of-home activities like music lessons; school sponsored or church related activities; social functions; medical and dental appointments; or meetings of the Boy or Girl Scouts, Indian Guides, Campfire Girls, 4-H, or other youth organizations. The civic and social involvement of the adult members is also increasing. Each of these place additional demands upon the resources of all family members.

Research also shows an ever increasing number of adult females within the family are entering and remaining in the labor force.[7] Walker and Walker's study shows that although the adult female is employed full-time within the labor force her assumption of household operational tasks does not diminish.[8]

Other research clearly indicates the time used for household operation by the homemaker who is not gainfully employed has not drastically changed since the 1920s.[9] The amount of time spent by the employed homemaker is less than the full-time homemaker. A study done by the University of Michigan indicates an average of forty hours per week is used by all homemakers in household operational tasks.[10] Thus work simplification is important to both the gainfully employed and full-time homemakers.

What does work simplification involve? In devising work simplification techniques you need to become aware of the relationship of space, equipment, materials and supplies, physical structure, and motion to the task being undertaken. The knowledge you have of these relationships, one to another, assists you in developing techniques to reduce or minimize resource consumption.

Have you ever stood working at a counter surface that was too low? How did you physically feel after working there for ten minutes? After thirty minutes? After an hour? Were you able to work at the same speed throughout the entire task?

Work simplification involves more than just completing a task. There are several components involved. Each one affects the overall task completion and the consumption rate of your resources.

Work Area

The rate of consumption of time and energy in task completion is affected by the work area. The work area is composed of the height, available space of the work surface, the location of the equipment, materials, and supplies being used. The work surface should be at the optimum height for the position you assume in task completion. This means if you are standing, the surface height should be slightly below your waistline. During the task completion there should be no necessity to bend at the waistline or hipline to complete any actions involved in the task. When in a seated position, your work surface should not require you to reach upward nor should there be excessive bending of the neck in order to view the activity in progress. Excessive bending at the waistline, in all probability, also indicates your work surface is too low. Both feet should rest comfortably on the floor. Good posture should be observed at all times.

Reach Area

Closely allied to the work surface is the location of the materials, supplies, and equipment. You have two reaching zones affecting your energy consumption. The maximum reach zone, shown in Figure 8.1, is created when your arms are

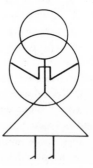

FIGURE 8.1. Maximum Reach Area. [Adapted from Naomi Shank, Make Your Kitchen Modern (Iowa State Extension Service, Bulletin P 62, 1948), p. 51.]

FIGURE 8.2. Minimum Reach Area. [Adapted from Naomi Shank, Make Your Kitchen Modern (Iowa State Extension Service, Bulletin P 62, 1948), p. 51.]

fully extended outward from the body to form a circle or arch. This circle represents the farthest you can reach without stretching or moving another part of your body. Any task, whether seated or standing, should be performed within your maximum reach zone. Tasks that extend beyond this area require additional movement and thus necessitate further energy and time expenditures.

The normal reach zone, shown in Figure 8.2, is formed by the circle extending outward from your body when your arms are bent at the elbows. It is within this zone that most of your work actually takes place. The specific task undertaken is performed here. Within this circle you have the optimum view and the most effective work motions.

Both of these reach zones have an effect upon your time and energy consumption. Any materials, supplies, and equipment necessary for task completion should be located within the maximum reach zone. The specific action occurs within the normal reach zone.

Although these two zones are important for task completion, they also play an important role in organizing work centers. Equipment, materials, and supplies used on a regular basis should be placed in these zones, and where possible on upper cabinets. You use less energy reaching upward than when reaching downward. Heavy equipment should also be stored in upper rather than lower cabinets, where possible.

Work Space

The amount of work space is another factor needed to complete the task. When you are typing a term paper, is your desk large enough to hold both your typewriter and all of the materials and supplies you need? What happens when you don't have a large enough work surface area? Lack of sufficient space often necessitates excessive physical motion whether you are standing or seated. These additional motions require more energy.

Equipment, Materials, and Supplies

Work simplification also involves the equipment, materials, and supplies needed. Suppose your task was to mow the lawn. How much energy as well as time would you use if your equipment consisted of a manual push mower? A motor-driven walking mower? A riding mower? The consumption rate of your resources to complete a specific task will be dependent not only upon the availability of equipment, materials, and supplies but also upon their working condition, accessibility, intended function, and storage location. Advancing technology has provided you with a wide variety of equipment. Use of this equipment may or may not reduce the amount of time actually consumed. However, for the most part, it does produce a better, more uniform product than when the task is manually done. The availability of this equipment has also created many changes in your shelter-sphere. Would you want wall-to-wall carpeting installed if vacuum cleaners did not exist?

The availability of equipment and the use of your resources will have little, if any, effect upon the reduction of resource consumption unless location of the equipment encourages its use, it is in good working condition, and the proper operational procedure is employed. Think about all of the equipment items you have. Where are they stored? How often do you use them? Where is rarely used equipment stored? The location of equipment is a factor in its actual use.

Frequently used equipment should be stored so it is readily available. Therefore it is located in either the maximum or normal reach zones. The size and frequency of use will determine the specific zone. The most frequently used equipment should, if at all possible, be stored within the normal reach zone.

To conserve both natural energy such as electricity and your time and energy resources, equipment should be kept in good working condition. When equipment needs repair or is not operating at its optimum level, more natural energy is required.[11] When this occurs you probably increase the expenditures of your resources to compensate for poorly functioning equipment in order to achieve the desired outcome.

Just as equipment availability has an effect upon task completion so, too, does materials and supplies. Like equipment, these should be stored within the maximum or normal reach zones.

Task accomplishment requires not only available equipment but also the necessary materials and supplies. You would not undertake the task of typing a term paper without making certain you had the typing paper. The extent to which your resources are used in task accomplishment is dependent upon the quantity and accessibility of needed materials and supplies.

Physical Structure

Although time is an external resource, your energy resource is an internally occurring one. Learning to effectively use your physical structure will minimize the extent to which time and energy resources are expended. This, in turn, will yield resources to be allocated for other uses. When this occurs, the production of the desired outcome and the capability to allocate for other purposes yields a higher degree of satisfaction.

Conservation of your resources is the goal of work simplification. Since task completion, for the most part, involves physical motion, work simplification techniques are developed to minimize energy expenditures as much as possible. To do this, you need to become not only "motion-minded" but also conscious of the various ways physical movement can increase or reduce energy consumption.

Management of your energy resources begins by studying the various aspects affecting the consumption of this valuable resource. You need to become aware of your physical structure and how your movements, stance, and other physical actions may increase or minimize your energy consumption.

Body Alignment

Your physical structure is designed to evenly distribute your weight over your legs. They are your primary support. As such you have a center of gravity. As you perform tasks, regardless of whether you are seated or standing, more energy is consumed when the body is out of alignment. Poor physical alignment results in an unequal distribution of weight. Additional energy is needed to maintain the body position. Continued poor alignment produces muscle fatigue at a faster rate. This in turn uses more energy. Keeping your body aligned is an important factor in minimizing energy consumption.

Posture

Throughout your life, teachers and parents have probably emphasized the importance of good posture. Although they probably were not aware of it, good posture minimizes energy consumption. Here, too, good posture should be maintained regardless of the position or movements of the body. Are you maintaining good posture right now? If not, you are using more of your energy resources than necessary. Poor posture often means that not only is your body in poor alignment but you are using muscles not intended to support your physical structure. As a result, you are not only consuming your energy at a faster rate but also placing a strain on your muscles.

Are there some tasks you perform where you tire easily? Do you maintain good posture as you work or are you "slumping"? As you attend classes, how do you sit? Classroom chairs or desks were designed for good posture. When you fail to maintain it, you use more energy and tire faster. At the same time, you may find it is much harder to concentrate.

Each time you increase your energy consumption to maintain poor posture you are using energy. This energy consumption means it will not be available for the completion of other tasks.

Body Mechanics

Your body is composed of a series of muscles, some larger than others. A study of these muscles and their function is important to minimize the use of your energy resources.

Each time you undertake a task you should be using the largest possible muscles to do the job. If you don't, you are consuming more of your energy than is necessary. To illustrate this, place a book on a flat surface. Now lift it by one corner using only your thumb and one finger. Can you feel the pull on your arm muscles? Hold the book in the air for a few mintues. Can you feel the pull on your shoulder as well as your arm muscles? Repeat this same action but this time lift and hold the book in the normal manner. Do you notice any difference? Now place the book on the floor. Bend from your waist to pick it up. You will notice the pull on your leg muscles. Return to a standing position. This time bend at the knee and hipline to pick up the book. Is there a difference here?

The first time you undertook these tasks you used smaller muscles; the second time, larger muscles were used. Work simplification involves learning to use the muscles in your body effectively.

Body mechanics also involves coordinating your muscles with the action taking place. To illustrate this, do the following experiments in your room.

1. Have someone sit in a chair with his back to you. Assume this represents a heavy desk you need to move across the room. Place your hands on the top of the chair back. Now move the chair forward. If at all possible try this experiment in front of a mirror. Examine your position. What muscles are you using?

2. In a standing position clasp a book in front of you using both hands. Swing the book from left to right to form a half circle in front of your body. Stop the swing when the book is back in front of you. Repeat this swinging motion five times coming to a full stop in front of your body after each full swing. Rest for two minutes.

   Now repeat the same motion with the book, this time swing it from left to right five times without stopping in front of your body until the end of the last swing. Compare your two swing motions. Which used the most energy? Why?

These two experiments and the preceding one demonstrate the correlation between body mechanics and energy consumption. In the first one you moved a simulated heavy object. Your body was not only out of alignment but you were using incorrect muscles to accomplish the task. In the second experiment you were stopping your motion after each action. In the second trial you were using a body rhythm to accomplish the task.

To minimize energy consumption during task accomplishment, use your knowledge of body mechanics. This means keeping the body in alignment, using the largest possible muscles, and developing and maintaining a paced rhythm throughout the action. Each of these play an important role in work simplification and the consumption rate of your resources.

Time and Motion

Minimizing the expenditure of both your time and energy resources are important. Although an emphasis solely on energy utilization will, in all probability, reduce to some extent your time expenditures, it alone will not accomplish the goal of work simplification.

Have you ever observed someone undertaking task action in an unfamiliar setting? What actions do you take when you change the sheets on your bed? As you clean off the top of your desk, what motions are involved? Work simplification involves effectively using your physical capabilities, to develop techniques to reduce both the time requirements and the number of motions needed to complete a task.

Work simplification means becoming motion-minded by examining the movements taken to complete a task. Reducing the movements and motions to the smallest possible number minimizes both your time and energy resource expenditures. There are two methods which can be used to identify the motions involved in task completion. The pathway chart involves recording the number of steps and the travel patterns taken by the individual to complete a task. The second involves the recording of the motions used to complete a task. Both of these methods were developed by Lillian Gilbreth.[12]

Pathway Chart

The pathway chart is used to graphically record the actual steps and travel patterns of an individual during the accomplishment of a specific task. By recording the travel pattern you are able to analyze where time and energy are needlessly used. Once completed it can also be used to determine possible aids, either physical or mechanical, which can be employed to minimize travel patterns.

Figure 8.3 is an example of a pathway chart. This method of task analysis is relatively simple to use. Begin by diagramming the setting for task accomplishment. As the individual completes the task, chart the travel pattern on the

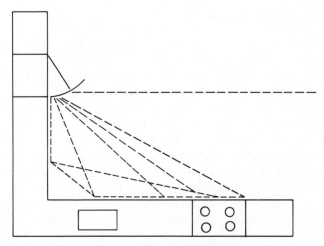

FIGURE 8.3. Pathway Chart for Vegetable Preparing and Cooking.

diagram. Be sure to trace the footsteps of the individual from start to finish. When retracing occurs, be certain one line does not cover another.

Once the task has been completed, analyze the travel pattern. Were steps retraced? Was the retracing necessary? Could some, part, or all of the retracing be eliminated? What aids or devices could have been used to reduce the retracing or to reduce retracing to a minimum?

A pathway chart can be a valuable tool in management. Although it was originally developed for industrial purposes, it has been readily adapted to the analysis of numerous operational tasks. It can analyze tasks regardless of where they are performed. As you determine your class schedule for the coming school term, examine your pathway chart. Are you retracing your travel pattern between buildings? Why? Could you eliminate some, part, or all of the retracing by using a different class schedule?

As you perform various tasks, the use of a pathway chart will also identify the use of other resources. After identifying the resources used, you can explore ways of reducing or minimizing their consumption. The pathway chart can also examine the sequencing of actions. Do the movements flow from one area to another?

Pathway charts are a management tool. Their use allows you to examine your travel patterns as you complete a task. Such an analysis can indicate possible reorganization of work centers and storage areas. It may also indicate the necessity of aids such as trays and rolling carts. In addition pathway charts can be used to examine the work flow. A pathway chart could also be used to analyze your room for study efficiency by examining room arrangement, shelving requirements, and other study aids.

Minimizing the number of steps required to complete a task reduces your consumption of time and energy resources. The pathway chart is a tool used for this purpose.

Time-Motion Studies

There are several different time and motion charts that can be used to analyze the movements during task completion. These, too, were developed by Lillian Gilbreth and others. Time and energy are consumed in walking, standing, or sitting. The motions of the body also consume time and energy. Time-motion studies identify motions and movements taken during task accomplishment.

The chart shown in Figure 8.4 is actually a compilation of several different charts used in the study of the motions and movements involved in the completion of a specific task. Figure 8.4 combines into one chart the (1) operational chart, (2) pathway chart, and (3) process chart.[13]

The purpose of time-motion study is to analyze the operations, movements, inspections, and delays used in accomplishing a specific task. An analysis of this record can be used to determine the possibility of reductions in motions and movements.

Steps	Movement	Operation	Narrative	Stop or Storage	Narrative
	○	○	△	□	
	○	○	△	□	
	○	○	△	□	
	○	○	△	□	
	○	○	△	□	
	○	○	△	□	
	○	○	△	□	
	○	○	△	□	
	○	○	△	□	
	○	○	△	□	

FIGURE 8.4. Time-Motion Analysis Chart. [Adapted from Irma H. Gross, Elizabeth Walbert Crandall, and Marjorie M. Knoll, Management for Modern Families, 3rd ed. (New York: Appleton-Century-Crofts, 1973), pp. 434–435.]

A study of this record will indicate if, where, and when motions and/or movements can be eliminated. A closer examination of these indicated areas should then be conducted to ascertain if elimination of the motion and/or movement will (1) have an adverse effect upon the desired outcome, (2) reduce the consumption of time and/or energy resources, and (3) necessitate the expenditure of other resources. Use of this recording procedure can also identify where or if mechanical apparatus can be substituted for an individual's time and energy resource. In addition these same records can be used to pinpoint other factors that are causing excessive expenditures of time and energy resources. These in turn might indicate the need to increase work surface area, relocate materials and supplies, adjust work height, or redirect the work flow.

This record provides more data than the pathway chart. It records both graphically and in written phrases the action taking place. Analysis of the action would seek to answer the following questions: Are there instances where the number of operations could be reduced? Would reducing the number of operations yield a product having a higher, lower, or the same standards? Would the reduction in operations also save time? Is the proposed reduction in operations logical? Many of these same questions could also be asked concerning the inspections taking place. Or questions regarding the delays: for example, what was the causal factor? Are the delays necessary? Were they an integral part of the action?

On the basis of the data and its analysis, the next step would be to modify the procedure used in the initial action. The task should then be repeated employing the modifications. Record the operations, movements, delays, and inspections. Compare the first and second trials: Did reductions take place in movements, operations, delays, and inspections? Were fewer resources consumed? How does the outcome of the second trial compare with the first? Did the outcome yield the same, higher, or lower standards for the product?

Time-motion studies can be a management tool. You probably have not considered the number of operations and movements you use in task completion. Yet each of these use your resources of time and energy. When reduced-use resource occurs, it is then available for utilization in other ways.

The graphic charting of task accomplishment can, in addition to those functions previously mentioned, be a source of evaluative feedback. Task sequencing can be graphically studied. Where the achieved outcome differs from the anticipated one, this record can be analyzed to point to possible causal factors. In the decision concerning routines and habits, it was noted that although these can be valuable management tools, they should be continually reexamined and modified. The recording of task completion is a tool to be used for this purpose.

Although the time-motion analysis chart is designed primarily as a tool to assess the expenditures of time and energy resources, it has validity in other ways. It can be used as a check on your planning and sequencing, as an evaluative measure, to indicate possible corrective action, and to assist in the analysis of routines, habits, and repeat-use plans.

Task Analysis and Scheduling

The time and energy spent in operational activities can also be reduced through task analysis and scheduling. Task analysis involves an examination of both the steps or procedures involved as well as the materials, supplies, and equipment needed to complete a task.

The analysis of specific tasks is another valuable management tool. Each task is assessed in terms of the steps taken or the procedures followed from initiation to termination. How many steps or procedures are necessary to clean your room or do your laundry? Although this has long been an accepted tool in business and industry, most individuals do not do task analysis. The time-motion analysis charting, as previously mentioned, is one phase of task analysis. This record indicates motion, movement, operations, inspections, and delays. However, it does not analyze the step-by-step procedures involved. Task analysis does.

Select a task you need to complete such as packing your suitcase to go home for the weekend. How many different separate steps are involved? Each of these lead to task completion or the desired outcome. Once each has been identified, you can begin to assess whether or not it is possible to either combine or eliminate certain ones. The sequencing of the steps might be examined to determine if they follow in a logical progression. The flow of action would also be analyzed. The analysis of the task is then another evaluative tool you can use in assessing the expenditure of your time and energy resources.

The time and energy spent in operational activities can also be reduced through scheduling. Some tasks may be scheduled to take place simultaneously; others are not. The knowledge gained from task analysis will be an enabler in task scheduling.

Planning involves sequencing and organization. Your knowledge of task analysis will enable you to sequence the steps leading to completion. In so doing, you are identifying the materials, supplies, and equipment necessary to complete the task. Organizing and securing these prior to implementation will not only eliminate unnecessary steps but will also enable you to eliminate delays. As a result, the expenditures of your resources is reduced.

Thus far you have examined some tools necessary for the rational development of work simplification. All of these are to no avail if they are not used to reduce the use of resources through task scheduling. Task scheduling incorporates the knowledge gained from task analysis, work production curves, physical structure and positioning, and the tools of work simplification. Each of these comprise the component parts of task scheduling along with other aspects affecting your productive work. Inherent within your productive work capacity are such factors as your attitude toward the task, the complexity of the task, the length of time required for completion, the degree of attention required, the anticipated derived satisfaction, and the input being received from the spheres of interaction.

Some tasks require a longer period of time to complete than others. The degrees of concentration and complexity vary. Your attitude about the task is closely allied to the satisfaction you anticipate resulting from its accomplishment.

Work simplification involves using the tools and developing techniques which will reduce resource consumption. It also involves understanding the other factors that affect both the outcome and the task completion process.

Task Scheduling and the Work Production Curve

It has been emphasized that your knowledge of your work production curve is an important tool in task scheduling. Tasks requiring a high degree of concentration or time and energy resources should be scheduled during the peak times of your work production curve. Tasks requiring minimal attention, time, or energy should be scheduled during low levels of the production curve. The factor of task complexity should also be correlated with your production curve. A highly complex task should not be scheduled during the low production period.

Although often not considered, your attitude toward the task and the anticipated satisfaction on completion are other aspects of concern. A task viewed as being disagreeable should be scheduled during peak rather than low periods.

When recognition is given to the work production curve, as tasks are scheduled into the time frame, the rewards are often evident in many ways. In addition to discovering that you are able to accomplish more individual tasks, you will also reduce the expenditures of your resources. The completion of the designated tasks and the reduction of resource expenditures will undoubtedly yield a higher degree of satisfaction. Each of these in turn enhances your self-perception.

Attention Requirements and Task Scheduling

Some tasks require your constant attention from start to finish. Others require only intermittent periods of attention and action. Task analysis can be a valuable tool here. Knowledge of the steps required for each task will enable you to determine the degree of attention each necessitates. In addition, task analysis will identify the optimum span of attention required at any given point.

When two or more tasks can be scheduled at the same time, it is referred to as *dovetailing.* You have probably done this many times but have not known the principles involved. There are numerous operational tasks that do not require your full and complete attention throughout the completion process. The tasks are accomplished by periodically giving them attention spans. Thus they can be scheduled concurrently. In so doing, your attention can be shifted from one task to another without any detrimental effects to the outcomes of either.

What tasks do you complete while you are doing your laundry? Once the clothing has been placed in either the washer or dryer, your attention is not needed for a set period of time. This time span can therefore be used to complete another task. This is an example of dovetailing.

Learning to use dovetailing can minimize resource consumption. In most instances you can probably dovetail more tasks and activities than you realize. Look over the demands you have for the next twenty-four hours. How many could be dovetailed?

Task scheduling is an important way to reduce the consumption of energy as well as time. Using dovetailing can enable you to meet more of your demands. However, too much emphasis on dovetailing can defeat the purpose. Assume for a moment you have decided to dovetail your laundry and library research. Although this may sound logical, if the library is located several blocks from your dorm laundry room, the time and energy you use moving from one place to another defeats the dovetailing process.

For dovetailing to serve its purpose, the tasks must be located in the same general area. In addition, the tasks must be such that your attention can easily shift from one to the other without producing any dire effects on either outcome. Dovetailing the tasks of writing the rough draft of a research paper and cooking something requiring more than occasional attention spans will probably have diverse effects on one or both of the outcomes.

Where dovetailing can be used it reduces resource utilization. Dovetailing is another valuable tool that can be used to meet demands. As you assess your demands for the coming week, which can be dovetailed and which ones cannot? Once you begin to purposefully seek tasks to be dovetailed, you will find you have more resources available for other demands.

Task Scheduling and Attitudes

Although often not considered, your attitude toward a particular task and the satisfaction anticipated from completion are important factors in scheduling. Are there some operational tasks you dislike doing? Why do you dislike these tasks? How and when do you do them? Are you a person who procrastinates completing a disliked task by delaying to undertake it as long as possible? Or do you do it to "get it out of the way?"

Over the years numerous studies have been conducted concerning the homemaker's attitude toward household operational tasks. These studies have clearly indicated the effect of the homemaker's attitude upon household management.[14] The preference and dislike of tasks is an important factor in household operation and management.

Steidl's study, done in 1975, examined the homemaker's attitude and perceptions of tasks as opposed to liking and disliking of specific tasks. This study found disliked tasks were associated with a lack of satisfaction, or the inability to achieve a sense of pride, accomplishment, or pleasure from completion. A disliked task was viewed as dull, monotonous, and routine.[15] Liked tasks were associated with being creative, interesting, and brought pleasure from accomplishment.[16]

Your attitude and perception of a task should be a consideration in task scheduling. Procrastination often occurs when disliked tasks are to be scheduled. All too often, these tasks are either put off to another time, or scheduled at a low worker productivity period. Whenever possible these tasks are often completely eliminated from the normal task scheduling until such time as procrastination can no longer take place. Procrastination can have dire effects upon the resource use. When the task can no longer be delayed to another time, the negative attitude towards it increases. Thus when the task is finally undertaken it may have increased in proportion to the length of the delay. Can you think of a task that you or someone else has continually put off doing? When this task was finally undertaken, did it necessitate a greater resource expenditure than it would have if procrastination had not occurred? Did the extent of the task increase in proportion to the length of the delay in undertaking?

Your values and standards as well as your attitude toward a disliked task will affect scheduling. Some homemakers schedule a disliked task just prior to one they enjoy. In this instance, the homemakers have something to look forward to while completing the disliked task. Other homemakers schedule disliked tasks first, or intersperse liked and disliked tasks throughout the entire schedule.

Care should be taken in scheduling tasks where a positive attitude is not present. A negatively viewed task when scheduled during a low period of worker productivity might have a detrimental effect on the outcome. Negative attitudes tend to increase due to the low level of productivity. These in turn often necessitate an increase in resource utilization. Thus the combination of attitudes and low productivity curve tend to compound each other.

Wherever possible the dovetailing of a disliked with an enjoyed task minimizes the negative aspects of the disliked one. The liked aspects transfer to the disliked one thus reducing its negative connnotation. Still another method of minimizing the aspects of the disliked task is to counteract it with a distraction such as listening to music while working.

You also need to examine the task to determine the causal factors creating the negative connotation. These factors might be lack of skills, inadequate space or equipment, environmental aspects, or the absence of a high degree of satisfaction upon completion. This analysis might pinpoint factors that could be eliminated, changed, or modified. Isolation of the causal factor(s) may enable you to change your perception from negative to positive. If this is not possible, you may at least be able to view the task in a different context.

The scheduling of disliked tasks can have an impact upon your total management. Procrastination does not eliminate a task; it only delays accomplishment. When all disliked tasks are scheduled at the beginning of the day, you have little if any incentive to accomplish the first since you know it will be followed by an equally disliked one. Even if you do accomplish all disliked tasks, the negative connotations you have accumulated and the additional resources consumed are such that neither the incentive nor the availability of resources remain to afford you the opportunity to undertake liked tasks.

Attitudes and motivation are prime factors in task scheduling. A higher probability of accomplishment is present when task completion is perceived in positive rather than negative terms. This perception is also directly related to the satisfaction anticipated from the outcome.

External Factors in Work Simplification

The accomplishment of operational tasks does not occur in a vacuum nor are they your sole endeavors or responsibilities. In all probability you are not able to start and complete a task solely on the basis of your own desires, scheduling, and time available. Work simplification involves not only using your knowledge and skills to reduce resource consumption but also recognizing some of the external factors affecting task accomplishment. Have you ever started a task and then been continually interrupted? This is but one of the external factors that affect task accomplishment. Other factors are the stage in the life cycle, the shelter sphere, and input received from the other spheres of interaction.

Interruptions

Interruptions in task accomplishment may originate from different sources. They may also vary in duration. Learning to deal with these is also a part of work simplification. Interruptions may originate from other members within the shelter sphere or from outside the sphere. How many different kinds of interruptions have you experienced in the last week? Disruptions can have an effect upon task completion and management. Time schedules should be flexible to allow for interruptions. Effective management means learning to deal with and anticipate these disruptions.

Interruptions can occur from many different sources. They might come from outside the shelter sphere such as telephone calls or unexpected guests. You may receive input from one or more of the spheres, such as a letter requiring an immediate response. Other interruptions may originate from other workers asking questions about procedures, requesting assistance, or expressing the need for further communication. An unanticipated event such as equipment breakdown, accident, or minor injury may also produce an interruption. Any of these disruptions in task accomplishment will affect the work flow and task accomplishment.

Family Factors

Each stage in the life cycle has its own distinctive demands. Combined with this are the factors of family composition and occupational status. Any or all of these will affect the action taking place.

During the beginning stage of the life cycle, work patterns and routines are established. Responsibilities and duties as well as role definitions are occurring. Each partner in the family is establishing household patterns. This may also be at a time when one of the partners is developing skills associated with tasks previously undertaken by another shelter sphere member. For instance the male partner may be developing skills to assist in household cleaning or grocery shopping. Although these may be somewhat familiar tasks, they may not have been his sole responsibility prior to this time. The female partner may also be undertaking unfamiliar tasks such as mowing lawns or assisting in home repairs.

The expanding stage of the life cycle experiences increasing demands following the birth of the first child. These demands continue for a prolonged period of time. New skills may need to be developed; alternative work patterns may need to be created. Time schedules and routines previously developed will need to be altered. Interruptions occur with an increasing degree of frequency.

As the children mature, a different goal priority may occur in reference to task accomplishment. Although task accomplishment may be the major goal, other goals may emerge such as teaching children to assume and accomplish tasks. This teaching-learning period necessitates allowances for the lack of refined skills, an increase in communication, and other adjustments created by the presence of an inexperienced worker.

The contracting stage of the life cycle may necessitate other changes. As the family membership declines task demands may be reduced. At the same time fewer individuals are available to assume task responsibility.

Physical changes may also occur that affect the homemaker's capability to assume task responsibility. As the body matures, energy levels and physical capabilities undergo a slow gradual decline. This decline will continue throughout the remaining years of life. The homemaker will find growing maturity means an increase in the resources required for task accomplishment. The accomplishment of a single task may require a longer period of time to complete, additional energy may be used to compensate for slower physical movements, or the number and length of delays may increase. The aging process is a gradual one taking place over a long period of time. In most instances the effects are not immediately discernable. Time schedules need to be altered to allow for the physical changes taking place. New work techniques need to be devised. Adjustments of work patterns will take place.

The composition of the family will also affect task scheduling. Increases or decreases in family membership are important factors to consider in task scheduling. A family composed of two adults and preschool children has a different task schedule than does the family composed of adults and teenagers. The assignment and responsibility for various tasks will vary in relationship to worker capabilities.

Changes in family size affect task accomplishment. Although there may be an increase in the number of individuals who are able to assume task responsibilities, the proportional size of various tasks may also increase accordingly. Consider what would happen to the task accomplishment in your shelter sphere if its membership were two or three times its present size. How many tasks would be increased? What would be the proportional increase taking place? How would these changes affect task scheduling and accomplishment? For instance how many loads of laundry would need to be done at one time? How many times during the week would someone have to do the laundry? What changes took place in your shelter sphere when you enrolled in your university?

The age of the family members is still another factor. A household composed of young children experiences different demands than one composed of teenagers. Although the basic tasks remain the same, the delays and interruptions as well as the number of members available for task assignment varies greatly. Routines, time schedules, and work habits are developed in relationship to the age range of family members.

Task accomplishment is also affected by the number of gainfully employed persons. When you finally attained the legal age for gainful employment outside the home, did you obtain a part-time job? Did this affect your task assignments at home? Although your employment may not have drastically altered the task accomplishment within your shelter sphere, the number of regular gainfully employed adults does. Tasks must be scheduled and accomplished during nonsalaried periods of the day and week. This may mean the homemaker's task accomplishment within the shelter sphere does not take place during the high peaks of the worker production curve.

Task scheduling must be done to coincide with the employment hours of the adult homemaker. Tasks necessitating high peaks of the worker production curve must be scheduled on nonsalaried days. How does your class schedule affect your task scheduling? Are there certain tasks that you schedule on non-class days?

The occupational status of the adult homemaker, too, is a factor in task scheduling and accomplishment. Some occupations have employment-related expectations. These must be added to task scheduling and accomplishment along with other operational responsibilities. Examples of these might be overnight travel, evening meetings, or social entertainment. Each activity will have its own effect upon scheduling and accomplishment. For instance, overnight travel may require adjustment of task assignments. In the absence of one of the adult homemakers, the remaining adult may have to undertake task completion. Other employment-related expectations such as mode of dress, the length and hours of the workday, or the social and civic involvement of the gainfully employed homemaker will also affect time and task scheduling as well as task assignment.

The gainful employment of more than one adult homemaker increases the occupational factor. In this case, task scheduling and accomplishment must accomodate the variables of both gainfully employed adults. When this occurs, weekends and evenings are often utilized for operational task accomplishment.

Task Disruption

The effect of task disruptions are varied depending upon the type of disruption being experienced and its duration. Coupled with this is your reaction to the interruption. In any case, your flow of work is terminated for a period of time.

Some interruptions are minor ones whereas others are not. In the case of minor interruptions of short duration, the flow of work ceases for only a short period of time. Generally your train of thought, rhythm of work, and the flow of the task accomplishment can be re-established quite readily. However, other kinds of interruptions make it difficult to reestablish the work flow, rhythm of movement, and train of thought necessary to continue the task accomplishment.

Dealing with interruptions is an important part of management. Developing an awareness of the importance of the interruption, learning to deal with it, and re-establishing the task accomplishment sequence are all a part of work simplification. Like many other aspects of the management process this is a learned skill.

Access to Facilities

The accessibility to needed facilities can be a determining factor in task scheduling. The facilities for your laundry task may be available twenty-four hours per day throughout the academic year. Suppose you could only use these certain hours on specific days of the week. How would this affect your task scheduling and accomplishment? Tasks that necessitate the use of facilities outside the shelter sphere must be scheduled and accomplished according to accessibility and not necessarily at the optimum time for the homemaker.

Restrictions may occur from within as well as outside the shelter sphere. Would you undertake a task that produced loud noise in the middle of the night when other family members are sleeping? Noise, vibrations, or other factors may affect when a task is scheduled and accomplished.

You may encounter situations where facilities can only be used during certain parts of the day. Suppose you and four other students rented an apartment off-campus. Although you are all living together, each functions separately and independently. You all share common areas such as bath, kitchen, and living area. As such you may be assigned certain hours when you may use the kitchen. This means your access to the kitchen facility is limited.

Have you ever tried to study in a poorly lighted area? Or tried to accomplish a task using outdated equipment? The physical attributes of the shelter sphere greatly affect task accomplishment and resource consumption. Excessive or limited space, inadequate or outdated equipment, hard floor surfaces, or inadequate ventilation are some of the physical attributes of the shelter sphere affecting work simplification.

The physical attributes of the overall atmosphere are a factor as well. Are there some places where you avoid working and others you prefer? Why? All too often the overall atmosphere where the task is to be accomplished receives little or no consideration yet it has a direct effect upon accomplishment. Are there some places which encourage and others which discourage work? This affects your task accomplishment as well as your studying capabilities. It is even further compounded when the task being undertaken is a disliked one.

It has been demonstrated that the shelter sphere can have an effect upon work simplification, task scheduling, and accomplishment. Although quite often this is not considered, nonetheless, it is a factor.

Work Simplification and the Management Process

The management process is combined with the principles and concepts of work simplification to aid you in achieving your goal or objective while reducing your resource consumption. The tools and techniques of work simplification should be incorporated as you use the management process. As you undertake the planning component of the management process, you establish the sequence of the action to take place. This sequencing should correlate with your worker production curve. Thus task scheduling is an integral part of sequencing. The pathway chart, task analysis, and time-motion studies serve as enablers for the sequencing and organizing done during planning.

The implementation component incorporates the techniques of work simplification. Since action is occurring, your knowledge of body mechanics, posture, and physical structure are vital. Implementation involves checking and adjusting. These two subcategories of the implementation component are enhanced when you use your knowledge of other factors and variables that might affect task accomplishment such as interruptions, equipment usage, normal and maximum reach zones, and task perceptions and attitudes. Although these are considered during planning, their true effect becomes more apparent as implementation takes place.

Evaluative feedback, the third component in the management process, should not be limited solely to the outcome or the accomplishment of the task. The pathway chart, task analysis, and time-motion studies are also a source of evaluative feedback. An assessment should be done of the task scheduling to ascertain the degree to which it correlated with the worker production curve.

Use of the management process to minimize resource utilization is an important part of work simplification. One does not exist without the other nor should one be used without the other.

Summary

Over the years business and industry have sought to increase worker productivity and profit margins through the use of work simplification. These same principles and concepts can also be utilized in the home and by individuals to minimize the consumption of valuable resources. All resources have limited boundaries. Work simplification recognizes the specific limitations of time and energy resources and seeks to reduce their use while achieving the greatest degree of satisfaction.

To reduce the use of resources several different tools and techniques can be effectively employed. These tools are worker production curve, time schedules, pathway charts, time-motion studies, and task analysis. The techniques of work simplification involve developing an awareness of body mechanics, good posture, and the normal and maximum reach zones.

Your capacity to accomplish tasks is affected by your attitude and perception of them and by the number and type of interruptions. Your like or dislike for a particular task, the stage in your life cycle, and any input being received from the spheres of interaction will also affect task accomplishment.

Work simplification involves correlating your task scheduling with your work production curve. The schedule you establish is compiled using the data obtained from the various tools and the resulting analysis. Each of these provides input during the planning component of the management process. During implementation your knowledge of your physical structure and body mechanics are utilized to accomplish the task. Evaluative feedback encompasses more than task accomplishment. The correlation of the worker production curve, the manner in which you re-established your action following interruptions, and worker productivity are all forms of evaluative feedback.

Using work simplification will enable you to minimize the extent to which resources are expended and to use this knowledge throughout the planning, implementation, and evaluative feedback components of the management process. The outcome resulting from work simplification is not only task accomplishment but also a reduction in resource consumption. These resources are then available for alternative uses. Effective management involves using work simplification in the management process.

ACTIVITIES

1. Diagram a pathway chart of your room. Using two different colors of ink or pencil, chart your travel patterns as you (a) get dressed and ready for class and (b) study for a test. Analyze the pathway chart to ascertain where or if you could reduce your travel patterns.
2. Develop a time-motion chart as shown in Chapter 8. Record on the chart the movements, operations, and such of another person completing a specific task. Analyze this record to determine a more efficient method of task accomplishment. Complete the task a second time and record the results on a time-motion chart. Analyze the findings and compare with the first chart.
3. There are probably several tasks that you dislike doing. Select the one you dislike the most and analyze why you dislike this task. Do a task analysis of the disliked task to ascertain if any modifications or changes would make the task more agreeable.
4. Select one task you frequently undertake. Complete a task analysis. Using this task analysis as a data base, determine
   a. Any changes you might make to conserve time and energy.
   b. Any way you could reduce the number of motions and/or steps required for completion.
   c. Any ways you could increase your worker productivity.
5. In Chapter 7 you recorded your time usage in a time log. Using this information as a data base, determine
   a. How many tasks did you dovetail?
   b. Are there other tasks that could be dovetailed?
   c. Any tasks that were dovetailed and should not have been?
6. What are the causal factors within your shelter sphere that affect your time and energy consumption? Which ones of these can be modified to reduce your time and energy expenditures? Which ones can not? Why are you unable to make modifications?
7. As you undertake any task completion you probably experience disruptions. Keep a record of all of the interruptions you experience during one day.

What are the major causes of these interruptions? What is the average duration of each? What are the effects of these interruptions upon your task completions? When these interruptions have differing causal factors, does this affect task completion?

8. You are familiar with the tasks needed to be completed within your campus shelter sphere. What would be the effect upon your management and the number of tasks to be completed if you were (a) in the expanding stage of the life cycle and (b) in the contracting stage of the life cycle?

JOE AND HARRY

Joe and Harry share a condominium in one of the new high-rise complexes near the center of the city. The living room, two bedrooms, and the kitchen are larger than those in their previous apartment. Their previous apartment was quite a distance from their employment. Three months ago they purchased this condominium primarily because of its location. Although the new apartment has basically the same number of rooms, the room arrangement is quite different.

Both Joe and Harry have tried to find the time to get "settled into" the apartment but there are still a number of boxes sitting in the living room corner and stacked in the kitchen. Joe is constantly complaining that he can't find what he needs other than what is located in his room. Harry is still trying to decide which wall to place the bed against.

Although each one has spent a considerable amount of time trying to unpack the remaining boxes, neither seems to get the whole job done. When one unpacks a box, he puts things away only to have the other complain about not being able to find the contents.

They have decided to devote this coming weekend to unpacking and overall cleaning of the apartment. Joe wants to be sure this is finally done since he will be leaving on a ten-day company trip on Monday. Harry wants to simply accomplish this goal because he is tired of spending the majority of his time every weekend unpacking, cleaning, doing laundry, and washing dishes.

Harry secretly wishes that they had stayed in their old apartment; his reasoning is that there everything had a specific place to be put whereas here there just isn't enough room to make everything fit. Joe keeps telling him that now they have more room and storage. Actually they do; the problem is that it is located in different places than it was in the previous apartment. This and the change in room locations are presenting problems to these two men.

This apartment offers many advantages to Joe and Harry. They no longer have to leave the building in the evening to do their laundry, a grocery store is just down the street, and they can both walk to work. Although they have not changed their work routines, they don't seem to be able to accomplish as much as they did in their other apartment.

Their goal for this weekend is to finish "settling in," doing the household operational tasks, and their laundry. Joe sincerely hopes they will accomplish all of this by Saturday evening as he would like to spend Sunday going over some reports before he leaves on Monday. Harry agrees with him simply because he is tired of spending all of his time in the apartment working.

Discussion Questions

1. What are the basic management problems Harry and Joe are facing? Which of these evolve around their values, goals, and standards?

2. Harry has told Joe that if they don't finish their tasks by Sunday afternoon's football game, they are going to stop and he will hire someone to come in to finish up while Joe is gone. Joe is opposed to this and has been from the start. His reason being they will have to do it after the person leaves if they really are to know where things have been put. Is this Joe's only reason? How valid is Joe's reason? What are his values?

3. Although neither man eats a large number of meals in the apartment at the present time, Joe would like to purchase some appliances and do more cooking rather than eating most of their meals outside the shelter sphere. Harry doesn't care as long as he doesn't have to do the cooking or much of the cleaning up of the kitchen. If Joe asked you for suggestions on which appliances to purchase, what would you suggest and why?

4. What plan would you develop for Joe and Harry so their goal of "settling in" their apartment can be accomplished this weekend? What considerations would be neccessary due to their individual values, goals, standards, and roles?

5. Identify the resources available within this shelter sphere. How could these be allocated and used more effectively? Analyze their present allocation and use of these resources. How would you rate their use: effective, average, or ineffective? Why?

GLOSSARY

Dovetailing A work simplification technique in which two or more tasks are scheduled and completed at the same time. The nature of each task allows the individual to alternately shift attention from one task to another.

Maximum Reach Area A circle formed by the extension of the arms and hands outward from the body; represents the farthest distance an individual is able to reach while in a stationary position, and the area in which all work is done.

Normal Reach Area A circle formed by the extension of the arms when bent at the elbow; represents the distance an individual is able to reach and comfortably work while in a stationary position.

Operational Chart A chart record of the movements, operations, and steps involved in the completion of a task.

Pathway Chart A chart record of the travel patterns and steps involved in the completion of a task.

Process Chart A chart record of the motions involved in the completion of a task.

Reach Area The distance an individual is able to extend hands and arms to obtain an object while in a stationary position.

Task Analysis A detailed examination of the steps, procedures, materials, equipment, supplies, time, and physical motions involved in the completion of a task.

Task Scheduling The designation of set periods of time during which a specific task or tasks is to be completed.

Time-motion Study A analysis of the time and motions involved in the completion of a task; used to determine energy consumption.

Work Area The surface upon which a task is completed, where materials and supplies are located, and the space in which the task is completed.

Worker Productivity The capabilities of an individual to produce a good, service, or perform an operational task.

Work Simplification The technique developed to reduce the time consumed and the physical motions in the accomplishment of a task while still producing the most desirable outcome or product.

REFERENCES

1. Irma H. Gross, Elizabeth Walbert Crandall, and Marjorie M. Knoll, *Management for Modern Families,* 3rd ed. (New York: Appleton-Century-Crofts, 1973), p. 671.
2. Ibid.
3. Ibid.
4. Cleo Fitzsimmons and Flora Williams, *The Family Economy Nature and Management of Resources* (Ann Arbor, Michigan: Edwards Brothers Press, Inc., 1973), pp. 285–289.
5. Ibid., p. 285.
6. Paulena Nickell, Ann Smith Rice, and Suzanne P. Tucker, *Management in Family Living,* 5th ed. (New York: John Wiley & Sons, Inc., 1976), p. 245.
7. "Working Women Joys and Sorrows," *U.S. News and World Report, Inc.* (January 15, 1979), 64.
8. Katherine E. Walker, "How Much Help for Working Mothers?" *Human Ecology Forum* (Autumn 1970), 13–15.
9. Katherine E. Walker, "Homemaking Still Takes Time," *Journal of Home Economics* (October 1973), 7–11.
10. Gross, Crandall, and Knoll, op. cit., p. 407.
11. Louise Jenison Peet, Mary S. Pickett, and Mildred G. Arnold, *Household Equipment,* 8th ed. (New York: John Wiley & Sons, 1979), pp. 16–17.

12. Gross, Crandall, and Knoll, op. cit., p. 436.
13. Ibid.
14. Rose E. Steidl, "Affective Dimensions of High and Low Cognitive Home-making Tasks," *Home Economics Research Journal* (December 1975), p. 122.
15. Ibid.
16. Ibid.

CHAPTER NINE

Your Money Resources

In all probability you are more aware of the limitations of your money resource than of any other resource. This knowledge is continually reinforced as you seek to meet the demands constantly being placed upon this limited resource. The major goal is to maximize utilization of this resource as much as possible.

Throughout your life you are going to have limited money while experiencing unlimited demands. As you participate in the marketplace and allocate this resource you will constantly be faced with making choices between your wants and needs. The decisions you make may have an effect not only upon your immediate financial situation, but your future status as well.

If you were to rate yourself using a one-to-ten scale with ten being the highest, how would you rate your money management skills? How much money did you spend yesterday? Last week? Last month? What possible demands might be placed upon this resource in the near future? Could you meet unexpected demands?

What would an examination of your spending patterns for the last week or year reveal about you. Just how do you use your money resource? Why did you choose to use your money resource in this manner? Although most people would agree that it is important, few really practice money management. There are numerous misconceptions concerning what really occurs in the management of money resources.

Unlike your resources of time and energy, replacement of your money resource generally necessitates action being taken. To replace your money resource, you may exchange your time and energy resources through employment to increase your money resource. This resource may also be replaced through investments. Or you might operate your own business using other resources to produce or increase monetary gains.

Money management is important for financial survival. To effectively manage money resources you need to be aware of money management concepts, the management tools, and the methods of disbursing money resources.

Money Management

Are you perhaps saying, "Hey, I have a budget and I stick to it." Or, "I don't have enough money right now to worry about budgeting." Or, "I do O.K.! At least I don't run out of money very often." Or perhaps, "Budgeting takes too much time and besides I don't need one." Or maybe, "I'll budget when I really earn some money. Right now I get by." If you voiced or thought such comments you, like many others, really don't manage your money resource. Nor are you really aware of the importance of money management to you now or in the future.

Money management is more than budgeting your income. Like other aspects of management it is a learned skill that should be continually practiced. It is true that money management involves budgeting. It also encompasses a great deal more. To manage your money resource effectively you need to know how your net worth, your expenditure commitments, your spending patterns, wants and needs, and your attitudes influence and direct money management.

As a college student you are preparing to enter a profession. To the business, industry, agency, or organization who becomes your future employer, money management is vital to continue to remain a part of the economic system. How effectively you manage your money resource will determine your participation in the financial world. It will govern the extent to which you are able to achieve your desired quality of life. In using money management you will not only economically survive, but you will be able to attain more of your wants and needs as you allocate and use this limited resource: money.

Income Concepts

Doesn't the term *income* mean money? Although most people tend to think of the term *income* as being synonymous with money, in reality, it means much more. Your income is composed of many aspects, one of which is money. Effective money management involves establishing your composite income not just your net or gross income. When you make money management decisions, you should be making them on the basis of your composite income not your monetary one. Decisions made solely on the basis of monetary income are based on insufficient data.

Money management decisions should be made using your composite income. As shown in Figure 9.1, your composite income is derived from a combination of your productive money, and hidden incomes. Each of these are important as you allocate your money resources to meet demands and achieve satisfactions through utilization.

Although your financial spending plan emerges and centers around your money income, the decisions made and the management that occurs results from the knowledge of your composite income. Knowledge of your composite income enables you to identify your total potential wealth—not merely your money income. Through this knowledge you can more readily determine available alternatives. In so doing more valid decisions result. Using a cost-benefit ratio, your analysis of opportunity costs will be more realistic. Complete awareness of your composite income provides the data base for money management.

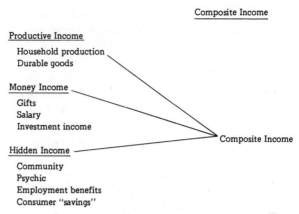

FIGURE 9.1.   Composite Income.

Productive Income

Your productive income is composed of the productive efforts of you and other members of the shelter sphere. This productive income may accrue from worker productivity or it may be composed of previous expenditures to purchase durable consumer goods.

Household Production Income

As an individual you have many talents and abilities as do the other individuals who reside within the shelter sphere. In all probability you may be actually performing some household production. You may not be cognizant nor perceive these productive endeavors as contributors to your income. When you do the laundry, wash your car, cook meals, or mow the lawn you are doing household production. Each time you combine your talents, skills, and capabilities with resources other than money to produce a good or service within the shelter sphere, your production is contributing to your money management. The contributions you make to the shelter sphere through household production enable you to redirect your money resource to satisfy other demands.

Although these contributions are often assumed to be a normal part of a family member's role, responsibility, and duty, the productive efforts of each family member contributes to the composite income. To better ascertain this, list all of the production you actually do on a regular basis. Now compute the costs involved if you had to purchase these. This aspect can be further amplified if you compute the cost of all of the production contributions of every person living in your shelter sphere.

Household production enables you to use resources other than money to obtain a good or service. You are therefore able to allocate your limited money resource to meet other demands, purchase additional goods, or consume services you cannot produce within your shelter sphere.

Durable Goods Income

As you have participated in the marketplace you have purchased tangible goods. Some of the goods are nondurable ones. In other words, they no longer exist. Examples of nondurable goods you might purchase are food, typing paper, pencils, and so forth. You also purchase durable goods that have lasted over a period of time such as your stereo, TV, or car. Each durable good represents a cash reserve that you can draw upon should the need arise. Although the cash value of the durable good may not be the same as when originally purchased, nonetheless, each does have a cash value.

Your productive income is composed of both your tangible durable goods and the productive contributions of the individuals within the shelter sphere. Each of these enable you to make choices and identify potential alternatives in the allocation and use of your limited money income resource.

Money Income

Your money income is composed of the wages or salary you receive from gainful employment as well as income derived from other money income sources. Your money income may be derived from one or a multitude of sources. Your salary or wages is probably the largest potential source of money income.. However, you also receive money income in the form of gifts from relatives and friends, earned interest, return from investments, or through the operation of a business enterprise. Money income is the accumulation of actual dollars. The financial spending plan you develop and implement is designed to direct the flow of this income.

Employment Income

Employment income is produced when you exchange your resources of time, energy, and employment skills for wages or salary. Your employment income, in all probability, will be a major source for money income. This will be true more in the future than it is at the present time.

Investment Income

Investment income is produced from previously earned income. It may accrue as earned interest from savings accounts, purchases of stocks and bonds, or other investments producing a monetary return.

Capital Gains Income

Capital gains income occurs from the profitable sale of property. These also produce a monetary return and thus are a part of your money income. Capital gains may also be derived from the profit margin accruing from the operation of a business enterprise.

Each of these sources provide varying dollar amounts. Each is a part of your money income. The accumulation of money income can be measured in actual dollars as opposed to your production income which has a degree of intangibility. Other sources of money income might be allowances, monetary gifts from friends and relatives, or rent accrued from the leasing of property or tangible goods. Regardless of the source, the actual dollar amounts can be seen and measured. The flow of this income can be directed more accurately than any other income.

Hidden Income

All too often when the aspect of money management is discussed or examined, individuals and families tend to overlook the hidden incomes available to them. These offer alternative choices in the management of the money income. Hidden income is composed of the community income, psychic income, employment benefits, and consumer "savings."

Community Income

Within your community are many resources you can draw upon as the need arises. These resources also represent a part of your composite income. You may not have thought of these in quite this manner but they are a part of your income.

Suppose a friend from your hometown was going to spend the weekend with you. You want this to be a special visit but you have only $5.00 and no other source to increase your money income. How could you entertain your friend spending only $5.00? What are all of the activities and facilities available within your university and the surrounding community you could use at little or no cost? Are there parks, recreational facilities, museums, and such within the community or university that are open to you? What are all of the activities going on in your university this weekend which you and your friend could attend at little or no cost? These are a part of your community income.

Many other services are provided by your community such as police and fire protection, public schools, or sewer and/or garbage collection. These, too constitute a part of your community income.

Although you may not have been aware of them, each of these contributes to your composite income. You might well be saying: "But I pay for these with tax dollars, how can they represent income?" These facilities are primarily supported by tax dollars. However, have you ever considered what the financial expenditure for each of these services and facilities would be if you had to totally self-assume their individual costs? How much would you have to pay for private police and fire protection for your home and family members if they were either not available or not supported by tax dollars? If your athletic teams were not supported in part through your student activity funds, how much would each ticket cost? Could you afford to purchase season tickets to your university's athletic events?

Community income contributes to your composite income. It provides services you might not otherwise be able to self-assume from your money income. These contributions also offer you possible alternatives to the allocation of money income.

Psychic Income

How do you feel when you purchase an important item? Each time you use your stereo does it produce satisfaction? Psychic income is the satisfaction that results from the ownership and utilization of goods and services. Although this type of income is difficult to measure tangibly in actual dollars, nonetheless it does represent a form of hidden income. It has value in that it offers you an alternative choice. You might choose to enjoy listening to your stereo rather than spending money income to go to a movie.

Employment Benefit Income

Through your employment or work-related situations you receive fringe benefits. These may consist of employee discounts, health care, and life insurance policies paid for by the employer, employee opportunities, or other derived benefits accruing from your job or position. These, too, constitute a part of your composite income.

If you are or have been an employee you are aware of different fringe benefits, such as discounts allowing you to make purchases at a reduced cost. Or perhaps in a food-related occupation, you might receive free or reduced-cost meals. You may have received other types of employee benefits such as your uniforms. Your employee opportunities might have increased your money income in other ways as well. Were you able to use company facilities at little or no cost? Did your employer install recreational facilities, pay tuition and books for enrollment in college courses related to your employment status, or provide and maintain the company-required uniforms as a regular part of the employment benefits?

Employment benefits received increase your spending power. Without employment benefits you would have to allocate and use part of your money income to obtain them. Thus they are a part of your composite income in that they contribute to your financial wealth.

Consumer "Savings" Income

How many different ways have you saved money in the marketplace? Perhaps you have purchased goods or services on sale. Or have you "bargained" with the merchant to secure a good or service at a reduced price? Consumer "savings" are also a part of your hidden income. Each time you "save" money by purchasing a good or service at a reduced or lower-than-retail price you are maximizing your money resource through consumer "savings."

If you choose to delay your purchase to a later date, you are also maximizing the allocation and use of your money resource. In essence this also represents a consumer "savings." By delaying your purchase to a later date, you have decided to reserve money income for future rather than current consumption. This decision should be carefully analyzed in terms of the present and anticipated economic conditions.

Although a delayed purchase may appear to be a "saving" this is not always true. The risk factor for delayed money income is dependent upon the current vs. future economy. The probability of the occurrence of either an inflationary or recessionary period must be carefully analyzed. In an inflationary period, income received along with prices increase. If income increases closely parallel those of the price rises, the risk factor is not as high. However, if prices increase faster than the income received, the risk factor becomes much greater. In an inflationary period delaying your purchase means you may be running the risk that the price of the purchase will increase faster than your income. Another risk is that your consumer dollar is worth less. Therefore, more dollars may be needed to make the delayed purchase than if a current purchase is made. Coupled with this situation, the purchasing power of the dollar may be reduced. In either one or both instances, a delayed purchase may yield a "dissaving" rather than a "consumer saving." In a recession, the purchasing power of the dollar is greater and prices are generally lower. However, you may not receive as much actual dollar income as in an inflationary period.

Thus the decision of whether to delay a purchase is dependent upon the current and anticipated economic conditions as well as the alternative choices which might be open to you if you choose to not expend this resource at the current time. Each of these factors will determine whether delayed purchase will produce positive or negative "savings" of your money resource.

Consumer "saving," whether it occurs as a result of purchasing at a reduced or lower price or through delayed purchasing, can increase the availability of your money income. When fewer dollars are spent in the consumption of goods and services, more dollars are available to meet other demands, wants, and needs. This maximizes your utilization of your money income. The satisfaction you receive is compounded. You initially receive satisfaction from the consumption of the purchased goods and services. Added to this, is the satisfaction you receive from "saving" your money resource to meet other demands, wants, and needs. Both your satisfaction and your spending power are increased. The increase in spending power results both from the actual dollar "savings" accrued from the lowered or reduced price and the available money income which can be allocated to meet another want, need, or demand. Since you do not pay taxes on the money you "saved" in this manner, you accumulate additional purchasing power. Maynes makes the following comment:

> Consumer "Earnings" Are Tax-Free. Among the least appreciated advantages of "earnings" (or "savings") from better purchase decisions is their favored tax status. Many people fail to appreciate the fact that such earnings are tax-free. They are ignorant, too, of the potential money value of this favorable tax treatment.[1]

Composite income, then, is composed of incomes in addition to actual dollars. The sum total of your production, money, and hidden incomes represents your composite income. The use of the composite income concept in the management of your money resource increases the alternative choices open to you. These enable you to choose among a variety of alternatives and plan your course of action accordingly. As your alternatives increase, you are able to make more valid decisions as to where and under what circumstances you will allocate your money income. These decisions are made on the basis of how demands can best be met. In order to meet a specific demand, you may choose to use your money income; or you may decide to meet the demand using an income other than money. Each time you use an income source other than money you are maximizing the money resource. Knowledge of this concept is vital to effective money management.

Using Composite Income in Money Management

Money management does not involve only money income—a point made earlier. Effective money management occurs when awareness of the composite income exists. Although the most evident part of money management is the financial spending plan, true money management occurs when decisions are made based upon the composite income. Decision making involves choosing between two or more alternatives. Inherent within decision making are the "opportunity costs" and the trade-offs that occur. Each decision you make concerning your money income involves opportunity costs and trade-offs.

In choosing to allocate resources to meet a demand, satisfy a want, or obtain a need you have lost the opportunity to use part or all of your resource in another way, or to satisfy a different want or need. In so doing, you have restricted or eliminated the availability of this resource for other opportunities. The resulting satisfaction may be either positive or negative.

What monetary decisions have you made recently? What did you receive when you used your money resource? Did you receive a good or service? When you made this decision to allocate your money resource you lost the opportunity to use this resource to obtain something else. What were your "opportunity costs?" As you made these decisions did you consider and examine your other alternatives?

Upon reflection, did you have other alternatives which would have yielded the same degree of satisfaction? Did your decision produce the satisfaction you desired and anticipated? What opportunities did you lose as a result of your decision? Would you change your decisions now? Why or why not?

All too often individuals view money management as involving only money income. In many cases, they further restrict their thinking to the funds that are available at any given point. In so doing, they neglect to consider their composite income. Thus decisions are made solely on the basis of current monetary status. This fallacy means they are not examining available alternatives and they are probably not considering the "opportunity costs" of their decisions.

Taking the time to identify available alternatives, possible trade-offs, and the opportunity costs are vital to the management of your money resource. The knowledge of your composite income will enable you to accomplish more valid decision making. Identifying and recognizing alternatives will help you in determining opportunity costs as well as potential trade-offs.

Your money income can be increased without spending additional hours at work or from any other source of money income. How can this be done? Using your production skills allows you to "trade" these and other resources to obtain goods and services. Your money income expenditures are reduced. This resource then can be allocated to purchase other goods and services.

Consumer savings also increases your money income. Your spending power is increased each time you are an effective consumer in the marketplace. Employment benefits further increase money income. Each time you utilize the fringe benefits of being a university student by participating in the free or inexpensive activities you are minimizing the use of your money income. Your spending power is increased since your money resource can be allocated for another purpose.

Money management occurs when you make logical decisions. Although your financial spending plan is developed and implemented on the basis of your money income, this plan had validity only when it has been developed and decisions are made using composite income as a data base.

Financial Planning

Financial management occurs when you make a concerted effort to develop and implement plans using your composite income as a base. The purpose of financial planning is to allocate resources to achieve your wants and needs. The objective of financial planning is to conserve all your resources, not only your monetary ones. The goal of financial planning is to achieve your desired quality of life.

Three different terms have been used herein. *Financial planning* is the development and implementation of a plan to allocate and use the resources inherent within your composite income. A *financial spending plan* is the development and implementation of a plan to allocate and use your money income. Money management involves both the financial spending plan and the *family financial plan.* Thus to achieve effective money management two separate planning components are developed and implemented. The first is the family financial plan. This plan is based upon your composite income. It is future- as well as present-oriented. Your financial spending plan is the second component. The data base for this is primarily your money income; however, your composite income and your family financial plan are additional sources of input.

As shown in Figure 9.2, each of these plans are linked to the other. Effective money management exists only when the planning and implementation of both occurs. Each is necessary if you are to achieve your desired quality of life.

Management of money resources occurs as you develop and implement your financial spending plan. However, this financial spending plan cannot be developed nor implemented unless you have a financial plan. To some, this may appear to be merely a matter of semantics; in reality it is not.

In developing a financial plan, you are looking forward to the demands, wants, and needs of the future as well as the current ones. Just as you anticipate future demands, so too, should you anticipate in the future increases, additions, and reductions of resources. As you graduate, new resources will be created. Other resources will be increased. The availability of still other resources will decline. Each of these must be recognized and incorporated in the money management process. Despite this you will continue to have a limited resource: money. It will not afford you the capability of securing all of your wants and needs nor of meeting your demands. To effectively manage your money resource, you will need to first identify your composite income. From this knowledge you can begin to assess your financial status. You then begin to examine the alternatives available, possible trade-offs, and opportunity costs of your financial decisions.

Let's look a little closer at this concept by examining your composite income. Using Figure 9.3, determine your composite income. This will be

FIGURE 9.2. Money Management Process.

Composite Income Sources	Dollar Value

Production Income

Household Production (List)
$_____
$_____
$_____
$_____
$_____
$_____

Durable Goods (List)
$_____
$_____
$_____
$_____

Total Productive
Income $_____

Money Income

Salary or Wages
$_____
$_____

Monetary Gifts
$_____
$_____

Investment Income
$_____
$_____
$_____

Capital Gains
$_____
$_____
$_____

Others
$_____
$_____
$_____

Total Money
Income $_____

- -

Hidden Income

Community Income
$_____
$_____

Psychic Income
$_____
$_____

Employment Benefit Income
$_____
$_____
$_____

Consumer "Savings"
$_____
$_____
$_____

Total Hidden
Income $_____

Total Composite
Income $_____

FIGURE 9.3.   *Individual Composite Income.*

achieved by listing all of the items within each category. Upon completion, establish a dollar value for every item listed. This dollar value can be determined by ascertaining the market cost for each item. Did you list cleaning your room as one of the items under household production? If so, multiply the time you use to complete this production endeavor by the market cost if you had employed someone to perform this service. The hidden income category dollar values can be computed in a similar manner. For instance, although a tax supported museum or recreational facility may not charge an admission fee, what would be the market cost if they did? Multiply this figure by the number of times you use such a facility. This same principle can be utilized to establish dollar values for each category. The sum total of each category is your composite income.

Assume your current cash funds are $25.00. Your family standard is to individually give gifts for each person's birthday. Your mother's birthday is next week. You haven't as yet purchased a gift for her. One of your courses requires the purchase of a laboratory manual (cost: $10.95). At the moment you don't have and should purchase notebook paper. You have a term paper due at the end of next week. You have enough typing paper for half of the final draft and no carbon paper. Last week you borrowed $3.00 from a friend with the promise of returning it no later than the beginning of next week.

On the basis of your composite income, what would or could you do? What are your alternatives? What trade-offs can you make? What are the various opportunity costs of each of your alternatives?

You, like other individuals, face similar situations on a regular basis. Very often in seeking solutions to these kinds of dilemmas individuals tend to overlook or minimize the alternatives represented within the composite income. Instead they concentrate their thinking only in terms of their money income. In so doing, they fail to seek alternatives. Their financial management then is done on the basis of insufficient data.

Using composite income to solve or seek solutions to an evident insolvency as just outlined, not only makes you more aware of your alternatives and possible trade-offs but may also indicate additional alternatives not previously identified. Each time the composite income is used to make money management decisions, spending power is increased. As spending power is increased, you are able to secure more of your wants as well as attaining those needs necessary for human well-being.

The Financial Plan

Your composite income provides the data base from which the financial plan is developed. Your planning is done on the basis of this and input received from several other sources. This input includes that received from individual and family members, knowledge of present and anticipated demands, and individual and family held goals, values, and standards. Other sources of input include the immediate and distant spheres as well as the shelter sphere. This input is necessary to develop a viable financial plan.

The purpose of a financial plan is to bring about satisfaction through the attainment of your desired quality of life. This means using the management process to develop and implement a plan. You will note there are a number of component parts involved herein. The management process is the tool. The data base is the composite income. And the ultimate, long-range goal is your desired quality of life. Each of these component parts must be recognized and involved if your financial plan is to be viable.

Financial planning begins by identifying your desired quality of life and then the short-range, intermediate, and long-range goals that will lead to this desired quality of life. Financial planning is directed toward future attainment and achievement as opposed to current or present day attainment and achievement.

The second phase of financial planning is directed toward examining the alternatives and resources needed to achieve these goals. Trade-offs and opportunity costs as well as the risk factors are considered and assessed. The data contained in the composite income is important in this aspect.

The third phase in financial planning is to develop a plan on the basis of your goals, your composite income, input received, and the analysis of trade-offs, opportunity costs, and risk factors. The financial plan serves a twofold purpose. It gives direction to the future. As such it encompasses both current and future goals, and resource allocation. At the same time it becomes a data base along with your composite income for the development and implementation of your financial spending plan.

Once the financial plan has been developed, the management processes of implementation and evaluative feedback are undertaken and completed. The financial plan you develop will reflect not only the financial stability you anticipate in the future but also your anticipated lifetime pattern. As such it mirrors not only your financial plans but your future plans as well.

Goals and Financial Planning

Short-range, intermediate, and long-range goals are an inherent part of any plan. Setting priorities is vital too. Financial planning, if it is to be viable and yield the desired degree of satisfaction, must be done on the basis of realistic, well-defined goals. These goals reflect your desired quality of life. However, they must be realistic and well defined. Although many children may grow up aspiring to be the President of the United States, few are realistically able to attain this goal.

It has been emphasized that the financial plan originates from your short-range, intermediate, and long-range goals. Although it is true that many of these goals may appear to center around tangible and materialistic consumption, your desired quality of life encompasses intangible aspects as well. Consequently, the financial plan should reflect both the tangible and intangibles. It should not be thought of solely in the context of consumption.

A financial plan is long-term planning. Therefore it begins through identifying the components that comprise your desired quality of life. What do you envision your life to be in ten years? What do you anticipate will be your life style? Where will you be living and working? What type of position will you be assuming within your profession?

In the answers to these questions can be found your desired quality of life. Now identify the goals that will direct your forward progress to achieve what you envision lies ahead of you. As these goals develop, they need to be given priorities and to be sequenced. In turn, you may discover that your goals will become more clearly defined and clarified. How clearly you define and clarify each will determine the success you will attain through your financial plan.

There are different methods used to identify, define, and clarify your goals. One is to start with your short-range goals and work forward to the long-range ones. Another is to reverse the process, starting with the long-range ones and work backwards to the short-range one. Still another is to isolate the component parts of your desired quality of life and then identify the goals necessary to achieve each.

Figure 9.4 demonstrates the latter method; herein your goals, their priority, and sequencing are more clearly identified, defined, and clarified. At the same time you can readily relate each level of goals to the component part of the desired quality of life you are seeking to achieve. Thus the direction you

Short-range Goal	Intermediate Goal	Long-range Goal	Quality of Life Standard
Savings account to achieve down payment	Purchase home and make mortgage payments	Complete home mortgage payments	Home ownership
College degree	Enter profession Work toward professional success	Upward professional movement Attainment of desired professional status	Achieve success in chosen profession
Develop investment plan	Invest money resources Seek investment opportunities having high rate of return	Continued investment Examination of retirement plans	Financially stable retirement

FIGURE 9.4. *Financial Goal Given Priorities to Attain the Desired Quality of Life.*

are taking and the rational are known. As implementation takes place, the processes of controlling, checking, and adjusting are continuous and on-going.

The component parts of the desired quality of life shown in Figure 9.4 are representative of only a few you probably view as being a part of your future. Remember your desired quality of life encompasses more than just the financial aspects. Each aspect has an influence upon your financial plan even though a particular component may not directly involve monetary expenditures. For example, how valid would your financial plan be if you did not include the component of attainment of your chosen profession? Although the measure of your success within your chosen profession may or may not involve the monetary standard of a predetermined salary, the securing of a professional position will necessitate the expenditures of money resources. These expenditures might include an advanced degree, civic participation, wardrobe modification, and other related items and endeavors.

The identification, definition, and clarification of the goals needed for development of the financial plan must be sequenced. The guidelines for sequencing of the management process also apply here. Goals should be sequenced in a realistic and meaningful pattern, each one leading to the next. Figure 9.4 demonstrates a method of sequencing your goals. The sequencing must occur within each level as well as between goal levels. In other words, short-range goals are sequenced internally. At the same time however, these short-range goals must be sequenced to correlate with intermediate goals. Since the attainment of all the components comprising your desired quality of life will not occur simultaneously, there must be correlation among and between goals of varying levels.

Alternatives and Resources in Financial Planning

Decisions must now be made to allocate the needed resources to attain the different identified goals. These decisions, if they are to be valid, must have as a base an awareness of all available data. This data, in part, comes from an analysis of the possible alternatives, trade-offs, opportunity costs, risk factors, and resource availability. Also relevant is the continued flow of input you are receiving from the spheres of interaction.

Alternatives are an important part of financial planning. Taking the time to identify them may mean the difference between status quo and real financial growth. In identifying alternatives you are better able to ascertain not only the needed resources but also the extent of consumption necessitated within each choice.

Alternatives point to potential trade-offs. Each also serves as a vehicle to isolate probable opportunity costs. The assessment of alternatives enables you to analyze the risk factors. As risk factors become apparent, you can begin to seek methods of reducing them to an acceptable level.

On page 210 you were faced with a possible insolvent financial situation.

One alternative would be to make a long distance telephone call home to

1. Inform your mother your gift would be late.
2. Tell her the telephone call was her gift.
3. Indicate you were using your skills and abilities to make her a gift.
4. Explain your insolvent situation and hope she understands.
5. Ask your Dad to include your name on his gift.
6. Ask your Dad or another member of the family to purchase a gift and you'll pay them back at a later date.
7. Ask someone to send some money to resolve your current financial situation and then purchase a gift for your mother with the funds you have currently.
8. Send a nice card to mother.
9. Although previously you had observed the family standard of presenting individual gifts to family members, you seek to change or modify this in some manner.

Only some of the alternative choices you have are listed; there are many others. What would be the opportunity costs, used resources, trade-offs, and risk factors for each of those listed?

All resources have limitations; some have more than others. Identifying the alternatives assists you in determining the existence and extent of each resource needed for each choice. Inherent within this process of assessment of resources is the determination of whether specific resources will be exchanged, transferred, protected, produced, saved-invested, or consumed. Although this is important throughout all of management, it is readily apparent in financial planning.

In seeking to identify resource utilization two factors become paramount. One is the manner in which the resource will be utilized such as exchanged or transferred. The other is the manner in which the resource is replaced and the requirements necessary for replacement.

In financial planning, utilization of resources may have a far reaching effect. This aspect must be closely correlated with alternative choices and will have a direct bearing upon the consideration and selection of alternatives. In exchanging one resource for another, your cash reserve may not be drastically effected because it is possible to reverse the exchange process. Partial or complete consumption of a resource could affect your cash balance; or you might decide to deplete a current resource in order to protect another one, to produce additional resources at a later date, or to voluntarily transfer one or more resources.

Resource replacement should also be a consideration in choosing among alternatives. Some resources such as time and energy are readily replaced necessitating little or no real effort on your part; others are not. Some require the expenditure of your skills, talents, abilities, and such in order for replacement to occur. Your money income, in most cases, represents this type of resource replacement. How readily the resource can be replaced and the procedures necessary for replacement will affect not only the alternative selection but also the opportunity costs. For example, when the replacement of money income necessitates the partial consumption of time, energy, talent, and work capability, you have lost the opportunity to use these resources for other endeavors and actions. Consideration of the risk factors in each instance must be done.

When choosing among alternatives the possible trade-offs must also be analyzed as well as opportunity costs and risk factors. Refer back to the alternative choices shown on page 210. What trade-offs might be possible? How would these trade-offs affect your financial insolvency? Would the trade-offs have any effect upon the opportunity costs and/or risk factors?

Financial Planning

Thus far you have explored the theory of financial planning. The development of the financial plan begins by assessing your current situation and establishing a time span for the implementation of the plan once it has been developed.

In seeking to ascertain the time span of the financial plan, Burton and Petrello suggest financial planning be done in terms of goal projection for the future. They further indicate the financial plan be formally developed in terms of a calendar year and informally to include those goals projected for beyond the current calendar year.[2] Consequently, these authors suggest the development of a yearly formal financial plan. Coupled with this plan should be informal financial planning which extends beyond the current year and reflects the projected future goals such as the anticipated purchase of another car in two or three years.

Although the financial plan you develop will encompass the time span of one calendar year, it should reflect the projected attainments which are seen as being a part of your desired quality of life. Your financial plan then is specifically developed for a time span of one year but has implications for several years hence.

Another aspect of financial planning is the determination of where you are right now. What is your net worth? The term *net worth* is used to express your current financial status. Although the term *net worth* may be a familiar one, have you actually computed yours? You have assets and liabilities. The difference between your assets and liabilities is your net worth.[3]

Your assets are composed of the market value of your tangible goods such as your car or stereo, stocks and bonds, the cash value of life insurance policies, and any money you have in your checking or savings accounts. Your liabilities refer to any debts you have incurred such as car payments, student loans, or credit accounts. To compute your net worth, you subtract your liabilities from your assets. Your net worth may be positive or negative.

Your net worth represents your financial status at any given point in time. It has many uses in financial planning and money management. Within money management, your net worth indicates the monetary value or the cash reserves you could draw upon. A positive or negative net worth demonstrates your financial solvency or insolvency. Financial institutions use your net worth to determine whether or not to extend credit. This is also used to measure the amount of dollar credit they are willing to extend. Using the form shown in Figure 9.5 compute your net worth.

The financial plan you develop will incorporate the data from your current and projected goals, your composite income, and your net worth. These are the tools used in the establishment of the financial plan.

The first step in development involves identifying and setting priorities for both current and projected goals. Note that priorities should be set by years. In other words, what are your financial goals for this year, next year, and in the coming years? Remember that the financial plan will be developed for this current calendar year but must reflect the years ahead.

From the net worth, you are able to determine liabilities which must be included in the financial plan. Here again, the current and coming years must be considered in the overall plan. The data contained in the net worth form serves two functions. The first is to identify your liabilities and the time span when each must be resolved. For instance, installment purchases will have a different time span than a real estate mortgage. Your net worth statement also indicates the assets you can draw upon should the need arise.

The composite income statement provides valuable data for your financial plan as well. This statement will provide information concerning possible alternatives and trade-offs that you could make.

The financial plan is developed using all of the data and within the time span of one year. Shown in Figure 9.6 is a general format for a yearly financial plan.

Although this may well appear to be synonymous with the financial spending plan, it is not. The financial plan is developed using general categories. The dollar amounts are anticipated expenditures for yearly time spans. The spending plan, on the other hand, is developed for a shorter period of time.

As you begin to determine your expenditures and payment of your liabilities for the coming year, you may find your expenditures, as anticipated, will exceed your money income. Here is where the composite income statement can be a valuable tool. Using this tool and the data from the financial plan statement, you can begin to assess where alternatives lie and to make choices. As you

FIGURE 9.5. (Opposite) Net Individual or Family Worth [Adapted from Robert H. Burton and George J. Petreillo, Personal Finance (New York: Macmillan Publishing Company, Inc., 1978), p. 93.]

Net Worth

ASSETS

Current Assets (List)	Dollar Value	
Cash on hand	$ _____	
Savings accounts	$ _____	
Cash in bank	$ _____	
Prepaid life insurance premiums	$ _____	
Life insurance surrender value	$ _____	
Common stocks (List)	$ _____	
	$ _____	
	$ _____	
Preferred stocks (List)	$ _____	
	$ _____	
	$ _____	
Bonds (List)	$ _____	
Total		$ _____

Fixed Assets (List)		
Car	$ _____	
Stereo	$ _____	
Furniture	$ _____	
Real estate	$ _____	
Jewelry	$ _____	
Total		$ _____
Others	$ _____	
Total		$ _____

Total Assets $ _____

LIABILITIES

Current Liabilities	Dollar Amount	
Finance companies (installment purchases)	$ _____	
	$ _____	
	$ _____	
Outstanding bills (List)	$ _____	
	$ _____	
	$ _____	
Total		$ _____

Fixed Liabilities		
Real estate mortgage	$ _____	
	$ _____	
Personal loans	$ _____	
	$ _____	
	$ _____	
Insurance premiums	$ _____	
	$ _____	
	$ _____	
Taxes outstanding	$ _____	
	$ _____	
	$ _____	
Total		$ _____
Other Liabilities	$ _____	
	$ _____	
Total		$ _____

Total Liabilities $ _____

New Worth $ _____

FINANCIAL PLAN FOR _____

Year _____ to Year _____

Income Sources	Dollar Amounts		
Salary, wages	$ _____		
Earned interest	$ _____		
Others	$ _____		
Total Gross Income		$_____	$_____
Income Deductions			
Income taxes	$ _____		
Social Security	$ _____		
Retirement fund	$ _____		
Others	$ _____		
Total Deductions		$_____	
Total Net Income			$_____
Fixed Expenses			
Real estate mortgages	$ _____		
Installment loans	$ _____		
Insurance premiums	$ _____		
Personal loans	$ _____		
Employment dues and fees	$ _____		
Individual family allowances	$ _____		
Others	$ _____		
Total Fixed Expenses		$_____	
Remaining Balance			$_____
Flexible Expenses			
Food	$ _____		
Clothing	$ _____		
Personal Care	$ _____		
Household operational expenses	$ _____		
Transportation	$ _____		
Savings and investments	$ _____		
Others	$ _____		
Total Flexible Expenses		$_____	
Remaining Balance			$_____
Other Miscellaneous Expenses			
Contributions	$_____		
Entertainment	$_____		
Gifts	$_____		
Others	$_____		
Total Other Expenses		$_____	
Remaining Balance			$_____

FIGURE 9.6. Yearly Financial Plan.

attach dollar amounts to the various categories, you can also begin to determine potential trade-offs that must be made now and in the future.

Have you found that once your expenditures are listed, the remaining balance is relatively small? If you are like most individuals and families today, this situation is not unique. Completion of the financial plan statement should readily convince you of the need to develop and implement it. Although most individuals are aware of their general inability to manage their money income, it is probably not until they complete a financial plan statement that they realize the true extent of their discretionary funds once fixed, flexible, and other expenses are allocated. Discretionary income will rise only when you actively seek to identify and use alternatives.

As you examine the financial plan, perhaps some terms need to be defined. *Income sources* represent all of your potential sources of income. These may include your salary, wages, tips, allowance, earned interest, or any other source of money income. The total of these represents your gross income. The term *gross income* refers to the total amount of your income before any taxes or deductions are taken out of your paycheck. *Net income* refers to the amount of money income you actually have to spend. When you receive your paycheck you are aware it does not represent the total amount of your wages and salary. Items such as income tax, social security, workman's compensation, and others have been deducted. The amount of money remaining after deductions is your net income. Thus your net income is the actual dollars you have to spend, save, or invest.

Your expenditures are divided into three general categories. *Fixed expenses* represent those outstanding bills, loans, or payments that require the payment of a set amount of money at a specific time. The dollar amount has been established and remains the same for as long as the debt is owed. Many of these represent credit usage or financial obligations to which you have committed yourself for a set period of time. *Flexible expenses* are items you purchase on a regular basis but which have varying dollar amounts each time the purchase is made. Food consumption is an example of a flexible expense. In addition to fixed and flexible expenses, you have other miscellaneous expenses. These do not have a fixed amount and may or may not be purchased on a regular basis. For instance, do you have a specific dollar figure for entertainment? If you do, then these items would be listed in another category.

Using Figure 9.6, develop your financial plan for the coming year. The more realistic your plan is, the better will be your financial management. You should remember this financial plan will also serve as a data base for the development of your spending plan.

Financial Spending Plan

The financial spending plan is developed from the financial planning statement. The financial plan directs and governs your money management for a specific period of time, usually one calendar year. The financial spending plan is developed for a much shorter period of time. Although the general categories may be the same for both, the spending plan is much more detailed. The financial plan actually represents your anticipated expenditures for the coming 12 months. The spending plan, on the other hand, represents your anticipated expenditures for only one month. The data from the composite income, goals, and net worth will be valuable tools along with the financial planning statement.

The development of the spending plan begins in the same manner as the financial plan. You identify and set priorities for your current and projected goals. The difference here is the detailing of the goals and the time span. Goals will center primarily around the current year and possibly the current month although the projected goals will also be considered. You might have as one of your current goals a plan to repay a short-term loan, or save an established amount of money for a special event.

The next step is to use the information of the financial plan to establish the spending plan on a monthly basis. Although you may receive your paycheck more often than once each month, most outstanding bills, debt obligations, and such are computed on a monthly basis. Thus this time span is easier to use than a shorter one. If you decide to use a shorter time span you need to anticipate monthly bills.

Every individual has a specific method of developing a spending plan. Shown in Figure 9.7 is a general method that can be modified to suit your individual needs. As you compare this with the financial plan statement you will note the similarity between the two in respect to categories. However, you should note that although the general categories are similar for purposes of expediency and effective planning, more detail is found within each category than in the financial plan.

Although the spending plan format shown in Figure 9.7 is for only one month, it should be remembered that a spending plan is developed for each month of the calendar year. In seeking to specify actual dollar amounts for these categories, you like many others, may experience difficulty in determining an exact dollar figure. Your check record of previous expenditures can be a guide in ascertaining dollar amounts. Another source is your record of expenditures from previous months. No spending plan is infallible. There are always instances when unanticipated expenses occur. The composite income and your net worth can be utilized in these instances.

You have established your composite income, net worth, and your financial plan; the next step is to develop your spending plan. Start by computing your gross and net incomes for the month.

Using the disposable income as a base figure, record your fixed and flexible expenses. The remaining balance is then allocated to your other miscellaneous expenses. Once completed you have developed your spending plan for the month. This represents the first step in the money management process. The second step is implementation.

Record Keeping

The work you have done thus far involves the planning component of the money management process. The second component is implementation. Inherent within this stage (as with the application of the management process to meet any demand), is the controlling, checking, and adjusting that takes place during implementation.

The control phase of implementation is the expenditure of your money income. The spending plan serves as the guideline for the monetary outlay of your funds. Your money flows outward into the spheres of interaction. You control this flow by spending according to your established plan.

Checking takes place as you compare your actual expenditures to your spending plan. As this occurs you need to keep records of actual expenditures. These records are then used to make adjustments where necessary. These records and the adjustments you make become a source of input for future spending plans and ultimately the financial plan statement.

Evaluative feedback will occur throughout the implementation of the spending plan. As you begin to develop a new spending plan evaluative feedback occurs again. The final feedback is completed at the termination of the spending plan.

Record keeping is another tool used in money management. The tools you have previously developed are the signposts and guides directing your forward progress. Unless you keep financial records of expenditures any future plans you develop will be done using insufficient data.

Quite simply, money management involves recording your expenditures in actual dollar amount. This means you record expenditures for each category as the dollars are spent. Although there are many methods used for this purpose, the loose-leafed notebook affords the greatest ease and flexibility. Separate pages are used for each subcategory with divider sheets between general categories. As you make purchases, record the total amount on the specific page along with the date and place of purchase. An example of the grocery store record is shown in Figure 9.8.

These records of actual expenditures serve many functions. Aside from the dollar amounts and the date and place of purchase, total monthly expenditures can be compared with your spending plan throughout implementation. This comparison will indicate potential and needed adjustments. Continually checking actual against anticipated expenditures will clearly indicate when adjustments must be made to avoid excessive expenditures prior to the close of the spending period. They will also provide evaluative feedback at the termination point of the spending plan. Records of actual dollars spent can assist in identifying areas where your anticipated spending was too high or too low. This becomes a source of input for future spending plans.

Your record keeping provides other data as well. Through analysis of your

FINANCIAL SPENDING PLAN FOR THE MONTH OF _____

Income Sources

   Salary, wages $ _____
   Tips $ _____
   Earned interest $ _____
   Others $ _____

                                       Total Gross Income $ _____

Income Deductions

   Income taxes $ _____
   Social Security $ _____
   Employment dues and fees $ _____
   Retirement funds $ _____
   Others $ _____

                                       Total Net Income $ _____

EXPENDITURES

Fixed Expenses

   Real Estate mortgages
     or Rental fees $ _____
   Installment payments (List) $ _____
                           $ _____
                           $ _____

   Insurance premiums (List) $ _____
                           $ _____
                           $ _____

   Personal loans (List) $ _____
                           $ _____
                           $ _____

   Employment dues and fees $ _____
   Allowances (List by
     individuals) $ _____
                           $ _____
                           $ _____

   Others (List) $ _____
                           $ _____
                           $ _____

   Savings & Investments (list) $ _____
                           $ _____
                           $ _____

                Total Fixed Expenses $ _____

                     Remaining Balance $ _____

Flexible Expenses

   Food
     Grocery store $ _____
     Lunches outside the home $ _____
     Home delivery items $ _____
     Food away from home $ _____

   Clothing
     Personal clothing $ _____
     Care and maintenance $ _____
     Special purchases $ _____
       (school or employment $ _____
        related) $ _____

FIGURE 9.7. *Monthly Financial Spending Plan.*

Transportation
Commuting costs $_____
Gasoline $_____
Care and maintenance $_____
Special travel $_____

Household operational expenses
Laundry $_____

Utilities
Electricity $_____
Water $_____
Gas $_____
Telephone $_____
Others $_____

Home delivery items
Newspaper $_____
Magazines $_____

Cleaning supplies $_____

Equipment
Household $_____
Personal $_____

Care and maintenance $_____

Special purchases (List) $_____
$_____
$_____

Others (List) $_____
$_____
$_____

Personal care
Cosmetics $_____
Drugs and medicines $_____
Others (List) $_____
$_____
$_____

Other miscellaneous expenses $_____

Educational expenses
Tuition $_____
Books $_____
School related $_____

Contributions (List)
United Fund $_____
$_____
$_____

Gifts
Family birthdays $_____
Christmas $_____
Special events $_____

Entertainment (List) $_____
$_____
$_____

Others (List) $_____
$_____
$_____

Total Expenses $_____

Remaining Balance $_____

Grocery Store

Food

Month _____

Date	Place of Purchase	Total Amount
5/2	Store A	$ 37.22
5/10	Store B	10.12
5/18	Store C	42.60
5/26	Store B	6.18
5/30	Store C	19.26
	Monthly total	$110.38

FIGURE 9.8. Recordkeeping Sheet.

actual expenditures you can identify your buying weaknesses. There will be indications of where and how your expenditure reductions could be made should such action become necessary. This same data will also demonstrate your current spending patterns. You, like most individuals, are probably not aware of your buying weaknesses but eveyone has them. What do you impulsively purchase that you don't really need? When you are feeling down or really want to reward yourself, what do you buy? Regardless of what the item is, such purchases represent your buying weaknesses. Recognition of this will not eliminate your consumption in these areas, but it may act as a control on future spending.

Records also point to possible areas where spending reductions can be made if and when necessary. Do you know a number of college students who spend a great deal of money on additional food even though it is provided and they frequently eat in the dormitory? The consumption of food in this instance may represent a spending pattern that the student did not recognize. It may also indicate a point where spending cuts could be made if necessary.

Unless accurate records are kept for actual dollar expenditures within each of the subcategories the data needed for future spending plans is missing. This information is vital to future planning.

At this point, you might well be saying: "I don't want to spend all my time keeping records and making plans." Although this process may appear to be very time consuming and actually is in the initial stages, to be effective money management necessitates the development of these tools. You will find that once you have used and become familiar with these tools, their development and utilization will consume less and less of your time.

Record keeping does involve expenditures of your time and energy, yet technological advances have eliminated or reduced the demands previously placed upon these resources. Home computers are available and can be utilized in record keeping, as can calculators. As technology continues to advance further assistance will be provided. Regardless of these, however, record keeping will remain a necessary component of the money management process.

Business and industry as well as governmental agencies and organizations develop and use the money management tools similar to the ones you have been studying. Do you honestly feel you and your financial well-being have lesser importance?

Disbursement of Money Income

All too often individuals and families regardless of their stage in the life cycle have placed a stronger emphasis on the inward flow of money income into the shelter sphere rather than its outward flow into the remaining spheres of interaction. This concerted emphasis is a fallacy in and of itself. It is true that money management would not exist without this inward flow, yet effective money management involves both the inward and outward flow.

Closely coupled with this are individual attitudes and perceptions of the function of money. Another crucial factor is the manner in which money resources will be disbursed.

Thus far the study of money management has been directed toward your role in the development of concepts and tools inherent within this process. When the management of money resources involves only a single individual the question of the disbursement methodology does not arise. However, as the shelter sphere changes to include other individuals who may or may not be gainfully employed outside the sphere, this question will arise and must be resolved.

The methodology employed to determine disbursement of money resources and the culminating decisions that will result are of paramount importance to money management within the sphere. Studies have shown this aspect is one of the prime causal factors of marital discord. Deep-seeded in this discord are conflicts concerning role perceptions, value hierarchies, attitudes, and feelings toward money. The resolution of this lies in communication among individuals. Each individual has personal attitudes and feelings regarding money, its importance, and function within the shelter and family spheres. Closely aligned to this are male-female role perceptions.

What should money enable you to achieve or attain in your lifetime? Should money be spent to bring pleasure or the satisfaction of ownership? Or is it more important to save rather than spend money? What purchases have you seen other college students make that you felt were a waste of money? Should you decide to marry, would you or your spouse assume the major responsibility for the disbursement of your money income? Will you have separate or joint checking and savings accounts? Should one member make all of the major financial decisions, or should these decisions always be joint ones?

Although every individual has his or her own attitudes and feelings concerning money and its management, few young couples as they prepare to share the future actively communicate these to each other.

The methodology of disbursing money income is changing, and in all probability will continue to change in the future. Technology has brought about changes in business, in industry, and in the home, and has affected the management of money resources. It is anticipated that these changes that have gradually emerged over the years will rapidly advance in the future. Closely aligned with these changes are the newly emerging roles of individuals within the social structure. As each of these changes is viewed within the context of current economic conditions, the disbursal of money resources to achieve effective money management becomes even more imperative.

In previous years the disbursement of money income occurred through the use of one of five systems: the dole, allowance, democratic, fifty-fifty, or equal salary. The advent of computer technology has changed the validity of these systems. Prior to our modern technological society, money income was disbursed utilizing either actual cash or check writing as a method of payment. Today many families no longer devote several hours each month to the tedious task of writing checks for the payment of outstanding bills. Instead the bank computers have been programmed for this purpose. The extent to which the computer is programmed is dependent upon the desires of each family unit. Some families have elected to include all fixed and selected flexible expenses; others have only fixed expenses paid. There is also the option of determining when a separate outstanding debt payment will occur. In this instance, a telephone call activates the computer which then disburses money income. A growing number of individuals and families utilize the direct deposit concept for wage payment. Through direct deposit their wages are automatically credited to their account. No actual dollar exchange takes place. Other innovations are the automated teller machines often located in shopping malls and grocery stores. These enable customers to withdraw funds when necessary. Automated clearing houses transfer funds from one account to another or across geographical areas. Each of these is an integral part of the electronic funds transfer system.

The advent of computer technology has and will continue to necessitate a greater emphasis upon money management principles and concepts as the electronic funds transfer system becomes more and more a part of our daily lives. Most individuals and families are not aware of the extent to which it has already influenced their money management and their daily lives. The methods of bill payment just indicated are but a small part of the total system. The concept of the *cashless society* may be familiar to many, yet the extent to which it currently exists or the impact it will have upon money management in the future remains unclear.

Summary

The financial status of families and individuals within today's economic world necessitates the application of the management process to the allocation and utilization of money resources. This can be accomplished only through a concerted effort of on-going money management. Every individual and family experiences demands being placed upon this limited resource. Participation in the economic marketplace means choices must be made. Money management is the key to the achievement of the desired quality of life.

Money management necessitates the development of the tools inherent within the process. These are the composite income, the net worth statement, the financial plan, the spending plan, and the methodology of money disbursement.

The composite income is composed of your productive, hidden, and money incomes. Each is used to ascertain the alternatives available, potential trade-offs, opportunity costs, and the risk factors as decisions are made.

The net worth statement is an assessment of your financial solvency at any given point. This tool is used to indicate solvency and cash reserves to be drawn upon in a financial crisis. It also indicates your progress toward your desired quality of life.

The direction and path you intend to take financially in the coming year is reflected in your financial plan—your anticipated spending within one calendar year. It encompasses your short-range and intermediate financial goals while considering your projected future goals.

The spending plan is developed for a one month time span. It is the most detailed of all of the money management plans. As a guideline, it directs and details your anticipated immediate spending.

Each tool serves an individualistic purpose within money management. The absence of one negates the value of those remaining. Each one is developed during the planning component of the management of money resources.

As implementation occurs, the various plans are utilized along with record keeping. The recording of actual dollar expenditures serves as a check and balance while providing evaluative feedback. Comparisons are made between actual expenditures and anticipated ones. These evaluative instruments used throughout the implementation and evaluative feedback are components of the money management process.

As the electronic funds transfer system becomes an ever increasing part of the economic system, individuals and families must develop not only the skills needed to activate the computer terminals but also increase their money management skills. The continued movement toward a cashless society makes it imperative that effective money management be continually undertaken.

Money management is a necessity if the individual and/or family is to achieve their desired quality of life. It's your money, why not manage it wisely?

CASE STUDY: BOB AND SYLVIA

Bob and Sylvia plan to be married in three weeks. Discussions on money management have taken place since they have become engaged. Each is aware of the other's salary and they have often talked about their financial future but always in general terms. Despite this, neither is truly aware nor completely involved in the money management of the other. With the wedding so close at hand, they have decided that they should sit down and establish their joint financial status.

In order to plan their financial future, they decided to separately record their financial status and expenditures. Here is what each recorded:

Bob's yearly salary is $14,650. He has $837.23 in his checking account and $185.10 in a savings account. His apartment rent is $275 per month. His other monthly expenditures include: car loan payment, $150; credit account payments, $20.00; car insurance, $36.00; gasoline and car maintenance, $41.50; and clothing purchases and care, $24.00. He usually spends about $90 per month for groceries, $40 for lunch during the week, and $85.00 for entertainment.

Sylvia lives at home and pays no rent from her yearly salary of $12,890. However, her car loan payments are $162.00 per month and her car insurance is $36.00 for the same period of time. Her other monthly expenditures are: gasoline and car maintenance, $54.00; lunch during the week, $30.00; credit account payments, $38.00 and $65.00 per month which she gives to her parents for her share of food and rent. With the wedding so near, she has averaged $150.00 per month for clothing. Her checking account now has a balance of $416.19 and her saving account totals 455.16.

ACTIVITIES

1. On page 210 is the case study of Bob and Sylvia. From the information given, develop their financial statement. Using the financial statement and the information given, develop a spending plan for this couple.
2. You are preparing for your professional career. You have certain anticipations for the future. On the basis of your anticipations, identify your financial position five years after graduation.
3. Compare your current financial position and spending pattern with the one you have just developed as your anticipated financial position in five years. What are the differences? What has created these differences? Did you anticipate your change in life style? How does this affect your financial position?
4. Keep an exact record of all of your expenditures of money for one week. Complete the following:
   a. Determine the categories of your expenditures and the sum total for each,
   b. Identify your strengths and the areas where you could improve your money management.
   c. Indicate the categories where you feel you are spending too much money and the reasons why.
5. You are to develop a financial spending plan for three families. The disposable income for each family is $1,592 per month. Indicate what you feel would be the assets and liabilities of each family.

Family A: Young couple who are planning to be married in one month. Both are recent college graduates. There is no measurable household inventory.

Family B: Married couple with two preschool children. The wife is expecting a third child in four months. They own five rooms of household furniture.

Family C: Married couple in their mid 40s. Two children of the family are both in college. This couple live in an eight-room house with ten years still to pay on the mortgage.

6. Using the same couples in question 5, make any necessary adjustments in the financial spending plans for each family when the following happens to each family:

Family A: The wife becomes pregnant and is unable to work outside the shelter sphere.

Family B: The wife has twins and the family inherits $25,000.

Family C: The husband retires on Social Security and his pension fund. His original monthly salary is reduced by 33 per cent.

SAM AND LOUISE, AND BILL AND KATHY'S DECISION

Sam and Louise have been married for seven years. Their oldest child is in school but the younger one is not. Louise wants to return to her old job as a secretary in the fall when the youngest child enters school. Sam is working for a local firm. His disposable income is $1,000 per month. If Louise returns to her previous position she will make $640 per month before taxes.

Although Sam would prefer that Louise not work full time, he does want her to be happy. They have decided to sit down and logically decide whether or not they will really be making more money if Louise returns to her prior employment. They list their current monthly expenses:

Rent	$250	Car insurance	$31.50
Food	265	Life insurance	95.00
Car payments	122	Lunch for Sam	40.00
Clothing	40		

Bill and Kathy are members of a dual income family. Their two children are the same age as Sam and Louise's. Kathy has continuously been employed outside the shelter sphere since their marriage. Their expenses are as follows:

Home mortgage	$360	Car payments	$260
Food at home	300	Utilities	195
Lunches	80	Clothing	120
Day Care Center	160	Car insurance	55
Life insurance	190	Gasoline and Car	
Entertainment	60	maintenance	210

Bill's salary is $1,200 per month while Kathy's is $996 per month. Kathy is seriously considering terminating her employment. Both she and Bill are concerned about what this would do to their life style and financial status.

Discussion Questions

1. Two families described here have different decisions to make. Not all of their actual expenditures is given in the data. You must determine the remaining expenditures for each family. What other items would be included and what would be the possible costs for each?
2. Is each family currently living within their income? What are the assumptions you have made to arrive at this decision?
3. Assume you were advising Sam and Louise. What would be your decision? Would this family be further ahead financially if Louise did not resume her prior employment status? How much, if any, would Louise actually con-

tribute to the money income of the family if she was employed outside the shelter sphere? Does she have other alternative choices?

4. What would be the effect upon Bill and Kathy's financial status if she terminated her employment outside the shelter sphere? Can they financially afford for her to terminate her employment?

5. Develop a financial spending plan for both families. One plan should be developed for their current financial position and another financial spending plan on the assumption that (a) Louise returns to her employment status and (b) Kathy terminates her employment. Compare the two financial plans for each family and then the two families.

GLOSSARY

Assets The market value of durable goods, investments, cash value of life insurance policies, and the sum total of all checking and savings accounts.

Capital Gains Income The monetary return produced from profitable sale of real property or the margin of profit from a self-owned business.

Community Income The income derived from tax supported community services, facilities, and public benefit programs.

Composite Income The sum total of the productive, hidden, and money incomes used in the family financial planning for money management purposes.

Consumer Savings Income The income derived from reduced consumer spending or reduced money expenditures for retail goods and services.

Discretionary Income The monetary amount remaining for family expenditures after all fixed and flexible expenditures are paid.

Disposable Income The monetary amount remaining from employment income after taxes and other income deductions are removed. This amount represents the actual dollar amounts of employment income available to spend in the marketplace.

Durable Goods Income The monetary value of all nonconsumed goods within the shelter sphere. This represents a cash reserve that could be drawn upon should the need arise.

Employee Benefits Income The income accrued from employment-related benefits such as discounts, health care insurance, recreational facilities, and so forth.

Employment Income The earned income derived from employment outside the shelter sphere.

Fixed Expenses Expenditures having an established monetary amount for which payment is due at a specified time.

Flexible Expenses A recurring expenditure that does not have an established, specific dollar amount.

Financial Statement A detailed statement of the individual and/or family unit's financial well-being at any given point.

Financial Management A plan developed by the individual and/or family unit to allocate resources within the composite income in order to achieve wants and needs as defined in the desired quality of life.

Financial Spending plan The development and implementation of a plan to maximize the allocation of money resources in order to achieve individual and/or family wants and needs.

Hidden Income The sum total of income resources available to the individual and family unit from community income, psychic income, employment benefits, and consumer savings.

Household Production Income The monetary value of those goods and services contributed by the productive income of the talents, skills, and abilities of the family members within the family and shelter spheres.

Income Sources All potential sources of money income such as wages, salary, tips, allowance, earned income, and gifts that are available to meet expenditure demands.

Investment Income The money accrued from investments that produce a monetary return.

Liabilities The sum total of all debts or monies owed to individuals and/or financial institutions by the family unit or an individual within the family unit.

Money Income The sum total of employment income, investment income, and monetary gifts received by the family unit and available for allocation and use.

Net Worth The monetary figure representing the difference between the assets and liabilities of the family unit, showing the degree of financial solvency of an individual and/or family at any given point.

Money Management A process whereby resources are allocated in order to economically attain the wants and needs that comprise the desired quality of life through the use of financial planning and financial spending plans.

Productive Income The sum total of the household production income and the durable goods cash reserve.

Psychic Income The income derived from the satisfaction of ownership of durable goods for which an exact dollar amount may not necessarily be established.

Record Keeping A written record of the exact dollar expenditures during the implementation of the financial spending plan.

Record Keeping sheet An expenditure sheet developed for each catagory of the financial spending plan upon which is recorded the date, place, and amount of all dollar expenditures.

Trade-off The process whereby one available resource is substituted for another.

REFERENCES

1. E. Scott Maynes, *Decision-Making for Consumers An Introduction to Consumer Economics* (New York: Macmillan Publishing Company, Inc., 1976), p. 7.
2. Robert H. Burton and George J. Petrello, *Personal Finance* (New York: Macmillan Publishing Company, Inc., 1978), p. 93.
3. Roger LeRoy Miller, *Personal Finance Today* (New York: West Publishing Company, 1979), pp. 138–139.

CHAPTER TEN

Individual and Family Management

Management is done by individuals. However, the management process is used by business, industry, governments, institutions, agencies, organizations, groups of individuals, and families. Although the goals, aims, purposes, and objectives of each will differ, the principles and concepts remain the same. Regardless of the structural composition, each is striving to attain desired goals. Several have a more complex organizational structure than others, yet each utilizes the management process.

As an individual you undertake the management process throughout your daily life. Although your management is individualistic, you are also a member of the family unit residing within your shelter sphere. As a member of this family unit, you are concurrently involved in the management occurring within this sphere. In other words, managerial action is taking place simultaneously on two different levels. The decisions made and the managerial action taking place at each level are sources of input upon each other. Individual and group management differs one from the other. In each instance there are factors that affect the managerial action taking place and the decisions made. Thus far you have looked at your individual management and the factors that influence and affect it. However, since you also undertake managerial action as a member of a family unit, you need to understand how each influences and affects the other.

No individual lives completely isolated receiving no input from other spheres and individuals. Although you undertake management as an individual, your managerial action provides input into the various spheres of interaction. As such, this input is an influencing factor upon the management process of other individuals and/or groups.

Your management may provide input as a group utilizes the management process. Or it may be input into another individual's managerial process. Regardless of whether the management process is being undertaken by an individual or a group, the principles and concepts remain the same. Thus the differences lie not in the process and context but rather in the input received, the extensiveness of the process, and the factors that will affect the managerial action taking place.

Individual Management within the Family Sphere

As an individual you undertake the management process. At the same time you may also undertake management as a member of a collective group. The same is true for each member of a family. In other words, both individual and family management is occurring. This management may be undertaken as a collective group or it may be done separately by individual members of the group. In either instance, both involve the management principles and concepts.

The management that you undertake is influenced by the managerial action occurring around you in the various spheres of interaction. Conversely, the management being undertaken in the spheres of interaction is influenced by your managerial action. The greatest impact of these reverse influences is experienced between the individual and family spheres. Although individual and family managerial action differs one from the other, the decisions made, the planning done, and the implementation that occurs use the management process. Therefore, the differences between individual and family management lie not in the process employed but rather in the demands occurring, and the extensiveness of the process.

Thus your individual management is occurring within the spheres of interaction. This means that although you undertake individualistic managerial action, concurrent managerial action is taking place in other spheres. You may or may not be actively involved in this simultaneous management. Where involvement does occur, your participation will vary depending upon the given situation and the procedures taking place. Regardless of the extent of your active participation, the on-going process will be a source of input upon you just as you are input into the various spheres.

You are an individual. As such, you have values, goals, standards, resources, and a desired quality of life. On the basis of these you make decisions and use the management process. At the same time, you are receiving the input of the values, goals, standards, resources, and desired quality of life from your family sphere. Although the majority of your activities at the moment may accrue from your individual management decisions, you are a member of this family sphere. As such, the input you receive affects your individual management.

How many times have you wished you could completely control your life without any input from others? How often have you changed or modified your plans because of other people? Have you ever thought of what you would do if you didn't have to work for a living? Didn't have to account to anyone for your actions or behavior? Wished you didn't have to conform to rules and regulations?

Fortunately or unfortunately, this Utopia doesn't exist. Imagine for a moment what the world would be like if everyone "did his own thing"; if there were no codes of acceptable behavior, no rules and regulations, or no one telling you what to do. As an individual you are experiencing a continual flow of input from your spheres of interaction. This input flow affects your management. No other sphere has as much influence on your managerial action as does your family sphere.

Your managerial action, for the most part, takes place within the framework of your family sphere. It is here that you have the greatest input. From this comes the greatest input upon you. In the next few pages, you will examine this flow of input and output as well as the differences that occur between individual and family management. Each of these systems is unique. The uniqueness of each influences and affects the management taking place in the other.

Your managerial action occurs within the individual sphere. It is here your value hierarchy, goals, standards, and roles are established. It is also within this framework that individual decisions are made and the management process is undertaken. Here, too, input is received, decoded, and action undertaken. The input being received from the remaining spheres is of varying strength and necessitates diverse response. The impact of this input has shaped the person you have become and will continue to do so in the future.

As you receive this input, you undertake management within the individual sphere. Your evidences of your management then flow outward as input into the family and other spheres. In Figure 10.1 can be seen this continual flow of input and output taking place between you, your individual, and your family spheres.

In most instances, individual and collective group management are occurring simultaneously. Although the principles and concepts remain the same in both instances, differences and commonalities exist. These accrue from the aspect of collective group as opposed to individual actions; yet each is related one to the other.

To ascertain the commonalities and differences betweeen individual and family management, the principles and concepts will be discussed separately. Each is explored from the standpoint of both the individual and the family to demonstrate the interrelationship between the two.

Values

You have a value hierarchy as does each member of your family. At the same time, your family as a collective group has a value hierarchy. The family's hierarchy represents those values held in common by all members.

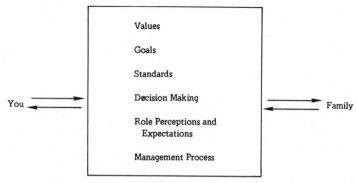

FIGURE 10.1 Flow of Input and Output Between You and Family Spheres.

Your family held value hierarchy was and is the original source of your individual hierarchy. The same is true for each member of your family. As an individual you have refined and clarified the values within your hierarchy. As you and other family members did this the collective values held by the family as a total group evolved into a family held hierarchy. This hierarchy was a source of input upon the role you self-assume and those which are assigned to you by other members of the family unit.

What are the common values held by all members of your family? What differences have you observed between your values and those of your family? Do your values occur in the same hierarchy as those of your parents? As you think about the common values held by every member of your family, would each one define the parameters in exactly the same manner?

As a young child you accepted and adopted the values of your parents and others within your kinship network. Through the process of maturity, past experience, and input received from your spheres of interaction, you have defined and refined these initial values, your role perceptions, and role expectations until they have become uniquely your own. Each member of your family has gone through the same process.

As you progressed to the current status of your value hierarchy, your family was a source of input upon you. At the same time, you were a source of input upon others. This continual flow of input from one family member to another yielded a value hierarchy. Thus two value hierarchies exist, your family hierarchy and your individually held one. There are times when the family held value hierarchy takes precedence over individually held ones. There are also instances when the opposite is true.

Family and individually held value hierarchies differ. Family value hierarchies are a composite of values held in common by all members. Reflect upon your family's value hierarchy. How clearly is each value defined? Do you feel these values tend to be more generalized as opposed to the specificity of your own?

Individually held value hierarchies tend to be more clearly defined than those of the family. This hierarchy tends to contain more specific values than the family hierarchy.

How closely does your value hierarchy match that of your family? In most cases, values highly prized by family members are also highly prized by you. However, their specific ranking within the hierarchy may vary to some extent. Family values are ranked in regard to family held goals and priorities. These mirror and reflect family expectations and the collectively identified desired quality of life. Your values, too, are ranked in accordance with your goals, priorities, and role perceptions. This may or may not be identical to your family's. Although the hierarchies will, in all probability, closely resemble each other, there still remains individual and distinct differences between the two.

Goals

Are your goals the same as those of your family? Where are the differences and similarities? What has brought about these differences and similarities? Every individual within the family unit has goals. At the same time, the family, as a collective unit, has goals. Family goals occur as short-range, intermediate, and long-range. Like individual goals they originate from the value hierarchy. The difference, here, is that these goals stem from the value hierarchy held by the family unit rather than individuals. Individual goals provide a direction or a sense of striving toward an objective. The same is true for family goals. Goal attainment, however, is done as a total group. The differences between family and individual goals, thus, lie not within their formulation, depth, or dimension but rather in the scope and attainment process.

Family goals often represent the sum total of individually held goals. They extend to include all family members as opposed to one individual. Your goal is a college degree. Your family's goal is the same. However, it may involve more than just your college education. Your family's goal may be much broader encompassing a college degree for all of the children within the family unit. Therefore although your goal is individualistic, it is also a part of a much broader family held goal.

Family goals tend to center around the entire group. The establishment of these goals culminates from the input of all members of the unit. As you look at your family's goals how would you compare their complexity to that of your individual goals? In all probability they are more complex. This complexity stems from the broader, more encompassing scope of the family held goal. Since more individuals are involved in goal attainment, the complexity of the goal is increased. This complexity necessitates more extensive planning.

During implementation, several individuals are involved in the forward progress of goal attainment. Implementation then necessitates more extensive communication. The checking, controlling, and adjusting occurring as the attainment of the goal is sought takes on a greater degree of importance.

Family goals differ from those of the individual. They are complex and broader in scope. They are established from input received from diverse sources. As such they correlate very closely with, and reflect the goals held by each individual family member.

Standards

How many different standards are you aware of within your family unit? How closely do your standards correlate with those of your family? Does your family have specific standards for various managerial procedures? Are there standards for individual members as well as collective group ones?

In all probability many of your standards originated from within your family sphere; as such these reflect the life style patterns of your family. However, some of these standards have been modified by you to reflect your particular life style patterns.

Family standards are developed from the life style observed within the shelter sphere, the surrounding culture, and values and goals held by the family unit. Most families have more standards than they realize. There are standards for household operational tasks, child care, individual and group behavior, role expectations, and many more. At the same time, each individual within the family has standards.

Although your standards reflect those of your family, they may differ to some extent. What standards does your family have for lawn care, auto care and maintenance, or work areas of the garage or workshop? How do these standards compare with yours? Compare your standards for the cleanliness of your room with other members of your family. Are there differences?

Some family standards may be more rigid than your individually held ones. Since these standards involve the general well-being of the entire family, a greater degree of consistency and rigidity may be necessary than for yours. Is your evening meal consistently served at approximately the same time? What would occur in your household if this standard were much less rigidly observed?

As you compare your standards with your family's, what other differences do you observe? There are probably instances where your standards are higher or lower. Are there instances where your standards are more flexible than those of your family? Why does this occur?

The input from all family members establishes family standards. Thus the capabilities, skills, and values of all are incorporated in family standards. Coupled with this is the diverse input being received from the spheres of interaction.

Each individual has some standards that are identical to family held ones. At the same time, some individually held standards are modifications of family ones. In either case, some are flexible while others are inflexible. Standards, whether individually or family held, are viable measures of the progress toward goal attainment. As a criteria, each measures the extent to which values are observed and goals are achieved.

Decision Making

Are there differences between the decisions made in your family unit and those you make? Are these differences created by the number and categories of the decisions or does the difference occur from the methodology used to make the decisions?

How are decisions made in your family? Are some decisions made almost entirely by one person? Do some, such as those involving money management, become the primary responsibility of only your parents? Before making a decision, are there some which necessitate more extensive examination and analysis of alternatives than others?

The decision making taking place within the family sphere is comparable to yours. The major differences lie in the methodology used, the primary responsibility, and the scope of the decision. The categories of decision making and the use of the decision-making process are identically the same regardless of whether an individual or a family decision is being made.

How decisions are made within the family sphere differs greatly among families. The responsibility for decision making may be vested in a patriarchal, matriarchal, democratic, or shared system. In the patriarchal or matriarchal systems the father or mother respectively dominates and controls the decision-making process. A democratic system of decision making necessitates the use of the family council in which all members share equally in the process. Shared decision making may occur when all adult members are involved in the process, or when decisions are shared only between the parents. The responsibility for the decision making may also be delegated to the individual having the greatest degree of expertise in a given area. Thus, the responsibility for decisions shifts from one individual to another depending upon which has the greatest expertise to produce the greatest degree of satisfaction for the collective group. Which one is used in your family sphere? Which one would you prefer when you establish your own family sphere? Why would you select one over another?

The scope of the decisions made within the family sphere may have more far reaching effects and a greater risk factor than those you make. Family decisions encompass all aspects of the family and shelter spheres. Rules, regulations, and policies for individual and family codes of behavior and the life style patterns are established here. Still other decisions are concerned with resource allocation, household operation, child rearing, occupational status and endeavors, social involvement, and community participation. Although family decisions can be divided into the same categories as your own, they involve and incorporate all aspects of the family's management in addition to individual managerial actions which are simultaneously occurring.

Inherent within these decisions are various risk factors. Some decisions have a higher degree of risk than others. Although families most commonly relate risk factors to economic decisions, other decisions contain a relative degree of risk as well. Compare the risk factors of the decisions you make to those of your family. What are the risk factors for your decisions? How do these risk factors compare with the risk factors of your family's decisions? Which incurs the higher degree of risk? Why is this true?

Resources

Your family sphere serves as a resource reservoir for you and all members of your family as individuals and as a composite unit. Although you may not have thought of the individual members of your family in quite this way before, you have and probably will continue to draw upon them and your shelter sphere as you allocate and use resources.

Within the family unit the resource reservoir is much greater than it is for individual members. This reservoir consists of the total resources of each family member as well as those within the shelter sphere.

The resource reservoir within the family sphere is much greater than those of the individual member, yet the demands being placed upon the family unit is greater than the demands experienced by an individual. Select one of your family resources and identify all of the demands placed upon it during a single day. Your parent's skills, abilities, and talents are a valuable resource for the family. How many demands other than employment are made by each family member? What responsibilities place further demands upon these resources? The same is true for all of the resources within your family and shelter spheres. At times you experience difficulty in meeting the demands placed upon your resources. Compare the difficulties of meeting the demands placed upon your resources to those on your family resources.

Resources, their allocation and utilization are a vital aspect of management. Individuals and families must make decisions and allocate resources to meet the demands placed upon them. Although resources occur in greater abundance within the family unit than for the individual, the demands upon their use originating from the spheres of interaction are greatly increased.

Role Perceptions and Expectations

How does your self-assumed role compare with the role perception and expectations your family has of you? Is there a difference between a parent's role perceptions and expectations of you, and the role perception placed upon you by other family members? If you and either your brother or sister were to compare your role perceptions of one of your parents, would you anticipate a great deal of similarity or a wide difference between these two perceptions?

Every family has role perceptions and expectations for each member of the family unit. At the same time, role perception has been established for the family unit by the society in which it functions. This family role perception within the spheres of interaction governs the social orientation, the extent and degree of community involvement, and the participatory functions the family views to be its responsibility and/or duty within a given social culture and structure. A family who views its role as being a leader among the families in the community anticipates total involvement and commitment to the civic happenings, the social structure, and the governance procedures. These role perceptions and expectations include all members of the kinship network as well as the family unit. The origin of these perceptions and expectations incurred from this role may be of long standing or of short duration. Nonetheless they direct the family's function and the extent to which the family interacts within the various spheres. In addition to this, they determine the extent to which these spheres are defined and established.

Thus the individual undertakes management for himself. At the same time, each individual undertakes management as a member of a collective group. The management of one becomes input upon the other. The components of management, while they remain the same, are enhanced or deterred by the managerial action of the other. The individual effectively manages when he or she is cognizant of the management action of the family unit. The family effectively manages when cognizant of the individual's management. Both of these managerial actions to a great extent take place within the confines of the shelter sphere. These actions then become output into the remaining spheres of interaction. These same spheres in turn produce input into the managerial action of the family, shelter, and individual spheres.

Factors Affecting Family Management

Although the application of the principles and concepts are the same for individual and family managerial actions, there remains certain inherent differences between the two. Studies have shown that such factors as the stage in the life cycle, educational attainment, and occupational status affect the managerial action taking place within the family sphere.

Each of these has a direct bearing upon the components of managerial action as well as the demands being experienced during any given point. Demands vary with the stages of the life cycle. Educational attainment has a direct bearing not only upon the managerial action but also upon the extent to which it is employed. The occupational status of the family members involves other demands that relate to managerial action. To ascertain the extent of influence upon family management, each factor is presented separately.

Stages in the Life Cycle

Several different stages in the development of the family have been proposed by various authors. Although Bigelow's eight substages revolve around the educational and economic growth of the family unit,[1] the three major stages as established by the Family Life Conference are used herein for matters of clarification.[2] These are the *beginning, expanding,* and *contracting* stages of the life cycle.

Although families differ one from another, research has shown there are within each stage of the life cycle inherent characteristics that affect the managerial action taking place. The stages in the life cycle occur and are measured not in terms of years but rather as changes occur within the family structure and composition. These changes necessitate reexamination and possible alteration of the existing life style patterns. They produce new demands and/or events within the family and shelter spheres.

Managerial action results as the family seeks to meet these demands and events. Each stage in the life cycle has characteristic events, demands, and happenings which denote the termination of one stage and the entry into another. The progression of the family through these stages is also marked by changes in the managerial action taking place.

Beginning Stage

The family enters the *beginning stage* of the life cycle at the close of the marriage ceremony. This period in the family life continued until the birth of the first child. Some refer to this stage of the family development as the "period of establishment."[3] Others refer to this as a time of "getting acquainted,"[4] or as a "period of adjusting."[5]

In essence, this stage of the life cycle is a period of time in which the marriage partners are becoming knowledgeable about each other and their new partnership, establishing their family and shelter spheres, and adjusting to their newly emerging family life patterns. Within this stage managerial patterns are developed which will become the foundations for future management. There is no specific time span for this stage of family development. It may last one year or longer. The termination of this stage lies not in years but rather when the birth of the first child occurs.

Fitzsimmons, Larery, and Metzen[6] refer to this as the foundation stage in respect to the economic development of the family. Other fundamental managerial patterns also occur. The methodology employed in decision making, dominance patterns, task responsibilities, communication lines and interaction, household operational routines and habits, and other managerial processes are being analyzed and aligned in respect to individual role perceptions and expectations.

The relationships developed during this stage will affect many aspects in the future. Nickell, Rice, and Tucker[7] indicate the goals established during this stage ". . . will influence their way of living and the manner in which they use their resources of time, material goods, skills, energy, and income throughout married life." To quote Gross, Crandall, and Knoll:

> Although it may appear that the major adjustments of the young couple at this time are in the area of personal relationships, there are many managerial problems to be faced. Long term goals, habits of work, division of responsibility, and other patterns which will remain relatively fixed throughout marriage are determined now.[8]

Referring to this as an adjustment stage, Fitzsimmons and Williams indicate it ". . . . involves establishing mutually satisfying approaches to problem solving, habits of decision making, power structure, role definitions, and ways of communicating and interacting."[9] They further state:

> The adjustment stage of the family life cycle is completed when a way of living has been established which, for both, is as satisfying as can be realized with the resources on hand. The way of living will include some agreement as to the family's aims or goals.[10]

As the young couple seek to change their status from that of two individuals to a family unit, decisions are continually being made which encompass almost every aspect of their daily lives. In addition they are establishing a home, developing household routines and habits, solidifying long-range goals, becoming established within an occupational endeavor, defining individual role perceptions, and identifying the family held value hierarchy. Lines of communication and interaction as well as the dominance or power structure will emerge. The patterns established in this stage, although possibly modified as the family moves through the other remaining stages, will remain entrenched as an integral part of the overall management.

The resources of the young family may be limited in some respects and abundant in others. Money income is but one example of a limited resource. For most young couples a heavy drain is placed upon their monetary resources as they seek to establish their new life together. Dual incomes are often necessary for economic survival. The substitution of their talents, skills, and capabilities is often used as a viable alternative to their scarce money resource.

The necessity of dual incomes may result in extensive demands placed upon other resources in addition to time and energy. The young husband and/or wife may find that the multiple roles being assumed within the family and shelter sphere when added to employment-related responsibilities and duties leave little discretionary time or energy for desired and often needed entertainment or avocational endeavors. A counter situation may also occur. When the demands placed upon resources far exceed the anticipated demands prior to the actual marriage, frustration and stress may result. Many young couples are not completely familiar with the operational demands of households nor of the actual expenditure patterns of the other one until this time. This in turn often produces marital discord.

The beginning stage of the life cycle might well be identified as a period of searching as well as establishing. Each individual is searching for an identity as an individual within the family and as a member of a family unit. Each individual has entered the partnership with his or her self-assumed role perception. Each also had expectations of the other person's role within the family unit. As time passes these roles and expectations are anticipated to be performed by the other partner. Unless and until these perceptions and expectations are communicated in a meaningful and useful manner, this search will continue. As the communication and interaction lines are established, these roles and expectations solidify into behavioral patterns that are accepted and mutually agreed upon by the members of the partnership.

The efficient utilization of the management process during this initial development of the family unit can minimize, to a great extent, what many young couples find to be a frustrating time. This developmental period forms the foundation of the family unit. It is within this time span that decisions are made, goals are identified, values are established, and the ability to communicate and interact takes place. From these foundations laid during the beginning stage of the life cycle will come the patterns of the family's future development. Although the young couple seeking to create their family unit may not quite view it as such, nonetheless, the life style patterns and the management performed herein extends far into the future. As the family unit continues to develop and pass through other developmental stages, the patterns established here will continue to be expanded upon.

In the closing phase of this stage, the family and shelter spheres begin to solidify. An atmosphere of permanency and stability emerges. Roles, goals, standards, values, communication, and interaction lines are established. The shelter sphere begins to reflect the growth and maturity of the family unit.

Expanding Stage

The *expanding stage* in the life cycle is called by Perry and Perry the ". . . busiest part of the family life cycle."[11] It begins with the birth of the first child and terminates when that same child permanently leaves the shelter sphere to establish his or her own family unit. During this time several events are taking place in respect to the family and shelter sphere.

Although the establishment of the shelter sphere occurred in the beginning stage of the life cycle, the family unit begins to accumulate an inventory of tangible goods during this time span.[12] The shelter sphere begins to mirror the economic growth of the family unit. Reflected within this sphere are the tangible components that the family unit has identified as being a part of their desired quality of life.

Prior to entry into this stage managerial actions centered around the life style patterns of two adults. The birth of a child has a dramatic impact upon the managerial procedures established within the family and shelter spheres. LeMasters indicates entry into this stage of the life cycle represents the first real crisis or major event faced by the couple.[13] To quote Blood and Blood: "The child alters the power structure, the division of labor and personal relationships between the parents."[14] Melville feels few people are either prepared or knowledgeable concerning parenthood or its effects upon their marriage.[15] In his words: ". . . having a child is one of the few irreversible decisions that most people make in a lifetime.[16]

Management within the shelter sphere undergoes a process of change and modification. Although the birth of this child is eagerly anticipated, very few couples are truly cognizant of the demands that will occur as another member is added to the family unit. Hobbs found that young mothers reported not only personal but also managerial problems originating from this event. Personal problems centered around physical appearance, edginess, and fatigue. Managerial problems involved the changes taking place in routines and standards.[17] Dryer's earlier study found that young mothers reported problems involving lack of sleep, fatigue, doubts of parental capabilities, adjustments made within the shelter sphere and a reduction of the amount of time spent outside the home.[18] Young fathers, according to Dryer, reported problems relating to income reduction, adjusting to parent role, and changes in household routines.[19] Reinforcing this point, Hobbs found the father's personal problems included fatigue and edginess while managerial problems involved money management, alteration of previously established goals and plans, or work load increases within the shelter sphere.[20]

These studies clearly indicate the necessity for alterations and modification of previously established managerial patterns to reflect the new demands and input being received when this stage of the life cycle is entered. New roles are added to those previously identified and assumed by each member of the family unit in the earlier stage. Goals previously established may be altered, modified, redirected, or eliminated. New child-centered goals may emerge and be added to existing ones. Previously established standards will be analyzed and, where necessary, modified to correlate with current demands and input. As the child grows, values and their hierarchy are continually redefined and clarified. This becomes a teaching-learning experience for both parent and child. Decision making is cognizant of the presence of children within the family unit.

Modifications taking place within the family and shelter spheres can most readily be seen in the reallocation of resources specifically money, time, and energy. Demands upon income increase. During the initial entry point of this stage of the life cycle there is little correlation between the demands being placed upon income and its availability.[21] In addition, parents find limitations being placed upon the availability of time to spend together.[22] Communication between the couple diminishes and often relates primarily to the children. This creates stress in the relationship between parents.[23] The marriage, according to Perry and Perry, "'. . . becomes more businesslike and efficient."[24]

Evidences of the necessity to reallocate time and energy resources are found in the studies of Hobbs[25] and Dryer[26] previously cited. Blood and Blood indicate the female parent often experiences disrupted routines, expansion of household tasks, and the curtailment of social life.[27] As the family unit enters this stage some new mothers choose to terminate their employment outside the shelter sphere whereas others do not. Regardless of the choice, changes in the family's living patterns occur.

Walker found as each child enters the family unit, the number of hours spent in household operational tasks also increase.[28] To amplify this, Deacon and Firebaugh state the following: "The total time used for household work is 65 hours per week for families with a child under one year (regardless of number of children) and 42 hours per week families with the youngest child 12–17 years old."[29] According to Szinovacz: "Analysis of spouse's relative participation in specific household and childrearing activities further supports the assumption that female employment does not lead to significant more flexible and interchangeable family roles."[30] The fatigue, tiredness, and edginess cited in previous studies amplify the reallocation of resources to meet the increased demands experienced within the family and shelter spheres.

The reallocation of resources necessitated by the increase in the membership of the family unit is only one of several changes occurring as progression through this stage in the life cycle takes place. Role perceptions are modified by adults to encompass the parenthood role. Marriage, per se, no longer assumes the central role of the adults.[31] As the children grow, they too, assume roles within the family and shelter spheres. At different times in your life you have assumed a diverse number of roles within the spheres and you will continue to do so throughout your life.

Those adults employed outside the home must combine the parenthood role with employment-related ones. One or both parents may well encounter situations where role conflicts occur. Time and energy is being expended to meet the demands of both parenthood and employment roles and expectations. Thus little if any time remains for ". . the opportunity for intellectual and emotional exchanges."[32]

Input is continually being received throughout this stage from many sources. Although in the early phase of this stage social contact is curtailed, as the children mature the parameters of the immediate and distant spheres increase to include the social endeavors of the children as well as the adults. Nickell, Rice, and Tucker subdivide this stage into elementary, high school, and college.[33] The progression of the children through these three subdivisions increases the dimensions of the parenthood roles of the adults. At the same time, the roles assumed by each child is increasing. The parameter expansion taking place within the spheres of interaction affects the managerial action. Parents during this time often experience pressure inputs from church, school, relatives, neighbors, and other sources to have children conform to societal expectations.[34]

As the child enters and remains in the educational system, each begins to separate him or herself from the family and shelter spheres for progressively longer periods of time. During these times the child acts independently of the family and shelter spheres. Decision making which has been predominately the prerogative of the adult members now shifts to include the maturing child. Compare the decision making of your family now to that which took place when you were in elementary school. Although family decisions dominate within the shelter and family spheres, each individual is developing and exercising independent decision making.

This is also a period of time when upward movement takes place in the occupational endeavors of one or both parents. The occupational status momentum is also mirrored in the managerial actions within the shelter and family spheres. Although income increases, so too, are the expenditures of the family unit. Employment-related expectations may need to be incorporated into the managerial action as well as income expenditures.

Family held values are continually undergoing examination and definition. The input accruing from the expansion of the parameters of each of the spheres of interaction may produce value conflicts. This is a time when the maturing child is analyzing and establishing a value hierarchy. This process may be a "trying" one for parents. Value conflicts may also occur among the parents in respect to child-rearing procedures. Parents, too, are analyzing and redefining value structures on the basis of input received from the child's immediate sphere of interaction. As you reflect upon this period in your life you can probably identify times when there was a conflict between your values and those of your parents.

Throughout this stage in the life cycle the management occurring within the family and shelter spheres is a reflection of the input received, the interaction and involvement of each family member, and the spheres of interaction. Managerial actions are continually analyzed and modified as input flows into the spheres. Demands and events necessitate action. Although the family sphere is an integral part of your spheres of interaction, individual managerial action differs from that undertaken by a family unit.

Contracting Stage

Entry into the *contracting stage* begins as the first born child permanently leaves the family and shelter spheres. It is within this stage that the family and shelter spheres return to a childless state, employed adult(s) retire, and ultimately the death of both parents occur. In certain respects, the adjustments and modifications taking place within the family and shelter spheres closely resemble those of the beginning stage of the life cycle. In other aspects it does not.

Role perceptions are again redefined as the in-law and grandparent roles are added to those that already exist. The parents find they must adjust to a childless home and a different life style. Although input from the newly established family and shelter spheres of the children is being received, this input no longer has the impacting strength it once did in the previous stage.

The nuclear family is composed of two older adults. Plans and their implementation are primarily directed toward the goal priorities of these matured adults as opposed to a combined unit of adults and children. Nickell, Rice, and Tucker refer to this stage in the life cycle as a period of "vocational adjustment" and "financial recovery."[34] Parents are adjusting to the changes taking place in the lives of their children as well as their own status as a childless family unit.

During the first phase of this stage the employed adults are reaching the pinnacle of their earning power and professional status. Demands upon the earning power may continue to accrue until the last child attains his or her college degree and professional qualifications. At the same time, parents may be striving to secure their financial well-being through an investment plan prior to retirement.

Parental role perceptions must be altered in respect to their newly emerging status. The male parent begins to recognize that he has reached the upper most point of professional status he will probably achieve in his career. Thus there remains little if any goal attainment or rewards within his profession. He has ". . . no further chance to realize his youthful ambitions."[35] Although there are numerous evidences of the male parent's success in attaining the professional goals he has sought throughout the two previous stages, there are also continual reminders of the eventuality of his retirement from his "work life." The professionally employed female experiences many of the same reactions to the retirement period ahead. Although she views her retirement in the same manner as the adult male, the socially accepted role within society of the "retiree" does not impact upon her in the same manner as the retired male.

The adjustments necessitated during this stage are numerous. Within the shelter sphere the routines, habits, and living patterns established in the previous stage must be modified. Their childless state initiates the first of these modifications. Homemakers not employed outside the home find large blocks of unplanned time throughout the day. The duties and responsibilities of raising and caring for children is no longer placing demands upon their time and energy resources. The female parent often experiences more difficulty in making this adjustment to the childless state than does the male parent.[36]

The actual retirement from full-time employment is a highly prized goal for both individuals and families. Throughout the previous stages of the life cycle this goal has been continually sought and anticipated. The anticipated satisfaction to be achieved has been assessed and measured many times throughout the total employment life of the individual. This retirement from full-time employment outside the shelter sphere generally brings with it the second phase of the contracting stage of the life cycle.

Adjustment to the "jobless" state must be made by both adults regardless of the number who have been previously employed outside the shelter sphere. However, for the male parent whose employment has been synonymous with his major identity role, this may represent one of the most difficult adjustments in his life. His retirement from full-time employment has numerous implications to both his future and past living patterns. The role perception derived from his professional status no longer exists. The previously established employment routines, habits, and living patterns are no longer present. For him, it means a complete change in his daily life style. In essence his living patterns must be altered as he adjusts from an active to an inactive life.[37]

To both the male and female, retirement is anticipated and sought as a reward for the years of service to their profession. Although retirement trauma is anticipated and expected to occur when the male retires, many are not aware that retirement trauma is also experienced upon termination of professional employment for the female. Although they share similar traumas, society often views their retirement in a much different context. Many feel that the female's retirement actually produces only minor changes in her daily routines. This is not the case. Over the years in her professional capacity she has lead a full, active life. She, like her male counterpart, will experience a complete change in daily living patterns with its corresponding adjustments and trauma.

Retirement necessitates adjustments in household routines and life styles within the shelter sphere. At the same time, the older adults are also experiencing the aging process. Although demands upon these older adults decrease, the aging process affects the family and shelter sphere's management.

Resources, in some instances, become more limited while others become more abundant. Retirement from full-time employment often means a reduction in money resources. This is particularly true of the family unit who did not undertake preretirement planning. Since employment responsibilities and demands are no longer present, time resources are more readily abundant. This often results in extensive amounts of unplanned and noncommitted time. Over the years, the aging process will gradually become a constraint upon the energy levels available at any time for the older adult.

The physical limitation due to the aging process may also culminate in restrictions of other resources. Although an older adult may have the skills and abilities that could be used in leisure-time activities, a physical impairment such as arthritis or limited vision may limit or eliminate the use of these resources for personal satisfaction.

Decisions during this stage revolve around the establishment of the retirement life style. Many are comparable to those made in the beginning stage. The older couple must modify or alter routines to reflect their current living patterns. Other decisions include whether or not to remain in the currently established shelter sphere, the extent of involvement in the immediate sphere, and utilization of resources. Social interaction, once a prominent part of their lives, may be limited by monetary resources and/or the loss of friends and relatives through death.

This stage in the life cycle, like each of the others, affects the managerial action taking place. Role perceptions are modified in respect to the status of the older adults. Decisions are made, resources are allocated, and managerial action takes place. Each of these influence and affect the other.

Throughout the stages of the life cycle managerial action takes place. Inherent within each stage are characteristics that set one apart from the others. These same characteristics have a direct impact upon managerial action. The inherent characteristics, and the managerial response to demands within the various stages of the life cycle clearly demonstrate that both individuals and families utilize the principles and concepts of management. The difference then lies, not in the application of these principles and concepts, but in the factors that influence and provide input in daily living.

Other Influencing Factors

It can readily be seen that the stage in the life cycle is a mitigating factor in the management taking place. Other factors also affect managerial action being undertaken and the utilization of the management principles and concepts.

Education

The educational attainment of each individual within the family and shelter sphere will have implications not only upon the managerial action taking place but also upon how extensively and to what extent the principles and concepts of management are utilized to produce satisfaction. Deacon and Firebaugh indicate there are both short- and long-range effects of educational attainment. They further state that the capacity to apply these principles and concepts is directly related to an individual's educational attainment.[38]

Although for the most part, you accept this theory, in all probability you are not totally cognizant of the extent to which educational attainment affects effective management. A comparison of the lifetime earnings of individuals having differing educational attainment will readily demonstrate the increases in earning power accrued from increased educational attainment. The availability of monetary resources increases in proportion to the educational attainment of the family members. Although this increase produces a greater lifetime earning power, it also increases the capability to make more effective use of this valuable resource.[39]

In addition to the increase in earning power, Deacon and Firebaugh point to other effects within the family and shelter spheres which accrue from educational attainment. There is a direct relationship between the number of children and the formal educational attainment of the female parent. The extent of the female's formal education will also be a determinate factor influencing her participation in the labor force. Furthermore, there is an extent to which each participates in the spheres of interaction beyond the shelter sphere and this will be influenced by the educational attainment of both individuals.[40]

Blood and Blood indicate the extent to which the female interrupts her labor force participation for the birth and care of a child is influenced by her educational attainment. They state that the professional woman interrupts her labor force participation for an average of five years in order to give birth and undertake the care of the small child. Her eventual return to the labor force will depend upon the number of children born to the family unit. Each additional child reduces the probability of her return.[41]

The educational attainment of both parents is a factor in the managerial action taking place in the family and shelter spheres. Increased educational attainment provides the skills and abilities to make more valid decisions as well as increasing the resources and their respective availability within the family unit.

Occupational Status

The occupational status of the parents in the family unit will also have an effect upon the management within the family and shelter spheres. Fullerton indicates occupation rather than the family's heritage and culture has become the basis for placement within today's social stratification.[42] The status of today's family is based upon the occupational status of the husband and as such the family unit has a vested interest in his career status.[43] Thus the management taking place in the family and shelter spheres is directly related to the ". . . differences in goals, marital roles, and sex role expectations."[44] An examination of families having differing employment status will amplify these effects upon the managerial action.

Inherent within our economic structure are large corporations which employ thousands of individuals. The individual's employment status within these corporate structures have a direct influence upon the managerial action within the family and shelter spheres.

In many respects, the corporation becomes the kinship network to those individuals whose status lies in the upper managerial echelons. This corporate identity has implications to all members of the family unit. Fullerton found both husband and wife referred to the corporation in possessive terms such as "our group" or "our firm." Success to these families is measured in terms of upward promotion.[45] As emphasized, this identification with the corporation has ramifications to the managerial action. When choices must be made between family and professional career expectations for the male, the corporation ranks ahead of the family. In this respect his time expenditures revolve around his career rather than his family.

This does not mean, however, that the home and family life style are unimportant. Rather these domains are the primary responsibility of the wife who is expected to meet the social demands comensurate with her husband's promotional status. In addition to this, she is expected to provide an emotional support system for her husband.[46]

The managerial action within the family and shelter spheres is greatly influenced by the role expectations imposed upon the family unit by the corporate structure. These role perceptions include all members of the family unit not just the husband and/or wife.

The middle-class family differs from the corporate family. In the upper-middle-class family, the male parent has a career while in the lower-middle-class family he has a job.[47] The difference in the perception of the husband's occupational endeavors has a direct bearing upon how each family perceives the male's employment. Its implications are clearly demonstrated in the managerial action that results.

In the upper-middle-class family all members are considered to benefit from the male parent's career. Therefore adjustments and modification taking place within the family and shelter spheres are done with respect to this ideology.[48]

Personal satisfaction and fulfillment does not accrue from the male's employment in the lower-middle-class family. Managerial action, therefore, is directed toward fulfillment received from family interests, energies, and happenings in the future. Activities and endeavors are family-oriented. For this male his family, not his job, represents his highest priority.[49]

The skilled or blue collar family has still another perspective of the value of employment and the role of individual family members. Husbands within these shelter spheres have limited participation in the household operation. The father's role in the family is that of the disciplinarian and provider of the needed income to support the family. His emotional support system is often secured from outside the shelter sphere. All members of the family are task-oriented. The success of the wife is measured in her capabilities to operate the household and her child rearing activities. Her emotional support system generally comes from her mother and other female relatives. Social involvement is limited and restricted. Living patterns tend to be routine and conservative. Children's activities and endeavors tend to be closely and strictly monitored by the parents.[50]

Thus the decisions made, the establishment of goals, role expectations, and the managerial action within the family and shelter spheres are directly related to the occupational endeavors of the male adult within the family unit. Although the female adult may also be employed outside the shelter sphere, the life style, the living patterns, and the management center around the male adult's occupational status.

Deacon and Firebaugh identify health, race, and personality as other factors influencing management in the family and shelter spheres.[51] Although these do indeed have a bearing on the managerial action, the educational attainment and the occupational status of the male parent have a much greater impact.

The educational attainment of the adult members of the family unit can be correlated to the occupational status, yet one does not necessarily preclude the other. Some individuals, as pointed out by Fullerton, choose not to utilize their educational attainment within the corporate family structure. Other individuals elect to selectively emulate the characteristics of a particular social stratification group.[52]

Summary

Both individuals and family units use the principles and concepts of management throughout their daily lives. The greatest degree and the most extensive managerial action takes place within the family and shelter spheres. Although management results from input received from the remaining spheres of interaction, it is within the family and shelter spheres that both the individual and the family unit exercise the largest amount of control upon how and to what extent managerial action will take place.

Managerial action is taking place within both the individual and family spheres of interaction. Each person undertakes managerial action within his or her individual spheres. As a member of a collective group—the family unit— managerial action is also undertaken in the family sphere. Although within both spheres managerial action does accrue from numerous inputs and demands, the specific characteristics of each set one apart from the other.

In each instance the principles and concepts remain the same, yet differences in scope and application are apparent. The impact of the managerial action taking place within each is received, assessed, and acted upon by the other. The values, goals, standards, communication, and role perceptions established within each sphere are recognized. Each influences the development and utilization in the other.

External and internal factors affect the family unit's management and ultimately each individual's managerial behavior. Major factors affecting managerial actions and behaviors are the stage in the life cycle, formal educational attainment, and occupational status.

Inherent within the development of the family unit from inception to death are stages of the life cycle. Each of these stages have distinctive characteristics, mirroring the events and happenings as the family unit emerges and participates in the existing social structure. Life style patterns developed in the *beginning stage* of the life cycle form the foundation for the family unit's management. The birth of the first child pinpoints the entry of the family unit into the *expanding stage* of development. This event initiates the first of numerous modifications and adjustments of the previously established managerial patterns that continue throughout the future. As the children permanently leave the family and shelter spheres to establish their separate family and shelter spheres and a new family unit emerges, entry into the *contracting stage* for the parents begins. This final stage continues until the original family unit composed of the parents ceases to exist. This latter stage in the family's development necessitates the adjustments to retirement, a childless state, and old age. Each of these stages in the family's development requires further adjustments and modification in light of the events, input, and demands taking place.

Education and occupational status also affect the managerial actions and behaviors of the individual and family unit. The formal educational attainment has a direct bearing not only upon the managerial action but also upon the number of children born into the family unit, the participation of adults in the labor force, and the availability of resources. The occupational status of the adults within the family unit will have an important role in the identity of the family within a specific social stratification grouping; the employment-related expectations on both the individual's professional career and other family members, the derived satisfaction, allocation and utilization of resources, and the role perceptions of the family and individual members within the social structure.

Today's society in which the individual and family unit lives and participates in is a continually evolving and emerging one. This fluid evolution of society necessitates that if both the individual and family unit are to attain their desired quality of life, effective managerial actions and behaviors must occur. This necessitates effective use of management principles and concepts, which can occur only when each is cognizant and gives recognition to the external and internal factors that have a direct bearing upon their managerial actions and their lives.

ACTIVITIES

1. You are familiar with your managerial actions and behaviors and also those of your family unit. Contrast the differences and similarities between your management and that of your family unit. Examine the following closely:
   a. Resources.
   b. Decision making.
   c. Value hierarchy.
   d. Standards.
2. Listed are four family units. Identify the similarities in their management. What are the differences? Examine the values, resources, decision making, and the adjustments made.

   Family A: This couple has been married for three years. Their first child was born one month ago. The wife has temporarily terminated her employment outside the shelter sphere. This temporary absence from the labor force is anticipated to last for about five years.

   Family B: This couple has been married 20 years. She is not employed outside the shelter sphere. Their first and only child has just enrolled in college.

   Family C: Although the husband of this family unit retired last month, his wife plans to continue her professional career for at least two more years. They have four children. One child recently graduated from college. One is married and lives in the local community. The oldest child is employed in another state and the youngest is a sophmore in college.

   Family D: This couple who chose not to have children retired from their professional careers last month. Both were corporate executives.

3. What high ranking goal do you have which also ranks high as an immediate goal for your family? Clarify both your goal and your family's. Analyze each goal by answering the following questions:
   a. What similarities and differences do you observe between your goal and your family's goal?

   b. Which goal has the greatest degree of clarity? Why?

   c. Which goal is broader? Why? What are the causal factors?

   d. What values are evidenced in each goal?

   e. Identify the inputs upon each goal from the various spheres of interaction.

4. You, as an individual, and your family, as a collective group, have many standards. What are three standards common to both you and your family unit? Compare these three standards by answering the following:

   a. What commonalities and differences do you observe?

   b. Is your standard or your family's more specific? Why?

   c. Which of the two is more flexible? Why?

   d. What values are evidenced in the standards?

   e. Which standard was established first? What were the causal factors?

5. Although you may not as yet have experienced them, you have role perceptions and expectations for the adults of a marriage partnership. What role expectations do you have for both marriage partners in the following:

   a. Beginning stage of the life cycle.

   b. Parents of preschool children.

   c. Parents of teenagers.

   d. Parents of college students.

   e. Grandparents.

6. In question no. 5 you identified role expectations for both marriage partners. For either the male or female partner examine the extent which the role expectations change within the stages of the life cycle. What are the inputs being received which have necessitated these changes? What factors have necessitated adjustments and modifications in these roles?

7. You have made several decisions about your own life: your college major, the university you would attend, and the profession you would enter. Diagram the decision tree for your family unit to illustrate the decisions and alternatives that have been created as a result of the decisions you have made. Now diagram your own decision tree. Where are their similarities and differences?

THREE COUPLES

On a quiet street in a older subdivision live three couples: Jack and Carol Green, Marilyn and Keith Brown, and Karl and Mona Smith. Although these three couples share the same street, are neighbors, and the men are golfing partners, their lives are quite different.

Jack and Carol Green are nearing the end of the expanding stage of the life cycle. They have two children. Jim, their oldest, is a senior at a university in another part of the state. Jenny, their youngest, is a sophomore at a university in the Southwest. Jack is a high school principal. He has held this job for the last 15 years. Carol did work outside the shelter sphere before the children were born but hasn't since then. She keeps herself busy with volunteer work in the community. Jim is engaged to be married soon after he graduates. He anticipates being employed somewhere in the South.

Marilyn and Keith Brown have a five-month-old son. Keith is a production manager for a local firm. Marilyn was an executive secretary but has terminated her employment for the present time. They hope to have at least two more children. Marilyn plans to reenter the labor force after all of the children are in school. They have been married five years.

The Smiths, Karl and Mona, are grandparents. Their four children are married and have families of their own now. Although they would like to see their 15 grandchildren more often, all of their children live outside the state. Traveling by car to visit their children and grandchildren often involves overnight stays in motels. Mona and Karl both recently retired when Karl reached his sixty-fifth birthday. Mona really would have preferred to continue working two more years until her sixty-fifth birthday, but Karl talked her into retiring along with him. He was the plant foreman for over 30 years. She was the head of the secreterial pool for 20 years. Neither has any physical disabilities other than the normal ones associated with their age.

All three couples are friends. The men are golfing partners and the women like to play bridge in the afternoon. Mona looks upon the Browns as an extension of her own family. She treats the entire family as if they are her children and grandchildren. Since Marilyn's parents are both dead she has no living family members in her kinship network. Carol is busy with, as she calls it, her charity work. She often tries to persuade the other two women to participate with her but hasn't been able to do so yet. It is not unusual to find the Smiths, Marilyn and the baby, and Carol, when she is home, spending the afternoon together.

Discussion Questions

1. Identify the specific characteristics of each family. What differences, other than age, are there in the families? What are the similarities?

2. Each family has specific resources that are common to all, and others that are distinctly their own. Identify the resources of each family unit. What changes in resources have occurred over the years within each family unit?

3. Each of these families is experiencing demands upon their resources and their management. What demands is each family experiencing? How are these demands different? Which ones are common to all three families? Why?

4. Each family is experiencing periods of adjustments. What are the specific adjustments being made within each family? From the information given, you have some knowledge of their value hierarchy. How are these values affecting the management taking place, the adjustments and modifications, and the newly emerging role perceptions and expectations?

5. Describe or predict the future for each of these family units. What do you anticipate will occur within each of the family units in the next 5, 10, and 15 years? What affect will these changes have on the other two families? As you predicted the anticipated future of these three families, your response was based upon certain assumptions. What were these assumptions and to what extent were they influenced by your values?

GLOSSARY

Beginning Stage of the Life Cycle   The first developmental stage of the life cycle that begins with the establishment of the marriage partnership and terminates with the birth of the first child.

Contracting Stage of the Life Cycle   The last developmental stage of the life cycle that begins when the first child permanently leaves the shelter sphere and terminates with the death of the family unit parents.

Dual Income Family Unit   A family unit in which both of the adult members of the marriage partnership are employed outside the shelter sphere.

Expanding Stage of the Life Cycle   The second developmental stage of the life cycle that begins with the birth of the first child and terminates when this same child permanently leaves the shelter sphere.

Kinship Network   The extended members of the family which is composed of those members related to the nuclear family unit but who do not reside in the shelter sphere.

Nuclear Family Unit   Those family members who reside in the shelter sphere and are a part of the marriage partnership.

Stages in the Life Cycle The three major developmental phases of the family as defined by the family life conference. These three phases are the beginning, expanding, and contracting stages.

REFERENCES

1. Howard F. Bigelow, "What Are Usual Family Patterns?" *Journal of Home Economics* (January 1950), 27–29.
2. Family Life Conference, Washington, D.C., May 1948.
3. Irma H. Gross, Elizabeth Walbert Crandall, and Marjorie M. Knoll, *Management for Modern Families,* 3rd ed. (New York: Appleton-Century-Crofts, 1973), p. 51.
4. Paulena Nickell, Ann Smith Rice, and Suzanne P. Tucker, *Management in Family Living,* 5th ed. (New York: John Wiley & Sons, Inc., 1976), p. 20.
5. Cleo Fitzsimmons and Flora Williams, *The Family Economy Nature and Management of Resources* (Ann Arbor, Michigan: Edwards Brothers Press, Inc., 1973), p. 183.
6. Cleo Fitzsimmons, Dorothy A. Larery, and Edward. J. Metzen. "Major Financial Decisions and Crisis in the Family Span," North Central Research Publications Number 208 (Lafayette, Indiana: Purdue University Agricultural Experimental Station, 1971).
7. Nickell, Rice, and Tucker, op. cit., p. 20.
8. Gross, Crandall, and Knoll, op. cit., p. 51.
9. Fitzsimmons and Williams, op. cit., p. 51.
10. Ibid.
11. John Perry and Edna Perry, *Pairing and Parenthood* (San Francisco: Canfield Press, 1977), p. 299.
12. Nickell, Rice, and Tucker, op. cit., p. 20.
13. Gross, Crandall, and Knoll, op. cit., p. 58.
14. Bob Blood and Margaret Blood, *Marriage,* 3rd ed. (New York: The Free Press, 1978), p. 438.
15. Keith Melville, *Marriage and Family Today* (New York: Random House, 1977), p. 325.
16. Ibid., p. 309.
17. Daniel F. Hobbs, "Parenthood as a Crisis, A Third Study," *Journal of Marriage and the Family* (August 1965), 370.
18. Everett D. Dryer, "Parenthood as a Crisis: A Re-Study," *Marriage and Family* (1963), pp. 196–201.
19. Ibid., pp. 198–199.
20. Hobbs, op. cit., p. 370.
21. Perry and Perry, op. cit., p. 299
22. Ibid.
23. Ibid.
24. Ibid.
25. Hobbs, op. cit., p. 370.

26. Dryer, op. cit., pp. 198–199.
27. Blood and Blood, op. cit., pp. 442–444.
28. Kathryn E. Walker, "Homemaking Still Takes Time," *Journal of Home Economics* (October 1969), 621–624.
29. Ruth E. Deacon and Francille M. Firebaugh, *Home Management Context and Concepts* (Boston: Houghton Mifflin Company, 1975), p. 70.
30. Maximiliane Szinovacz, "Women Employed: Effects on Spouse's Division of Household Work," *Journal of Home Economics* (Summer 1979), p. 43.
31. Perry and Perry, op. cit., p. 300
32. Ibid.
33. Nickell, Rice, and Tucker, op. cit., p. 20.
34. Ibid., p. 21.
35. Perry and Perry, op. cit., p. 300.
36. Ibid.
37. Ibid. p. 302.
38. Deacon and Firebaugh, op. cit., p. 83.
39. Ibid.
40. Ibid. pp. 83–84.
41. Blood and Blood, op. cit., pp. 307–308.
42. Gail Putney Fullerton, *Survival in Marriage Introduction to Family Interaction, Conflicts, and Alternatives,* 2nd ed. (Hinsdale, Illinois: The Dryden Press, 1977), p. 253.
43. Ibid., p. 473.
44. Ibid., p. 498.
45. Ibid., pp. 472–478.
46. Ibid.
47. Ibid., p. 498.
48. Ibid.
49. Ibid.
50. Ibid., pp. 504–512.
51. Ibid., pp. 74–83.
52. Ibid., p. 498.

CHAPTER ELEVEN

Management of Other Family Units

T he society in which you live and function is composed of individual and family units. If you walked down the street in your home community would each shelter sphere house only the family units in varying stages of the life cycle as described in Chapter 10? Are there perhaps some family units who have special characteristics setting them apart from the family units previously discussed?

Think about your community and the families who reside there. Are there single-parent families, families having a handicapped member, or families where both parents are employed full-time outside the shelter sphere? In all probability, your community, like most in the nation today, have all of these categories of family units residing there. Are you or some of your classmates married students? Have some married couples made the choice not to have children? Are there senior citizen families?

Although progessing through the developmental stages of the life cycle, each of these family units have distinguishing characteristics that set them apart from the nuclear family unit.

These distinguishing characteristics affect the family and shelter sphere management. An examination of these characteristics and their impact upon the management of each family follows.

Dual Income Families

The current labor force is composed of single and married male and female workers. Every individual strives to attain educational goals and anticipates entry into the labor force. The male homemaker anticipates his participation will continue from entry until retirement. In previous years, the female homemaker anticipated that her participation in the labor force would terminate either when she married or when she became pregnant with her first child. To most families, the full-time employment of the female was viewed as being temporary rather than permanent.

Some female homemakers today choose to continue this concept of full-time employment. However, there is an increasing number of female homemakers who are entering and remaining in the labor force regardless of their roles as wives and mothers. This trend and its implications for both the family and society are reflected in the following statements.

> Women are swelling the work force at a rate of almost 2 million every year—a phenomenon that is beginning to transform everyday life in the United States.

263

Ginzberg predicts that the desire of women for jobs ultimately may alter the lives of every American: "It changes the relationship of men to women; it changes the relationship of mothers to children." And the future of the suburbs may also be in doubt.[1]

Just what is the impact upon the labor force by working wives? The U.S. Departments of Labor and Commerce, and the National Science Foundation predict that by 1990, 43 per cent of the labor force will be composed of 54 million women. The 1978 data reveals that of the 38 million women in the labor force, 19 per cent are single, 56.4 per cent are married and 24.6 per cent are divorced, separated, or widowed. Fifty-three per cent of all women who are or wish to be employed in the labor force are mothers of preschool or school-age children.[2]

Why is the participation of women in the labor force increasing at such an astounding rate and what are the factors that affect the woman's employment outside the home? Brown states:

> Recent studies indicate that the likelihood of a wife's working is increased by family economic pressure, by her level of employability (as indexed by educational attainment and/or prior work experience), by her status as the head of a household, and by a labor market environment that provides equal opportunities regardless of sex.[3]

Other factors that will influence the woman's participation in the labor force, as cited by Brown, are the number and ages of the children in the family unit and whether or not adults other than parents reside within the shelter sphere.[4] "For the working woman herself, a job means independence, a sense of accomplishment and—most important—money. Economists say that women are working primarily to keep families from falling behind in the race with inflation."[5] Gross, Crandall, and Knoll indicate the extent of the woman's participation in the labor force is affected by "(a) the woman's age or stage in the life cycle, (b) her husband's income and (c) the wife's educational level."[6] Still another reason the female enters and remains in the labor force may be to provide the financial support for the family unit due to a physically impaired spouse who is unable to remain in the labor force.

Regardless of the rationale for her participation in the labor force, the female member of the family unit has become an established part of the labor force. This participation has an effect upon the family unit and the management occurring within the family and shelter spheres.

Although it is obvious that the management within the family and shelter spheres must be altered to include the female's work-related roles and expectations, even those families who are conversant with the situation are not completely aware of the extent to which the managerial actions and behaviors are modified. Although it is anticipated these modifications do occur, the nature and extent of these may not be totally visible nor evident. These modifications encompass resources, role perceptions, decision making, and managerial actions.

The managerial behavior of the dual income family differs from that of the nuclear family only in respect to when the modification ultimately takes place. In some instances, the entrance into the beginning stage of the life cycle and dual income status are initiated at the same time. When this happens the management patterns developed incorporate the dual employment status. There are, however, instances where dual income status is undertaken at a later date such as in the expanding stage. When this occurs, modification of previously established managerial patterns are much more extensive.

Brown's assessment of the dual income family unit has many implications for future family units, for example: dual income families tend to have fewer children. He also found that not only are women who actively participate in the labor force marrying later in life but many remain unmarried.[7] Her decision concerning whether to marry and at what age may be based upon the knowledge that although she actively participates in the labor force, once a woman chooses to marry, her husband's occupational status may dictate to a large extent her future professional endeavors, geographic location, and social standing within the community. It is unfortunate but true that although she may actively participate in the labor force until retirement, she is still not considered by the majority of the population to be a wage earner.[8]

These trends and their implications for the future family structure should be closely observed. Increasing numbers of women are entering and remaining in the labor force and this can have far reaching implications not only to the traditional family structure but also to the growth and prosperity of the nation.

The input from the woman's participation in the labor force varies in accordance with her occupational status. The established family must modify managerial action to correlate with the additional input being received. The impact of this input will be somewhat governed by whether the woman's employment is full time or part time. Probably the most extensive impact is seen in the child care managerial actions.

Children are being raised by surrogate parents. This may involve baby sitters, day-care centers, nursery schools, relatives, friends, or school systems. The increasing numbers of child care institutions are further evidence of the growing female participation in the labor force. Studies also show that child care is the one area where the male parent is more likely to assume added responsibilities as opposed to any other area of the household management.[9]

Another major area of change involves the household operational tasks. A *U.S. News and World Reports* article indicates the male parent is assuming some household tasks;[10] however, Szinovacz states that ". . . although husbands of employed women help with household chores, the responsibility for managing the household remains with the wife."[11] This same study also found no evidence of major changes in activity patterns of spouses or role perceptions.[12] On the one hand it appears that the male does contribute more time to the household operation, but the employment status of his wife does not mean he will assume proportionally more time or equalized responsibilities.[13]

Role Perceptions

The role perception of the male and female parent in a dual income family undergoes a subtle but evident change. Brown found the wife's employment meant she no longer had to depend upon her family for social status, ego gratification, or stimulation. In fact, her employment status was her ego gratification.[14] Her employment often means she must juggle the responsibilities of home, parent, and work.[15] This may, at times, produce conflicts between her job and her home.[16] In addition, there are the guilt feelings concerning surrogate parent child care.

The continued outside employment of the female parent necessitates the development of new roles for all family members. It is perhaps not voiced, but many husbands view their wife's employment as a reflection on their ability to adequately provide the financial support for the family.[17]

Szinovacz reports an increase in the egalitarian role among families having dual income earners.[18] Yet this same study indicates no evidence of a change in the female's role expectations. It would therefore appear that although the husband accepts his wife's employment status he still expects her to assume all the other roles previously established within the marriage partnership.

The employed female must also be cognizant of the attitudes of other individuals. Some males are not comfortable working under the leadership of a female. This may be openly or covertly expressed. The female is also often viewed as the "second" wage earner in the family. Therefore, her income is used to purchase luxuries rather than necessities. Whereas this may or may not be true, some of her colleagues who are the major source of support for their family units resent her presence. Undoubtedly her employed status will be questioned by her nonsalaried female peers who may ask why she prefers employment rather than the traditional female homemaker role. Others may view her labor force participation as a form of competition with her husband. In addition others may perceive it as a mechanism to escape from the duties and responsibilities of marriage and motherhood.

Regardless of the reason for the female's participation in the labor force, the role perceptions of all family members will be modified to include this input. The extent to which the adjustments occur will depend upon the stage in the life cycle and the length of her workday.

Resources

Probably the most noticeable effect upon the availability of a family's resource is the increase of the money income. When the female member of the family is employed outside the shelter sphere, the family's income is increased by 38 per cent.[19] This increase has two different effects upon the family unit. The first is the tendency to increase the family's standard of living. The second is that it reduces the economic dependency of the wife on the husband's income.[20]

When monetary resources increase in the dual income family unit, other resources, particularly time and energy, are affected. Fullerton found that although the female parent worked a 40-hour-week outside the home, she still spent 30 hours per week in household tasks and child care.[21] The employment of the female outside the household does not diminish or reduce the task load within the family and shelter spheres. It has been found that the only real reduction in the female's workload within these spheres occurs when household operational tasks are completed using outside assistance such as the kinship network or employed help, as opposed to the increased assistance from the husband.[22] In other words, the contributions of the husband and children to reduce the workload of the employed female within the family and shelter spheres does not appreciably increase when she enters the labor force. Thus household operational tasks often are completed at night or on the weekend when she is relatively free of her employment responsibilities. The utilization of time and energy in this manner yields very little discretionary time or high energy levels for other family demands.

Consider for a moment the female parent's work curve on a weekday. Compare the time she is generally undertaking household operational tasks with the probable energy levels that exist at the time the task is being undertaken. In all probability her work curve would indicate low energy levels during the evening hours. Yet this is the time when she is undertaking the household operational tasks normally done by the nongainfully employed homemaker. The latter does these tasks during the daytime hours when energy levels are much higher. Obviously the household operational tasks completed during lower energy levels require increased expenditures of energy than if these same tasks were completed when energy levels were higher. It is possible the increase in energy consumption will also result in additional time utilization for task completion.

Another demand upon time and energy resources involves scheduling. Since only weekends and evening hours are available, task scheduling must occur during this time. The female's time schedule must include not only task completion but also the other family time demands such as school programs and social activities. These constraints upon the female's time and energy often mean she has little, if any, of either resource remaining to satisfy her personal wants and needs.

The female employed outside the shelter sphere is expected to meet not only the time demands of her employment and household status, but her role-related ones as well. This often means she is the one who remains at home when repair service is needed for major appliances or equipment. She, too, is generally the one who remains at home when a child is ill or has a scheduled medical appointment.

Despite the fact that the female's continued participation in the labor force places a heavy drain on her time and energy resources, the satisfaction, stimulation, and ego gratification accrued from this activity may become resources. The independence and sense of accomplishment obtained from utilizing her talents, abilities, and skills in the professional career are viable factors as the woman chooses to enter and remain as a contributing part of the labor force.

The decision of whether or not to become a dual income family is continually being made. In some cases economic necessity is the basis for the decision; in other instances, it is not. Regardless of the reason, the family who elects to become a dual income one should recognize both the obvious and subtle changes that will occur within the family and shelter spheres.

Single-Parent Family

Throughout the nation there is an ever increasing number of single-parent households. The rising divorce rate has been a major contributor; other causal factors are the death of a spouse, separation but not divorce, or women who have never married. Regardless of the causal factors, these family units have become a significant part of communities across the nation. Craig reports that in 1975, 13 per cent of all families were female headed households. This represented a 61 per cent increase from 1960 to 1975.[23] By 1979, one out of every seven or slightly over 14 per cent of the family units were headed by single females.[24] In many of these female headed households income levels are at or below the poverty line.[25] Conversely only 2 per cent of the single parent families are headed by males.[26]

Although the single status of the head of the household is a distinctive characteristic of these family units, there are other characteristics setting them apart from the nuclear family unit. The parent is a part of the labor force, therefore as in the dual income family, child care must be done by surrogate parents. Studies also indicate these family units tend to be more isolated but probably more extended.[27] The causal factor for this isolation stems partly from society's reaction to the female headed household and partly from the lack of sufficient income resources.[28]

Role Perceptions

The establishment and acceptance of role perceptions for the single parent is at best a difficult and often frustrating endeavor. The single parent must somehow combine the parenting role with the psychological and emotional needs of an adult. In undertaking the parenting role, the single adult must be cognizant that he or she must assume the total responsibility for the discipline, supervision, child care, decision making, and community participation done in the nuclear family by two adults. In addition, there are the psychological and emotional needs of the adult. Then, too, the single parent must meet the role expectations of an employee and the homemaker roles within the shelter sphere. Thus the single parent is expected to identify and develop a self-assumed role that is a combination of all these roles. This is indeed a heavy burden.

The expectations and assumptions made by the surrounding social structure may have an impact on this definition and establishment of the parenting role. In many instances the surrounding social structure raise doubts concerning the single adult's capabilities to assume the parenting role. This is particularly true for the female headed household.[29] Questions are raised as to the female parent's ability to provide sex role models for children, particularly sons. Other assumptions involve the capability of the female parent to exercise adequate discipline, to provide economic support for the family unit, and to fulfill the domestic functions of the household.[30] Each of these assumptions and expectations will affect the family's status within the local community.

As the adult within this family unit is defining and establishing the parenting role recognition must also be given to the psychological and emotional needs that cannot be completely satisfied by the parenting role. These needs include social interaction, male/female companionship, leisure-time and recreational endeavors. The sole responsibility for child care limits and/or restricts the avenues by which the single parent can satisfy these needs. Frustration may develop from the conflict between the desire to satisfy both the psychological and emotional adult needs and the parenting role.[31] The combination of society's perception of the single-parent family, the psychological and emotional needs of the adult, the assumption of the parenting role, and the inherent self-doubts of the divorced or separated parent over the inability to sustain a marriage relationship often produces a loss of self-confidence and self-esteem.

Although the single-parent family created by the death of a spouse experiences to some extent social ostracism, society more readily accepts this family unit than it does the one originating from divorce, separation, or a nonmarried mother. Regardless of the initiating circumstances, the single-parent family probably remains isolated from the kinship network and its emotional support system. "Because of this, the single parent family has less flexibility to adapt to crisis."[32]

Thus the single parent is often perceived as lacking authority, power, and status. The family's prestige within the community is weighed and assessed by the expectations and assumptions projected upon it and its members.

Resources

One of the most critical issues facing the single-parent family is the effective allocation of resources within the family unit. The availability and extent of resources is immediately reduced when one parent, for whatever reason, is no longer a member of the shelter sphere. This immediate reduction of resources has both an immediate and long-range effect upon the ensuing managerial actions. When the newly emerging role perceptions of both the adult and children are combined with the reduction of critical resources such as home, energy, and money, the problems of the single-parent family are compounded. Several things are happening concurrently. The demands of family life style and child care are suddenly transferred from two individuals to one. Also there are the reasons that have necessitated the separation or divorce. Adjustments to a new family life style are undertaken. Decisions are being made in respect to employment, the possible relocation of the shelter sphere, and daily living patterns. The critical extent of resources impacts upon the family and shelter spheres. Choices among alternatives must be carefully analyzed in reference to the reduction of critical resources. The remaining family members within the shelter sphere must draw upon individual resources to assume responsibilities and duties of the parent who is no longer present.

As emerging roles are modified and others are established, new skills will need to be developed. The skill development may require additional expenditures of energy and time until each becomes an integral part of the family's overall management.

The roles assumed by the single parent now encompass all aspects of the family and shelter spheres. The responsibility for household operational tasks, child care, home maintenance and repair, meal planning and preparation, and all the financial aspects of the family unit are assumed by the single parent. In all probability these responsibilities are combined with employment-related roles and expectations. The single parent experiences the demands similar to those of the female within the dual income family in addition to having the sole responsibility for the home and family. Each one often competes against the other for the time and mental attention of the single parent.[33]

"Time management becomes critical."[34] In most instances, the single parent is not financially able to reduce the household workload by employing outside assistance or using the support system of the kinship network. In order to meet the demands of both the family and shelter spheres as well as those of employment, hours previously devoted to sleep and personal time are instead devoted to trying to meet these needs. Since this parent has practically no discretionary time, his or her participation in social and community activities is often limited to those which involve the children. This further contributes to the isolation and social ostracism often imposed upon the single parent family by the community.

Many women who head single-parent households do not have the educational expertise nor the skill competencies to effectively manage their households. Prior to becoming single parents they probably relied quite heavily on male family members. First their fathers and later their husbands made major decisions, particularly financial ones. These women probably do not possess the skills needed to reduce home maintenance and repair costs. Conversely, few males are truly familiar with the skills and competencies involved in household operation, meal planning and preparation, or child care. The absence of these skills and competencies often results in mismanagement of critical resources.

The female who heads a single-parent family, in all probability, will not have the monetary resources of her male counterpart. Despite the passage of the 1963 law governing equal opportunity employment, statistics show the female median income will be 58.9 per cent of the median income of males.[35] The majority of women who head such households probably lacks the educational skills to attain higher salaried positions. This lack of educational skills relegates the single-parent female and a high percentage of all the female labor force to employment in predominately service, blue collar, or clerical positions.[36]

"To compound the problem, female family heads (and women in general) are often faced with discriminatory practices that reduce their income-effectiveness."[37] When the female's lack of financial management skills and in some cases, poorly developed consumer buying skills, is coupled with these discriminatory practices, the end result may be a costly drain on monetary resources—a drain she can ill afford.

Hungerford and Paolucci report these discriminatory practices often involve securing "consumer and mortgage credit," "basic health, major medical and income disability insurance," and auto insurance.[38] In addition to these, the female often has poorly developed consumer skills such as "purchasing cars, negotiating contracts, filing income tax forms, and selecting legal advice."[39] Each of these impact upon her already dire financial position.

The single parent, like the dual income family, is forced to modify managerial actions and behaviors in light of the current situation. However, the demands placed upon the critical resources for the single parent are much greater than those experienced within the dual income family. The constraints upon resources, when added to the other demands inherent within the family and shelter spheres, often produce stress, anxiety, and frustration. They may be further magnified if the single parent lacks access to an emotional support system, community sponsored child care facilities, or formal education to attain high salaried employment. These afford little opportunity for the single parent to satisfy personal wants and needs while still meeting the demands of employment, shelter spheres, and the individual family members.

Handicapped Family

Twenty six million Americans face life with some type of handicap. Another 500,000 will become disabled each year.[40] Approximately 12 per cent of these are women who have physical handicaps which limit their activities in some important way.[41] The principle cause of handicaps are faulty vison, arthritis, paralysis, and circulatory disease.[42]

The handicapped family unit, like others, discussed within this chapter, have special characteristics that set it apart. This family unit, too, makes adjustments and modifications within the family and shelter spheres with respect to these characteristics.

The nature and extent of these modifications and adjustments will be dependent upon several factors. The first is whether the handicap is a temporary or permanent one. The duration of the temporary physical impairment is a determinate factor. Suppose you were physically impaired for three weeks. How would this affect your life patterns? What adjustments would you have to make? Would these be different if the duration of your physical impairment was six months? Although numerous adjustments would be necessary in either instance, the duration of a temporary physical impairment has a direct bearing upon the adjustments undertaken within the family and shelter spheres.

A permanent physical impairment necessitates numerous adjustments within the family and shelter sphere. The permanency of this occurrence ultimately means continuous and on-going modifications will occur as the family unit moves through the stages of the life cycle. Within the shelter sphere adaptations to enable the physically impaired person to function as independently as possible will be more extensive than in the case of a temporary impairment. The stress and frustrations experienced by all family members will have different implications for the future. Changes in living patterns within the family sphere will also be dependent upon the permanency and duration of the impairment.

The second factor involves the type of physical impairment and the limitations it places upon the individual's life style patterns. The adjustments necessary for an individual confined to a wheel chair are quite different than those for an individual with visual impairment or one who is ambulatory.

An important factor is which family member is physically impaired. The adjustments and the effect upon the family are quite different if the handicapped individual is a parent as opposed to a child. Although the physical disability of any family member places a hardship upon all other family members, the physical impairment of the female adult denotes fewer social connotations than does the impairment of the adult male. The role expectations of the female adult are such that it is socially acceptable for her to remain within the shelter sphere.[43]

Deacon and Firebaugh indicate that the presence of a handicapped child within a family unit affects the managerial processes. There is a reduction in goal agreement between the parents.[44] Other effects noted are an increase in the tension surrounding the parenting role and an increase in ". . . the difficulty of managing a home in a manner consistent with the family goals."[45]

Although there are numerous instances of the handicapped adult female, in all probability the handicapped individual is more likely to be the adult male. Nagi's study of the handicapped adult found the majority were over fifty years of age, had an educational level of six to eight years of formal schooling, were predominately while males, and lived primarily in private homes. The handicapped individual tended to suffer from two or more distortions at the same time.[46] A study of their previous employment found it was in one of the following: service related occupations, craftsman, operator, or as a nonfarm or mine laborer.[47] The probability of future employment in the labor force is dependent upon the skills, formal educational attainment, and the nature of the handicap. A high degree of skills and formal education increase the probability of return to the labor force.[48]

The age of the individual and the specific family situation are additional factors. The young person adjusts much easier to the permanency of a physical impairment than does the older adult. The specific family situation also has a direct bearing. Families with limited income, minimal educational attainment, and inadequately developed management skills experience a greater degree of difficulty in making the necessary adjustments and modifications within the family and shelter spheres.

Traditionally, the adult male is the major wage earner of the family; this factor alone foretells the impact upon the family unit. When combined with the data concerning his employment status prior to the onset of the handicap and the probability of his reentry into the labor force, the impact upon the family unit, its well-being, and its future management is extensive. Probably the hardest adjustment to make for both the individual and the family members is the acceptance of the handicap and all its implications to the family's life style patterns, the shelter sphere, and to the future.

Role Perceptions

Each individual establishes and defines his or her role based upon a value hierarchy. Inherent within this role establishment are the relationships of the individual to those peer, family, and reference groups which have become a part of daily living. As these roles are being established numerous criterias are used to assess the validity of the role in relationship to the existing social structure.

One criteria is the relationship of the individual to other members of the family unit, i.e., father, mother, son, daughter, brother, sister. Other criterias include the contributions made by the individual to his or her respective groups and society in general, and the perceived acceptance of the individual's role within these groups.

The role status of the individual within the family unit does not change due to physical disability. The parent or child still remains as the parent or child. What does occur, however, is the modification of that role. This is somewhat governed by the extent to which the disfunction affects the continued capability to assume the role and its modification.

Recognition of the implication of the disability and its acceptance as a permanent part of the family's living patterns will play a major part in the modification taking place. This acceptance and recognition takes place for both the individual and the family members.

All family members are affected by the modification of role perceptions. Each family member modifies his or her role with respect to the degree of impairment. In some instances, one or more of the family members may find themselves ". . . automatically placed in the caretaker role."[49] According to Green: "It means being a surrogate parent and experiencing all the complex emotions that entails: love, anger, resentment, guilt, frustration, pity, and anxiety."[50] Not all families find they must assume the caretaker role. However, when the shifting of responsibilities to others within the shelter sphere occurs, the role perceptions of both the handicapped individual and others are modified.

The advent of physical impairment also affects the individual's role perception. This individual, young or old, male or female, must re-establish a role perception on the basis of what has happened. In so doing, he or she must deal not only with self-perceptions but also the roles assigned by family members and society. This is not an easy task at best. A modified role for the handicapped person will emerge in time. The criteria you use to establish and validate your role are identical to those employed by the physically impaired person.

The handicapped individual may use a variety of defense mechanisms in an attempt to deal with the physical impairment. These might include dependency, the power to manipulate others, or seeking attention[51] as well as assumption of the "sick role."[52] In order to understand why the individual might utilize one or more of these defense mechanisms compare your role perceptions with the disabled person. The disability may have closed some employment avenues. Other family members are assuming the responsibility for tasks and duties once completed by this person. Persons outside the shelter sphere experience difficulty in responding in a normal manner to the handicapped person. If the disability is a severe one, this individual may not have sufficient formal education nor the vocational skills to return to previous employment. Thus he or she may no longer have any form of occupational status.[53] Yet many of these are the aspects which have formerly been sources of ego gratification and reinforced role perceptions.

In addition there are the changes that must take place in daily living patterns. Surrounding the handicapped person are the obvious physical changes that have occurred within the shelter sphere. As this individual seeks to function within new surroundings, standards will be modified,[54] long-term implications must be kept carefully in mind[55] throughout decision making, and a strain is placed upon the resource reservoir of the family unit.

The physically impaired person is not the only member of the family unit who is undergoing role modification. Each member of the family unit modifies self-assumed roles as a result of the impairment. The extent of these role modifications will be dependent upon the nature and extent of the impairment as well as which member of the family is physically impaired. Calhoun reports that mothers of handicapped children are ". . . more likely to think of their roles in interpersonal terms; they see themselves as managing tensions among different family members."[56] In respect to other family members, ". . . parents sometimes expect the siblings to assume an inordinate amount of responsibility for the care of the handicapped child."[57] She amplifies this further:

Sex differences have been found in the demands parents place on brothers and sisters of handicapped children. Grossman reports that brothers are usually not expected to assume major responsibility for the physical care of the handicapped children but that sisters, especially those from lower-class backgrounds, frequently are expected to assume major shares of this responsibility.[58]

Calhoun also indicates that the rank of the handicapped child in the birth order and the total number of children in the family unit are factors affecting role assumption. When the handicapped child is the youngest in the birth order or there are a large number of children, there tends to be fewer role problems.[59]

When the physically impaired person is one of the adults within the family unit, modifications are also undergone. The nonimpaired adult may need to assume one or more of the responsibilities of the impaired adult. Children, too, undergo role modifications. The extent to which each family member modifies individual roles will be governed by the type of impairment and the age of the impaired person.

As these role modifications occur caution should be exercised as to which role should be assumed by the nonimpaired person. For example, a parent, whether physically impaired or not, can still undertake the parenting role. Minimizing or eliminating this role assumption can have a detrimental effect upon both the impaired person and the family unit.

As role modification occurs, each family member must recognize the stress and frustration which is an integral part of the family and shelter spheres. The periods of stress and frustration will vary throughout the stages of the life cycle and will be dependent to some extent upon the specific impairment. It is not unusual for an adult who assumes the major responsibility for an aging parent to at times feel extremely frustrated for having to assume the surrogate parent role, or for a nonimpaired child to resent having to assist in the physical care associated with either a handicapped sibling or parent.

The role perception that ultimately emerges within this family unit is dependent upon the acceptance of both the individual and the family unit of the disability and its implications. Numerous studies have shown a close correlation between the individual's acceptance of the handicap and his or her ability to successfully participate in society. The same correlation applies to the family's acceptance of the situation. In both instances, these will have a direct bearing upon the role perception of the disabled person and those around him or her.

Resources

The allocation and use of the resource reservoir to meet demands is sometimes a difficult and arduous task for the nonhandicapped family unit. When a handicapped person is a member of the family unit these demands must still be met along with the demands incurred by the disability factor. The type and degree of these additional demands will be governed by the type of the disability and which family member is impaired. The handicapped family has much in common with other family units in this chapter. They, like the others, face serious demands upon the allocation and use of resources. Probably the three most critical resources for this family unit are time, energy, and money.

The demands upon the family's resources can originate from several sources. A severely handicapped individual may require the purchase of special equipment, appliances, and clothing. If the impaired individual was previously the major wage earner, the reduction of income through loss of employment has both immediate and far reaching effects upon the availability of this critical resource. Should both of these be combined with limited formal educational attainment and minimal employment skills, the probability of regaining the family's previous income level in the future is very low. The presence of a handicapped child within the family unit means additional demands are placed upon money resources. To the cost associated with rearing a nonimpaired child must be added all the financial strains of specialized household and personal equipment, clothing, and educational programs. The child's impairment may also necessitate the anticipation of periods of hospitalization throughout the child's lifetime. Calhoun also indicates the family may at some time be forced to determine whether or not the physically impaired child should be institutionalized.[60] Should this become necessary, an additional demand upon money resources may accrue.

The necessity for structural changes within the shelter sphere may range from minor to quite extensive ones. The nature and extent of the handicap will be a factor. The major purpose here is to allow the handicapped person to live and function as normally as possible. These structural changes may include the installation of ramps instead of stairs; enlarging traffic areas; relocation of rooms such as bedrooms and baths; hand railings; modifications in the height of kitchen cabinets, vanities, and other counter tops; and alteration of door entrances.

The expenditure of financial resources may also extend to include specialized equipment, alteration of current motor vehicles, recurring medical expenses, or special foods to meet dietary requirements. In addition to these, special clothing items may need to be secured.

Each of these place a heavy burden upon the financial resources of the family unit. Unfortunately, in most cases, the handicapped family has fewer reserves to draw upon than other segments of the population.[61] This factor together with the probable previous employment of the disabled individual ultimately means continual and on-going strains upon the financial resources of the family unit. There is no doubt that the handicapped family unit experiences many demands upon its resource reservoir.

Two other critical resources within the family and shelter sphere are time and energy. The expenditures of each of these for all family members increases. Every member will find that some of his or her time and energy resources must be expended to provide some form of assistance despite the severity of the handicap. A family member may be forced to allocate time and energy resources to assume the caretaker role. This may include providing assistance in arising and dresssing, preparing special diets, giving medication, or meeting special needs of the disabled person. The severity and type of impairment will determine the extent to which this role must be assumed. The extent to which role modification and the shifting of duties and responsibilities within the family unit are also factors governing time and energy expenditures of other family members.

The increased expenditure of time and energy is not limited solely to non-impaired family members. The handicapped individual as he or she seeks to function as independently as possible, also increases expenditures of these resources. The amount of time required for task completion will increase in proportion to the severity of the handicap. Tasks, once completed in short time spans, will require additional time usage. This increase is often accompanied by greater expenditures of energy. Muscles may have to be retrained to do a task once done with ease. Special equipment may be required to complete a task, to assist impaired muscles, or to aid faulty vision. New methods of completing a task may have to be learned. Each of these place additional demands upon time and energy resources.

Ultimately the disabled person will become an integral member of the shelter sphere and may possibly be able to reenter the labor force. The adjustment period and the process of developing new life style patterns require the expenditures of additional time and energy from all members of the family unit as well as the impaired person.

Work simplification techniques, programs for rehabilitation, and state and federal legislation provide alternative solutions for the handicapped individual and family members. The retraining of the handicapped person to assume employment in the labor force and increase in the formal educational attainment also offer potential solutions.

Regardless of which family member is impaired, the financial resources of the handicapped family experience continual and on-going demands. Unless the family is an affluent one, the demands placed upon this critical resource impact upon every member, the life style patterns, and the allocation of other resources within the family and shelter spheres.

Aging Family

As you have established your long-range goals and developed the master plan for your life, do either of these include retirement and the time when you will become a "senior citizen?" Just what does *old age* or *aging* mean to you?

If you are like most people, you tend to stereotype the aging family. In all probability you don't perceive of yourself as ever growing old. Unfortunately most individuals fear growing old. The fact that each individual will inevitably grow old is viewed with distaste and anxiety to the degree that they resent, deny, or repress their attitudes toward aging.[62]

Yet aging is a part of the life cycle. By the year 2000 it is estimated 29 million people will be 65 years of age and older.[63] Although the aging family has several commonalities with the other families discussed in this chapter, their age range is not the only characteristic that sets them apart from the nuclear family. Currently the vast majority of aging persons reside in urban areas, predominately within ten states. There are more older females than males.[64] Cutler and Harrootyan report that while the majority have completed some elementary schooling only 28 per cent have completed high school.[65] An even smaller percentage have one or more years of college.[66]

Retirement from active participation in the labor force according to Kimmel marks the event upon which the individual and/or family moves from middle to old age.[67] He further indicates that although retirement is often publically celebrated as a major event in the life pattern of an individual, it also means a shifting in social position.[68]

The advent of retirement and entry into the status of an aging family has different meanings. In any case, retirement means ". . . some disruption of long standing commitments and behavior patterns."[69] This is a period of time when the individual and/or family can look forward to freedom from occupational demands and extensive family obligations. Thurnber's study of individuals approaching retirement found travel was the most desired goal to be attained after retirement. Other desired goals were relocation, health care, leisure activities, and freedom from work and family obligations.[70]

Entrance into "senior citizen" status carries with it many connotations. Although society tends to equate retirement with old age, the individual and/or family reaching this stage does not. Although some approach this period in their life cycle with fear and dread, others eagerly anticipate it.

The manner in which the individual becomes and lives as a "senior citizen" is strongly affected by previous life experiences and the individual's personality. Kimmel reports that men who were bitter or saw themselves as being unable to attain goals did not adjust easily to retirement. Those who had positive self-perceptions or lived passive lives moved easily into retirement and looked forward to the freedom from responsibility.[71]

The aging family, like other family units in this chapter, have role modifications and critical resources. Both of these are brought about as the family unit shifts from a complex world involving professional endeavors to a less complex leisurely life.[72] There is a shift in decision making and values are reoriented.[73]

Role Perceptions

As the aging family enters this cycle in their lives, role modification takes place. Some roles are eliminated. Others are adjusted to coincide with the newly emerging life style. New roles may be assumed. Often accompanying the role modifications taking place within the family sphere are the role perceptions placed upon the aging family by both society and other members of the kinship network.

The current society tends to view entrance into the aging cycle as denoting a loss of power and status. This is reflected in the negative connotations often accompanying these expectations.[74]

The major role eliminated by the aging family is the work oriented one. The extent to which others are modified, new ones assumed and the impact it will have upon the aging family is dependent upon the sex, occupational status, personality, marital status, and how the individual views retirement.

Women tend to be less willing to move into this life cycle than men. Single and married women tend to plan for and anticipate retirement more than ,divorced or widowed females.[75] The individual's personality and sense of satisfaction regarding previous occupational activities aid in making the transition.[76] The male is still considered the head of the household.[77] His role shifts from that of a provider to a helper within the shelter sphere.[78] As he assumes the role of helper the question arises as to whether his wife will allow him to take a participatory role in her world.[79]

Kimmel reports those individuals having high incomes, education, and professional status tend to desire early retirement. He also found when retirement was chosen, roles associated with it were viewed more favorably.[80]

Role expectations for the single individual are often quite different than those of the married couple. If a male lives alone, he has to assume the household roles.[81] The children of the single aging individual tend to make overt attempts to include this parent within their shelter sphere rather than allow him or her to continue to live alone.[82]

New roles assumed by the aging family may involve community service participation such as civic or volunteer activities. Within the kinship network, they may become involved in the child care of grandchildren.

The role perception of the aging couple is modified by their change in life patterns, the expectations of society, and the extent to which entrance into this life stage is positively viewed. The individual who has a positive conception and accepts the biological changes resulting from the aging process will make positive role modifications.

Resources

As role modifications are taking place, so too are there changes in resource availability. The resource of time becomes more available as the necessity for time devoted to professional endeavors is greatly reduced or eliminated. In most instances money resources become fixed amounts and in all probability reduced. The biological process of aging begins to make itself felt in the reduction of energy levels. Other resources take on a greater importance.

The aging family's time resource becomes more abundant. As the availability of this resource increases, decisions need to be made concerning its allocation and use. Although you might view the loss of having to devote many hours each day to work-related activities as a major benefit, the aging family may not. The aging couple must not only determine how time resources are to be used but also define, in accordance with their value hierarchy, what constitutes leisure time and what is not.[83] Bernhardt and Kinnear's study found aging families spent their time reading books, sewing, attending ball games, going to movies, doing crossword puzzles, fishing, gardening, attending church activities, and eating meals outside the shelter sphere.[84]

The financial status of the aging family is a major problem.[85] Many of these families are living on fixed income amounts accrued from social security or retirement funds. Therefore an inflationary period presents a real threat to the aging couple because their buying power is reduced due to price increases.

In expending money resources, Waddell found the aging couple is highly susceptible to fraud and deception because they are ill-informed, lack confidence in their decision making, and often lack the opportunity to secure valid feedback.[86] In addition they make heavy use of mass transit systems, long distance telephone calls, taxi cabs, and laundromats.[87] Money resources are primarily allocated and used to meet basic needs.

Other resources become more important to the aging couple. The presence of a confidant is a valuable resource to the aging family. This resource aids in the loss of roles and the reduction of other resources. The loss of this resource has a significant effect upon the family unit.[88] Other resources which increase in importance are the social life, family, and kinship network. Although personal relationships are important, they begin to decrease as friends and relatives die. The loss of the spouse and the spouse role often produces loneliness, loss of affection, and the capability of shared tasks.[89]

The older couple may eagerly or reluctantly enter the aging cycle. Inherent within this process are role modification and changes in resources. In some respects, their life style closely patterns the beginning stage of the life cycle. New routines and life style patterns must be developed to reflect the changes taking place in their life. Their role modifications, effective resource allocation, and the presence of support systems can make this period in the life cycle truly golden years.

College Family

Following World War II many college and university administrators found that in order to meet the housing needs of their students, a different type of housing unit had to be constructed. The veterans from World War II were returning to the college campuses and they were bringing with them their families.

The need for married student housing began with these veterans and has continued.

Many college campuses, particularly urban and community colleges, along with specialized training schools have a high percentage of married students.[90] An ever increasing number of young couples are choosing to combine parenthood with the attainment of their college education. Although the vast majority of these students are under twenty-five, many colleges and universities are finding an ever increasing number of older women who are returning to or entering college for the first time.[91]

The college family may consist of two full-time students, one full-time student who is being financially supported by the other partner, or a student who enrolls in classes to increase personal knowledge. These students may be enrolled in graduate or undergraduate programs. Regardless of their status within the educational institution, there are inherent problems which exist and therefore set them apart from the other family units. Some are full-time students throughout the academic year. Others attend only evening or summer session courses. The actual status of the college student will have a direct bearing upon the management taking place. Regardless of the enrollment status of the college student, each is striving to meet the demands of being a student and the demands of a family member.

Role Perceptions

Many couples are deciding to simultaneously combine the roles of marriage partners with the goal of attaining a college education for one or both of them. Although the shared experiences of the academic campus are accrued benefits, the role expectations of society, parents, peers, and the marriage partners may, at times, instigate role conflicts not experienced by the single student or within the noncollege family unit.

The married student must assume the dual roles of marriage partner and student. Each marriage partner receives the emotional support from the other along with the satisfaction of the need for love and affection.[92] This combined with the family living patterns may mean the difference between whether or not the goal of attaining a college education continues to be sought.

Kelley indicates the drop-out rate for married students is high.[93] Many student couples when faced with the continued assumption of the dual roles of marriage partners and students over prolonged periods of time choose to terminate the educational endeavors of one or both partners. The rationale for this termination often lies in the conflicting roles of student and family member.

In addition to these factors, the married couple must assume the dual roles of student and family member. Inherent within the assumption of these two roles are many potential conflict situations. Most academic programs place heavy time demands upon any student. When these demands are combined with the necessity for financial support by employment beyond class hours, the married student experiences conflict. The married student, in addition to these roles, is also assuming the role of a marriage partner. Thus the probability of conflict is further increased. The increased demands of the roles of student, employee, and marriage partner often mean a reduction in the time available for their personal lives, relaxation, and a social life. When these needs are not met, the potential for conflict is further enhanced. Most college couples experience difficulty adjusting to two major responsibilities at the same time.[94]

The role perception of the married student is dependent upon several factors. Among these are the stage in the life cycle, the priority ranking of attainment of the educational goal, parental acceptance and support, the expectations of each marriage partner, and the expectations placed upon the couple by society.

The stage in the life cycle has a direct bearing upon the roles being undertaken during this time span. The college couple in the beginning stages of the life cycle experiences much different role assumptions than does the couple who are in the expanding stage. The couple within the beginning stage of the life cycle is experiencing not only the marital adjustments commensurate with the initial establishment of a family unit but also the demands of the student role. Kelley indicates the marital patterns established in the early development of the marriage will have a lasting impact on the marriage.[95] The college couple in the expanding stage of the life cycle must combine with the roles of student and marriage partner that of the parenting role. In this instance, this couple has much in common with the dual income family unit and experiences the same role perception demands.

The role perception of the married student will depend upon the priority ranking of the educational attainment goal. Although most married college couples view the attainment of a college degree as an investment in the future, and their present situation as temporary[96], the rationale for college enrollment will have an effect upon role perception. If for some reason, the attainment of the college degree was imposed upon one or both, the role of the college student may become secondary to that of the marriage partner. If on the other hand, the attainment of the college degree is a high priority goal, it may be placed ahead of the partnership role. Where the attainment of the college degree is of high priority for both partners, each is more willing to modify the traditional roles within the family unit during this time span.

Parental acceptance of the college marriage and the support given to it are also factors in the establishment of roles within this marriage. Although in most cases the parental ties are cut to some extent, the absence or presence of these support systems will have an impact upon the student couple. Where parental support is present in either emotional or economic terms, the role perceptions of the college marriage is greatly enhanced.

Closely aligned to this are the social expectations of society and the length of time remaining until the goal is attained. The advent of marriage within a society denotes the capabilities of the couple to be self-sustaining. Thus the couple is expected to be able to undertake the financial aspects of their life together. The college couple may find this expectation difficult to meet. Although it is common for both partners to be employed, with one being full-time and the other part-time, the acceptance of this situation may be difficult for parents and society, as well as the marriage partners. Despite the advent of equal opportunity for males and females, society still looks upon the male partner as the major wage earner. The male partner may also define his role as providing the economic support for the family unit. He may well experience self-doubts and question his role within the family unit if his wife's full-time employment is providing the major financial support during this time.

Where the termination of the temporary status appears to be in sight, the role perceptions are quite different than are those where goal attainment lies in the distant future.

How the individuals perceive their roles will have a direct influence upon the continuation of a college career. The college couple who places a high priority upon the goal attainment of the educational degree will modify current roles for the duration of the academic program. However, the married couple or the marriage partner who places a higher priority upon the roles within the family unit may not complete the goal attainment.

Resources

Across the nation, college couples are seeking to attain academic degrees utilizing the resources available within their family unit. In this respect, they share much in common with the family units. Time is a critical resource. Their financial resources can vary from practically nothing to being affluent. Energy resources, in most cases, are high. These are further augmented by the skills, talents, and abilities accrued from their increased educational attainment. In this respect, they are increasing their resource reservoir.

Most college students, regardless of their single or married status, would indicate that time, and possibly money are their two scarcest resources. For the college couples, time is a limited resource. The allocation of their time resource must include those responsibilities and duties inherent within the shelter sphere as well as those necessary to pursue their academic program. Most married students seek employment outside the shelter sphere to augment their financial reserves. Each of these necessitate the use of time resources. The demands placed upon the time resources of the student couple will depend to some extent on the number of roles being assumed. The college parent may also have to include time allocations for child care. In most instances, the college couple does not have the financial resources to employ outside assistance to reduce the workload within the shelter sphere.

The allocation of time resources within this family unit must be done in light of the demands of all family members and the roles each is assuming within the partnership. Time schedules are developed not only to encompass class schedules but also the other activities of the family members such as employment and the social expectations. If the family membership includes children, the school hours and related activities must also be included. Added to these are the task responsibilities associated with household operation. During this period in their lives, the student couple may find little, if any, discretionary time remains for either the family functions or to meet and satisfy the need for private and personal time.

Energy resources are high for the young couple yet they must be allocated to meet the demands of the various assumed roles. Like their time resources, the energy resources of this couple are continually drawn upon to meet the role expectations.

For most the financial resources are strained in order to meet the demands of both the family unit and college expenses. Economic support may be provided from employment, parental contributions, scholarships, personal savings, or a combination of these. In a study of students, 50 per cent listed money as a primary cause of tension in student marriages.[97] As the financial cost of a college education continues to rise, these couples will experience even greater demands upon their limited money resource. If a choice must be made as to which one continues to assume the student role, in most instances it is the male.[98]

Today's student couple employ a variety of alternatives to attain this academic degree. Some couples intersperse their academic studies with full-time employment. In this instance, both obtain full-time employment and save until sufficient funds are accumulated to allow them to return to the college campus. Academic studies are pursued until these funds are depleted. At this point, they return to full-time employment in the labor force until their savings allow them to return again to the college campus. Other students seek part-time employment while being full-time students. Still others elect to alternate their employment. One partner is employed full-time and the other attends classes for a period of time. At the termination of this time span, the employment and student roles are reversed. Other college couples choose to have one partner support the other for the duration of the academic program. In these instances, it is generally the husband who is the first to attain the academic degree. Following this, the husband supports his wife while she attains her degree. Regardless of the option chosen by the student couple, very few attain their college degrees without employment outside the shelter sphere.

The financial status of the student couple place limitations upon the allocation of this resource. Their first financial obligations are to meet the demands of college and family expenses.

The college couple, regardless of their stage in the life cycle, will experience role modifications and adjustments. The assumption of the student role will necessitate changes in the living patterns of the family unit, in the allocation and utilization of resources, and the decisions made. How each member of the family unit views the participation of the individual in the academic world will affect to a great extent not only the managerial actions and behaviors taking place but also the willingness of family members to make adjustments to the living patterns and the resource allocation.

You may currently be a member of one of the nonnuclear family units discussed herein. Or perhaps your future planning includes one of these. Although it may not be a part of your future plans, you may, at some time in your life, find yourself a member of a nonnuclear family unit.

Throughout the nation there is an ever increasing number of nonnuclear family units. Regardless of whether your future plans include the traditional family unit as discussed in Chapter 11 or the nonnuclear family unit discussed in this chapter, awareness of both and the effect each has upon management will help you determine the alternative choices you make now and in the future.

Summary

Throughout the nation there are family units in various developmental stages of the life cycle. Some of these family units follow the traditional concept of the family unit. Not all families, however, fit into this traditional mode. These families have special characteristics that necessitate different modifications and adjustments in the managerial actions and behaviors.

In each instance these family units share commonalities with the nuclear family as they progress through the developmental stages of the life cycle. Yet at the same time, their special characteristics set them apart.

Although commonalities exist, in almost every instance the critical resources are time, energy, and money. By necessity, each member within the family unit has adjusted and modified role perceptions. These role modifications have occurred because of special circumstances within the family unit. These roles of the members are not different, rather they have taken on additional depth in directions not required within the nuclear family.

Just as there are commonalities, so, too, are there differences. Each has a unique feature which sets it apart from both the nuclear family unit and from each other. In most instances the prime causal factor is the changing status of one or more family members. In the dual income family, both parents are employed outside the shelter sphere. The single-parent family results from the permanent absence of one parent. Physical impairment of a family member produces the handicapped family unit. The aging family emerges with the passage of time and retirement from occupational endeavors. The college family, although not a newly emerging family unit, is steadily increasing its members.

Each of these family units has an impact upon society. Their input is felt in communities across the nation. Their special characteristics set them apart. The input received from the spheres of interaction necessitate that managerial action be cognizant of special circumstances taking place within their family and shelter spheres. Although they are distinctly different from the nuclear family, they utilize the same principles and concepts of management. Their differences lie not in the use of the principles and concepts, but rather in the factors that have created their current life situation.

ACTIVITIES

1. Family units have different values, goals, standards, resources, and methods of decision making. There are numerous articles in current periodicals devoted to a real life account of one or more of the family units discussed in this chapter. Select one and answer the following questions.
   a. What are the family's values, goals, and resources?
   b. What role modifications were necessary?
   c. What is the current developmental stage of this family? What are the similarities and differences between this family and a nuclear family in the same developmental stage?
   d. Using one particular problem as a reference point, describe how this family used the management process to achieve resolution.
   e. If the same situation happened to you and/or your family unit, what role modifications would be necessary? How would this affect the resource allocation within the family and shelter spheres? Would your goals change? If so, which ones and why?
2. Each family in question no. 1 has resource reservoirs. Do the following for the family discussed in the article you read for question no. 1.
   a. Identify the specific resources in their reservoirs.
   b. Determine the limitations and availability of each resource.
   c. Indicate the demands upon these resources from
      1. Input being received from outside the shelter sphere.
      2. Input from other family members.
      3. Input from within the shelter sphere.
3. Each family experiences role conflicts. What types of role conflicts would you anticipate might occur within each of the families discussed in the chapter? What might be causal factors for these role conflicts? How might they be resolved? Are there some which would be more difficult to resolve than others? Why or why not?
4. The process and procedures used by families in decision making will vary from one family to another. Compare the decision-making process and procedure of the nuclear family unit to each of the family units discussed in this chapter. What are the commonalities and differences between each of these families? Isolate two probable causal factors for each family.

5. You have established standards for yourself, your shelter sphere, and your life style. Would any adjustments or modifications occur in these if you
   a. Became handicapped?
   b. Became one of the members of a college family?
   c. Became the single parent in a single family unit?
   If your response to any of these is positive. what modifications and adjustments would you make? Why would these be necessary? What would be the result upon your current and future management?

6. Establish what you would anticipate would be the tasks necessary for the daily and weekly household operation. Determine the amount of time needed to complete each task. Develop a time schedule for two of the following family units.
   a. Nuclear family where female parent is not employed outside the shelter sphere.
   b. Dual income family.
   c. Female headed single-parent household.
   d. Male headed single-parent household.
   e. Physically disabled male in a handicapped family.
   f. Physically disabled female in a handicapped family.
   g. College family.

FOUR FAMILIES

For the last two years four different family units have occupied the four apartments in one building of an apartment complex. During this time they have become friends as well as neighbors.

Lois and Ray have lived in this building the longest time. They are the same age as the other adults in the building. They have two children who attend the neighborhood elementary school. Ray was injured in an industrial accident five years after they were married. He has been confined to a wheel chair since then. His income is a small disability pension. Lois teaches math in a high school several miles away. She returned to teaching after Ray's accident. They were living in the building at the time and have remained there. Their apartment is located on the first floor of the building.

Jim and his two children live on the same floor. The children are the same age as Lois and Ray's and attend the same school. Jim is in his late twenties and is employed in a management position for a local industrial firm. His wife died in childbirth. He has never remarried. Although he occasionally dates, there is no specific woman in his life. He says he is too busy with his job to consider marriage right now. Jim's work does require that he travel more than he would really prefer. When he does go out of town the children stay with Lois and Ray or one of the other families in the building. Unfortunately these trips seem to come more often lately. Because of this he is considering hiring a full-time, live-in housekeeper. If he does both children will have to share a bedroom. The housekeeper will take the other one.

Jack occupies one of the two second floor apartments. He is referred to by the others in the building as their "swinging neighbor." He has never married and really doesn't intend to in the near future. "Too many responsibilities" is his answer when anyone asks or tries to match him up with a young woman. As the sales manager of a local car agency, Jack always has a new car and appears to have plenty of money to spend. His social life is quite full. On several occasions he has included Jim and would like to more often. Jim has attended some of Jack's parties but feels he should spend as much time with his children as possible.

Sarah, in her mid-twenties, is the newest resident in the building. She moved in shortly after her divorce. Her two children attend the neighborhood elementary school. Sarah teaches English in the same school as Lois. The two women share a car pool with two other teachers who live in the same complex. Although she receives some child support, Sarah still finds that most of the time she is experiencing financial problems. Her social life is quite limited. Although she likes both Jim and Jack, she openly expresses her adverse feelings concerning any serious "entanglement" and has refused to attend social functions with either one.

All four family units tend to help each other on many occasions. Either

Jack or Jim make it a point to be present when Ray has a doctor's appointment. One of the two men always goes with Lois to help get Ray in and out of the car. Ray often watches all of the children after school until the other adults return home in the evening. Jack assumes the responsibility for the care and maintenance of both Sarah's car and Ray's car. Jim is the coach for one of the Little League teams. Three of the children are players on the team. When Jim has to be out of town, Jack takes over the coaching duties. Sarah often plans special Saturday activities for all of the children.

Discussion Questions

1. Each of these four family units have common problems as well as special ones. What are the common ones shared by all of the family units? What are the special problems of each family unit?
2. Within this apartment building exists a special situation. In many respects these families are luckier than most in similar situations. Each of these families faces many demands upon their resources. Obviously one of their shared resources is the close relationship that has developed. What are the resources within each of the family units? Identify each family's resources. How available are these resources?
3. Each of these families is experiencing special demands in addition to those incurred by the nuclear family unit. Identify the demands for each family unit. What resources are being used by each family unit to meet these demands?
4. Three of these families have made major parenting role modifications. What were the modifications? How have these affected the management principles and concepts? What decisions are being made and how are they made?
5. Jack, Jim, and Sarah have all expressed in one way or another their unwillingness to marry or remarry. Why? Lois and Ray have remained married and are trying to create as near normal a household as possible. What have been the motivating factors in this endeavor? What do you anticipate will be the future of these four families? Do you foresee any changes in their present status? If so,, what and why?

GLOSSARY

Caretaker Role A role assumed by an individual for the physical, emotional well-being, and the economic support of another individual who is partly or completely unable to undertake those duties and responsibilities for himself or herself.

Consensual Union An alternative to a marriage partnership in which two adults of the opposite sex choose to live together in established family and shelter spheres as a mated pair without the legal marriage sanction of state laws.

College Family Unit A family unit in which one or more of the adults in the marriage partnership is enrolled either part time or full time in a college or university.

Dual Income Family Unit A family unit in which both husband and wife are employed in the labor force outside the shelter sphere.

Employment Full- or part-time participation in the labor force outside the shelter sphere which produces money income in the form of wages, salary, or business profit.

Female Headed Household A single-parent family unit in which only the adult parent is a female.

Handicapped Family Unit A family unit in which one of the members is physically impaired.

Male Headed Household A single-parent family unit in which the only adult parent is a male.

Parenting Role The role involving the duties and responsibilities of child care assumed by an adult.

Single-Parent Family Unit A family unit composed of one adult parent and a child or children.

Standard of Living The economic and social style of living desired by an individual and/or a family unit.

Surrogate Parent(s) An individual, agency, or institution that assumes the duties and responsibilities for child care in the absence of the parents of the marriage partnership or the parent of a single-parent family unit.

Wage Earner An individual who is employed outside the shelter sphere in the labor force and who receives money income for this participation.

REFERENCES

1. "Working Women Joys and Sorrows," *U.S. News and World Reports, Inc.* (January 21, 1979), 64.
2. Ibid.

3. David L. Brown. "Women in the Labor Force," *Journal of Home Economics* (November 1977), 21.
4. Ibid.
5. "Working Women Joys and Sorrows," op. cit., p. 64.
6. Irma H. Gross, Elizabeth Walbert Crandall, and Marjorie M. Knoll, *Management for Modern Families*, 3rd. ed. (New York: Appleton-Century-Crofts, 1973), p. 76.
7. Brown, op. cit., p. 22.
8. "Working Women Joys and Sorrows," op. cit., p. 68.
9. Maximiliane Szinovacz, "Women Employed: Effects on Spouse's Division of Household Work," *Journal of Home Economics* (Summer 1979), 44.
10. "Working Women Joys and Sorrows," op. cit., p. 69.
11. Szinovacz, op. cit., p. 43.
12. Ibid.
13. Ibid.
14. Brown, op. cit., p. 22.
15. "Working Women Joys and Sorrows," op. cit., p. 69.
16. Ibid.
17. Gail Putney Fullerton, *Survival in Marriage Introduction to Family Interaction, Conflicts, and Alternatives*, 2nd ed. (Hinsdale, Ill.: The Dryden Press, 1977), p. 26.
18. Sinovacz, op. cit., p. 42.
19. Karen E. Craig, "Gainful Employment for Women: The Facts" *Journal of Home Economics* (November 1977), 23.
20. Brown, op. cit., p. 22.
21. Fullerton, op. cit., p. 27.
22. Szinovacz, op. cit., p. 45.
23. Craig, op. cit., p. 23.
24. "Working Women Joys and Sorrows," op. cit., p. 64.
25. Ibid.
26. Nancy Hungerford and Beatruce Paolucci, "The Employed Female Single Parent," *Journal of Home Economics* (November 1977), 10.
27. Ibid., p. 11.
28. Ibid.
29. Ibid., p. 12.
30. Ibid.
31. Ibid.
32. Ibid., p. 11.
33. Ibid.
34. Ibid.
35. "Working Women Joys and Sorrows," op. cit., p. 64.
36. Ibid., p. 66.
37. Hungerford and Paolucci, op. cit., pp. 11–12.
38. Ibid., p. 12.
39. Ibid.
40. Alpha H. Jones and Lois O. Schwab, "Rehabilitation for Homemakers with Cardiovascular Involvements: Changes in Attitude and Abilities," *Home Economics Research Journal* (December 1972), 144.

41. Irene Oppenheim, *Management of the Modern Home,* 2nd ed. (New York: Macmillan Publishing Company, Inc., 1976), p. 295.

42. Ibid., p. 294.

43. Ruth E. Deacon and Francille M. Firebaugh, *Home Management Context and Concepts* (Boston: Houghton Mifflin Company, 1975), p. 75.

44. Ibid.

45. Ibid.

46. Saad Z. Nagi, *Disability and Rehabilitation* (Kent: Ohio State University Press, 1969), p. 41.

47. Ibid., pp. 41–42.

48. Ibid., p. 133.

49. Kinsey B. Green, "Coping Daily with the Handicapped and the Elderly," *Journal of Home Economics* (Fall 1978), p. 15.

50. Ibid.

51. Nagi, op. cit., p. 127.

52. Ibid., p. 124.

53. Green, op. cit., p. 16.

54. Oppenheim, op. cit., p. 298.

55. Green, op. cit., p. 15.

56. Mary Lynne Calhoun, "The Handicapped Child," in Lawrence G. Calhoun, James W. Selby, H. Elizabeth King (eds.), *Dealing With Crisis. A Guide to Critical Life Problems* (Englewood Cliffs, N.J.: Prentice-Hall, Inc., 1976), p. 97.

57. Ibid., p. 99.

58. Ibid.

59. Ibid.

60. Ibid.

61. Green, op. cit., p. 16.

62. Bernice L. Newgarten, "Grow Old Along With Me! The Best Is Yet to Be," In Trude J. Unger and Eugenia M. Parron (eds.), *Growing Up And Growing Old Part II: Adulthood and Old Age* (Lexington, Mass.: Xerox Individualized Publishing, 1975), p. 141.

63. Douglas C. Kimmel, *Adulthood and Aging An Interdisciplinary Developmental View* (New York: John Wiley & Sons, Inc., 1974), p. 256.

64. Neal E. Cutler and Robert A. Harrootyan, "Demography of the Aged" in Diana S. Woodruff and James E. Birren (eds.), *Aging Scientific Perspectives and Social Issues* (New York: D. Van Nostrand Company, 1975), pp. 55–56.

65. Ibid., p. 63.

66. Ibid., p. 64.

67. Kimmel, op. cit., p. 255.

68. Ibid.

69. Majda Thurnber, "Goals, Values and Life Evaluations at the Preretirement Stage," in Kennard W. Wellons and Paul K. H. Kim (eds.), *On Aging An Orientation to Social Gerontology* (Lexington, Mass.: Xerox Individualized Publishing, 1975), p. 97.

70. Ibid., pp. 98–99.

71. Kimmel, op. cit., p. 262.

72. Ibid., p. 258.

73. Thurnber, op. cit., p. 97.

74. Richard A. Kalish, *Late Adulthood: Perspectives on Human Development* (Monterey, Calif.: Brooke/Cole Publishing Company, 1975), p. 52.

75. Kimmel, op. cit., p. 258.

76. Ibid., p. 260.

77. Kalish, op. cit., p. 77.

78. Ibid., p. 62.

79. Kimmel, op. cit., p. 260.

80. Ibid., p. 258.

81. Kalish, op. cit., p. 84.

82. Ibid., p. 83.

83. Kimmell, op. cit., p. 265.

84. Kenneth L. Bernhardt and Thomas C. Kinnear, "Profiling the Senior Market" in Fred E. Waddell (ed.), *The Elderly Consumer* (Columbia, Md: Human Ecology Center, 1976), p. 247.

85. Cutler and Harrootyan, op. cit., pp. 59–63.

86. Fred E. Waddell, "Consumer Research and Programs for the Elderly: The Forgotten Dimension" in Fred E. Waddell (ed.), *The Elderly Consumer* (Columbia, Md.: Human Ecology Center, 1976), p. 313.

87. Bernhardt and Kinnear, op. cit., p. 247.

88. Kimmel, op. cit., pp. 317–319.

89. Kalish, op. cit., p. 83.

90. Robert K. Kelley, *Courtship, Marriage and the Family*, 3rd ed. (New York: Harcourt Brace Jovanovich, Inc., 1979), p. 80.

91. Laura Folland, Eunice Pickett, and Ruth Hoeflin, "Adult Women in College: How Do They Fare?" *Journal of Home Economics* (November 1977), 28.

92. Ibid., p. 234.

93. Kelley, op. cit., p. 237.

94. Ibid., pp. 234–237.

95. Ibid., p. 240.

96. Gross, Crandall, and Knoll, op. cit., p. 56.

97. Kelley, op. cit., p. 238.

98. Ibid., p. 239.

CHAPTER TWELVE

Management and a Changing World

Thus far the study of management principles and concepts has been devoted to you, as an individual and as a member of a family and shelter sphere. These principles and concepts are universal. As you have explored these in depth you have probably commented to yourself and perhaps to others that you were aware of and used these before you enrolled in this course. Although you were somewhat cognizant of these, by now you have not only increased your awareness but you are also better able to utilize them in your management.

Management principles and concepts are the universal tools used by business, industry, governments, families, and individuals. The purpose of management, regardless of who is involved, is to achieve a specified desired quality of life. This is achieved when values are recognized and clarified, standards are developed and used to measure progress, and decisions made are based upon a logical and rational assessment of the alternatives.

Management is a continual and on-going process. Effective management takes place when the individual not only utilizes the management principles and concepts but utilizes them effectively. The extent of effectiveness is based upon recognizing that although management is an individual process, it is influenced by the continual flow of input received from the spheres of interaction.

Inherent within this is the further awareness that no individual lives and functions isolated from the systems surrounding him or her. The society in which the individual manages is in a constant state of change. Therefore, if the desired quality of life is to be achieved the individual's management must continually recognize and adjust to the fluidity of the social evolution taking place.

The society in which you currently undertake management has changed in the past five years. It will change in the future. Reflect for a moment upon the changes you have seen in your lifetime. The extent of your awareness of changes and the adjustments you make will reflect your relationship in reference to others. To a great extent, it will also govern how satisfied you are now and in the future.

Although your society somewhat resembles itself as it was five years ago, there have been changes. The present society differs greatly from that of a generation ago. The future promises even further changes. What has brought about the changes in the past and what does the future have in store for you?

Advancing technology has had and will continue to have a tremendous impact upon society. Today there is an almost instantaneous communication network. This network allows you not only to hear but to see what is taking place almost anywhere in the world. This communication is not limited to the earth either. The happenings in outer space also can be seen and heard.

What does all this mean to you? Let's begin by looking at your profession and the future. Advancing technology has already brought about changes in the length of the workday and work week, the production of goods and services, and even the process of producing them. Computer technology has become an integral part of your life as well as business and industry.

Computer technology is used to complete many tasks in business and industry that were once done through manual labor. Computers and other electronic equipment now direct factory production lines, record current inventories, route materials and supplies to meet production needs, provide accounting and billing services, monitor air climate control systems, and serve in many other capacities. Similar systems are used on your campus for a multitude of purposes.

As you look around your classroom and your campus, what other evidences do you see of advancing technology? In all probability you can identify many such advances that have changed your environment and your daily life.

A comparison of current course offering with those of five years ago reveal evidences of these changes. Courses in computer programming, numerical control, computer graphics, and programming languages are common academic requirements for various majors.

The evidences of technology can be found in the shelter sphere too. Electronic computer toys for children and games for youth and adults are commonplace. Solid state thermostats and controls are used in both large equipment and portable appliances. In the home, computers can be used for household record keeping, such as financial records, inventories, insurance policies, and other legal document locations. These can also be used to monitor temperature controls.

Technology is a viable factor in other aspects. Microwave ovens can be programmed to undertake and complete a series of cooking procedures. Homes can be heated and cooled using solar energy. These are only two of the technological advances found in your home.

Synthetics is another example of advancing technology. More and more natural materials are being replaced by manmade products. Synthetics are found in cars, home furnishings, construction materials for both home and commercial buildings, and even in the clothes you wear and the food you eat.

Your life expectancy is much greater than your parents or grandparents. Advances in medical technology have not only given you a longer life span but have also given you the opportunity to live a healthier and more productive life.

These and other technological advances have brought forth changes in the society in which you live. Each in its own way will necessitate continual adjustments and modifications in your life style and your managerial actions.

Recognition must be given not only to these changes but also to the input each has upon management. Have you ever met someone who lives more in the past than in the present? Someone who cannot or will not accept the changes taking place.

Although no one can predict the future, current trends can indicate movement and implications of change. The assessment of these trends can help you to recognize that change is inevitable and to identify the possible adjustments and modifications that can be made.

Technology and the Labor Force

Participation in the labor force has undergone many changes in the past several years and many more lie ahead. Within the working world distinct changes are taking place in the composition of the labor force, in the occupational endeavors currently being undertaken, and in the duration of labor force participation.

As indicated in Chapter 11, although the family member employed outside the shelter sphere is still predominately the male adult, the numbers of females who are entering and remaining as an integral part of the labor force is continually increasing. This factor alone necessitates managerial changes in the family and shelter sphere.

From this has emerged the "flextime plan," the "school shift," the "split location," and the "split level jobs."[1] Melville refers to these as the "radical modifications of the work week."[2] The participation of the female in the labor force and the roles she assumes has been a major force in their development. Each of these were initially developed to enable the female employed outside the shelter sphere to continue to assume the responsibility of child care within the parenting role. The basic premise was to adjust the workday hours in such a manner to enable her to be physically present when the children were or to allow her to adjust work schedules to meet other family needs such as medical appointments. These plans thus afforded the female parent the capability of assuming the parenting role while satisfying her personal self-fulfillment needs in a professional career.

The *school shift* used by one industry was established for the mother of school-aged children. The mother's working hours are identical to her child's school day.[3] The *split location* is another method which allows the mother to work full time and still assume responsibilities for child care and household operational tasks. She can personally determine where employment responsibilities and duties will be undertaken. Depending upon the exact nature of these, the employee has the option of completing assigned duties at the business establishment or in the shelter sphere. Thus the employee not only has the freedom to select the location of the work duties but also the time period when the tasks will be accomplished.[4]

Other companies, recognizing that part-time rather than full-time employment is desired, have instituted either the *pairing of jobs* or the *split level jobs*. In the *pairing of jobs* one position is equally divided. Two individuals are employed to fill the one position. Each assumes the responsibilities and duties of the single position; however, each is employed only half of the working day.[5] *Split level jobs* occur when one position requires two different skill levels or competencies. Rather than employ one individual to assume the responsibilities of both, the position is divided into two half-time jobs.[6]

Although each of these methods was designed to meet the needs of the employed female who has responsibilities for child care, many males are discovering the advantages of these positions as a means of meeting some of their personal needs. College students who cannot or desire not to be employed on a full-time basis are availing themselves of these.

With the increasing emphasis on energy conservation, many corporations are closely analyzing and considering adopting a plan which some companies moved toward a number of years ago. This plan lengthens the working day by increasing the number of hours per shift but reduces the work week. Some educational institutions and businesses have gone to a four-day week. One firm has a three-day work week.[7]

In addition to the alteration of the work week and working shift, some employers are recognizing the needs of their employees and are making available various support systems and physical fitness facilities. These include recreational facilities, child care centers, and various programs designed to foster the well-being of the employee and his or her family. Other support systems are counseling services and drug, alcohol, and child abuse programs.

The emerging employment patterns serve as input on individual and family management. The reduction in the work week yields an increase in the amount of leisure time available for nonemployment-related activities.

The reduced work week may appear to be an advantage to the adults in the family unit, particularly the female employee, but we must consider the overall implications to the remaining spheres of interaction as well as the family and shelter spheres. It is possible that school systems and retail establishments will feel the impact of these changes. Pressure may be exerted to change the school hours to accommodate the working hours of parents. Retail establishments may be pressured to lengthen or alter their opening and closing times or to change the number of business days.

Within the shelter sphere planning and implementation will need to be re-examined in respect to the length of the workday and work week. Still another problem to be resolved is the use of the time not devoted to work-related endeavors. As reported earlier, studies clearly show that the participation of the husband in household operation does not appreciably change when the female enters the labor force. Assuming role perceptions remain the same, although the female may have a longer length of time in which to complete her household operational task, how does the male adult use his increased time away from employment?

Other studies demonstrate that as the length of the work week decreases, families tend to devote more time to recreational activities. What type of activities might be pursued if the adult family members work week produces a four day weekend? This may have implications for the recreational facilities of the community and the nation. What effect would this have upon the nation's economy? In addition, does this mean school systems will need to increase their course offerings to include courses devoted to leisure-time activities? Might these pursuits also increase the demands upon other resources, particularly money?

Although the reduced work week could possibly yield a reduction in surrogate child care, other impacts may be experienced. Assume for a moment both the employed parents could adjust their employment shifts so one parent was always available for the child care responsibilities. This would probably result in increased participation of the male adult but might also alter the relationship and communication between the parents. A discussion with parents who currently use this method of child care could provide some revealing answers.

Only a few inputs upon the spheres of interaction are discussed here. Using your career objectives and your long-range goals for the future as a reference point, what are other implications you would foresee happening to your life style if your work week consisted of three 10- to 12-hour shifts per week?

The impact of technology can most readily be seen in the employment field. Over the years labor once done through physical exertion is now done through automation. Computers are used in business and industry to control production lines, for quality control, and to undertake many actions previously done by humans.

The work-related endeavors of employees are changing as automated mechanisms are programmed to assume production tasks. The employee's role is becoming more and more one of monitoring machines rather than one of actual physical labor. As robotics and CAD/CAM systems become an integral part of industry, the job description of the employee will be altered.

On the other hand, jobs previously completed manually by the physical effort of an individual have been eliminated. This, in turn, has created new positions requiring different skills and abilities. This trend will undoubtedly continue in the future. Some studies predict that during your employment lifetime you will assume several different positions. This diversity will necessitate that you be retrained at least four times to assume the new positions. The need for retraining will stem from the elimination of current positions, and from the requirements of technological advances.

The necessity for job retraining could have one of several impacts upon your managerial action. The financial costs involved may be assumed by your employer, or you may need to self-assume these. If your employer assumes the financial costs, where and when do you undertake the retraining? Will this be achieved during or after your workday? Should you have to self-assume this financial burden, how will your resource allocation be affected? The question of when, where, and how retraining will take place will also be factors. Again, resource allocation is affected.

In addition to resources, role modification will need to be analyzed and

corresponding adjustments made. Although the role of student is readily acceptable to you now, will it be quite so easy to accept and adjust to in five, ten,
fifteen, or twenty years? Would this retraining be the same, easier, or harder
for you during each of these time spans?

The individual and the family benefit from employment. The most commonly thought of benefit is money resources, yet other benefits include a
feeling of self-worth, an occupational identity, and other ego gratification
aspects. Employment also gives you the opportunity to interact with individuals
outside your shelter sphere; to use your skills, talents, and abilities in a purposeful and productive manner; to attain self-satisfaction; and many others.

The employment picture, as it existed for your grandparents, has undergone the process of change initiating change in all of the spheres of interaction.
As these changes occurred, individual and family managerial actions were adjusted and modified to reflect the input being received. Even as you read this
textbook changes are occurring and will continue to occur in the employment
future of the individual and family unit.

You have a career objective. As you develop the skills and competencies
to attain your desired employment, some will be obsolete by the time you
reach and attain your entry level position. Others will require modification as
you enter your chosen field of specialization. Only with the use of effective
management will you be able to undertake the necessary modification and adjustments leading to self-satisfaction in your employment and in your daily life.

Technology and the Family

Just as technological advances have impacted upon the labor force, so
too can these advances be seen in many ways within the shelter sphere. We
discussed how telecommunications have enabled the family unit to become
a citizen of the world; how in-home computers have reduced the amount of
time consumed in record keeping. Year around temperature and humidity
control of the shelter sphere has enhanced the home environment. Continual
advances in food preparation and storage offer the family unit alternative
choices to the previously time consuming task of food preservation. Appliances
and equipment within the shelter sphere produce more consistent standard
products while reducing the physical exertion. The shelter sphere and the
living patterns of the family unit reflect the advent of technology.

The conservation of naturally occurring energy resources is of prime
importance to individuals, governments, and nations. Technology affords the
opportunity to search for and develop alternative energy sources. This has
produced new commercial products, alternative choices for home heating
and cooling, different home construction materials, and a concerted effort
on the part of individuals and families as well as business and industry for
energy conservation.

Gasahol is one of the new products being produced as an alternative energy source. Alcohol distilled from corn is added to gasoline to produce a mixture called *gasahol* used to fuel automobiles. During this process other products such as sweetners, starches, oil, and protein are produced. These additional products are used for human and animal food.[8]

The necessity to reduce the consumption of naturally occurring energy sources has produced innovations in the heating and cooling of both homes and commercial buildings. Several commercial firms have instituted a heat recycling process. Rather than exhaust heat into the outside air, it is recycled through the building's heating system.

Homes and businesses are being heated and cooled using solar energy. Solar One on the campus of the University of Delaware is but one example of these. Although the interior design of Solar One closely resembles a conventional home, there is a concerted effort to reduce energy consumption. This is evident not only in the construction features but also in the recycling of heat producing equipment.[9]

New construction materials for the insulation and heat preservation are also being developed. These materials, primarily composed of synthetics, are increasing heat retention capabilities. Other energy conservation developments include the establishment of EER (energy efficiency ratios) for construction materials and household equipment, heat retention materials, and electrical systems which enable the family to reduce equipment energy consumption by eliminating one or more programmed cycles.

Although energy conservation is of prime importance, other technological changes are also impacting upon the family unit. As the economy moves forward to a cashless society with the implementation of electronic fund transfer systems, the impact of this technological advancement will be felt in every aspect of society. The money management skills of the individual and family unit will need to be combined with the knowledge and skills of computer operation in order to safeguard the family's financial well-being. The speed at which money transfers occur will be felt and reflected in the marketplace as well as within the family and shelter spheres. Individuals and families will need to modify managerial actions and adapt their money management behaviors. New work incentives will become necessary to replace those accrued from receiving a paycheck. The full implementation of this system will mean that financial banking transactions once confined to specific hours of the day will be obsolete.

Food and food packaging will continue to change. Nutritionally equivalent substitutes and imitation foods have long been a part of your daily diet. As technology continues to advance new methods of food processing and handling will continually emerge. One company is packaging foods in individual serving pouches that have a shelf life of seven years. These single serving pouches have no special storage requirements and can readily be transported. Once opened they can be eaten either hot or cold. Complete meals can be purchased and stored on a shelf until needed. In addition to the individual meals, this company employs the same preparation and packaging techniques to produce institutional quantities of food items.

The advances in telecommunications enable individuals and families to communicate around the world. Educational endeavors are no longer restricted to a single classroom and teacher. The teacher may be in a geographical location widely separated from students, yet each is able to see, hear, and respond to the other. Television programs can be recorded and viewed later. Long distance conference calls are commonplace. Business and industry can transmit records and correspondence across the nation in a matter of hours.

These and other technological advances have and will continue to impact upon the individual and family unit. This impact will necessitate changes in managerial action. Although in some instances new resources will become available, existing ones may have more demands placed upon them. The decisions concerning resource allocation will continue to be influenced by technological advances. New or different skills will need to be developed or refined.

The changes occurring in business and industry are also impacting upon the family and shelter sphere. As employment positions are eliminated and new ones emerge, family living patterns will need to reflect these changes. The alteration of the work week will have a strong input into the managerial action taking place in the shelter sphere. As business and industry incorporates technological advances, the input being received within the family and shelter sphere will necessitate managerial responses. At the same time, the family unit must also respond to the input of technological advances accruing from the marketplace.

These advances, although they are gradual ones, will continually be a viable source of input upon the family and shelter sphere. The managerial action of the individual and family must reflect this input. The decisions made, the allocation of resources, the restructuring of value hierarchies, the setting of goals, and the utilization of the management process will be affected by technology. The effectiveness of the managerial action will be dependent upon the degree to which the individual and the family unit make corresponding modifications and alteration in light of the input being received.

Role and Social Change

Although you might not have thought about it in quite this context before, technology has brought about many sociological changes. No longer does the young child grow to maturity anticipating living a life style which mirrors that of his or her parents. This child anticipates a much different world in which to live and achieve personal satisfaction.

The roles each individual will assume during a lifetime are undergoing the process of change. The currently assumed roles are constantly undergoing modification to reflect each individual's status within society.

The roles assumed by each person are not static ones. Each role is continually redefined in regard to the current status and the social structure. The continual evolution of society provides input upon roles and necessitates an on-going evaluation and redefinition.

One of the roles undergoing the redefinition process is the sex role.[10] The male-female roles once clearly defined within the family and shelter spheres as well as within society are being questioned. In the initial development and settlement of the United States the female often worked side-by-side with her husband, yet her primary role was that of child bearer and homemaker. It was not until the advent of World War II that the employment of the female outside the home on a permanent basis became an accepted social behavior. The female employee is no longer viewed as an oddity. In addition, both the adult male and female no longer have clearly defined and specified worlds in which each is expected to live and function apart from the other.[11] Once the female's world consisted almost entirely of the family and shelter spheres, now it reaches out beyond these boundaries.

Although the roles of both males and females are changing, Melville feels the greatest changes are occurring in respect to the female's role.[12] He cites the woman's movement, female participation in the labor force, and the increase in job availability as some of the change factors. Other causal factors are the equalization of educational opportunities and employment status.[13] The female's role has been modified to include those of a wage earner, capable of self-support and financial independence from her husband.[14] This role modification means she is less reluctant to dissolve unhappy marriages.[15] Sawhill indicates the stereotyped homemaker of the past is rapidly becoming an endangered species.[16] Only 16 per cent of all American families currently occupy the status of the typical family unit composed of "an employed husband, a homemaking wife and children."[17] The causal factors, according to Sawhill, are increasing divorce rates, decreasing numbers of family members per unit, increasing opportunities for female employment, "changing attitudes and aspirations—especially among younger and better educated women," and the financial demands for economic survival.[18]

Melville states males are refusing "to re-define roles and share in housekeeping and child care."[19] They are nonetheless accepting and, in some instances, encouraging employment of their wives. Other noticeable changes are the attitudes of males toward female coworkers.

Other roles of the individual and family unit within the social structure are changing. Each individual has the option to choose his or her status: married or single adulthood, whether or not to have children, occupational career, and many other aspects of the life style. Parenting once clearly defined not only in terms of male-female roles but also as an obligation and responsibility of a married couple is now a choice. Couples are deciding if and when children are to be born to the union. Many no longer feel that child bearing is a serious obligation and responsibility necessary to insure the continuation of the family's existence.[20]

These changing role definitions have afforded the individual and the family unit a greater freedom to make decisions concerning their lives. Each individual has the opportunity to establish an adult role within society consistent with the desired quality of life and value hierarchy. This affords the individual the opportunity to undertake not only his or her specifically designed role in the family, home, and employment worlds but also to undertake changes if desired.

Value hierarchies are also being reexamined and given priorities. "Personal growth, happiness and fulfillment" have become high priority values.[21] These value priorities and the freedom to undertake role adjustments are evidenced in many ways. Formal educational attainment is increasing. Individuals are switching jobs and even careers. Once the switching of jobs from one company to another with any degree of frequency was considered to be detrimental, now the growing importance of personal fulfillment and satisfaction has removed much of this stigma. Individuals are turning or returning to formal education to make career changes. The rational, here again, is the importance of personal satisfaction.[22]

The increasing emphasis on personal satisfaction through the realization of self-fulfilling goals is but one evidence of the changes taking place in society. This and the advances made through technology have produced role adjustments and modification. In your lifetime you will modify the role you assume. Part of this modification will stem from the changes in your status as an adult, family member, and as an employee. Part will also result from the input received from your spheres of interaction. Still another will accrue from the social changes taking place in the world around you. As your roles are modified to reflect social changes, the role of the family changes too. Both will yield fundamental changes in family structures, family life, and the family union as you know it today.

Life Style Patterns

The freedom to choose those roles that bring about personal satisfaction and self-fulfillment have become input upon all aspects of society. These changes can be seen in the individual's relationship to society, the role of the family unit in the attainment of personal growth, and the depth and degree of individual rights and responsibilities. Further evidence can be seen in the emerging life styles, the modification of traditional roles, and in the concept of the marriage.

Lerner in his discussion of the family of the future points to several aspects of the family structure undergoing change. Some of these include the changing roles of the adult female, questioning the validity not only of having children but also the current child rearing practices, and the family's capability to instill realistic and meaningful values within the family unit.[23]

Lerner not only questions the previous roles placed upon the adult female within the family structure but also why she has for so long continued to accept and assume them:

> We have given the American woman a considerable burden to carry. She's the home manager, the purchasing agent, the logistics manager, the ambassador to the schools, the social negotiator, the chief educator, the taste maker, the culture carrier, the social conscience, the sexual fulfiller, the crisis manager, and the custodian of values—all of these together.
> The wonder to me is that she submitted to it at all and did it as well as she has and has survived it.[24]

Melville discusses the importance of the changing perception of the adult female within the family structure and its implications to the emergence of different life cycles. Most of today's females have completed their child bearing by the age of 26, have all of their children in school by their early thirties; and by their mid-forties these children have left the shelter sphere on a permanant basis. Ahead of these mothers lie many years of discretionary time which they will utilize to satisfy their personal fulfillment needs.[25]

Such factors, according to Melville, indicate the need for a closer examination and possibly redefining of the life cycles.

> Three features of the re-defined life cycle with far reaching implications for marriage and family are: (1) postponement of first marriage; (2) a longer postparental or "empty nest" period after children move out of their parent's home; and (3) an increasing number of potentially stressful transition points for adults as they move from one status or lifestyle to another.[26]

Both Lerner and Melville view the family unit as being in a state of evolution. Although neither view the family unit as becoming obsolete, both see changes taking place that require a closer examination of the traditional roles of family members.

As your status changes from a college student to an employed adult, role perceptions will be modified. As you determine your role in society and the direction your life will take, you will be faced with several choices. Undoubtedly one will involve your future adult status in respect to the formation of close relationships with other adults. Your choice may be a traditional marriage partnership, or one of the alternative forms of the marriage setting, or it may involve one of the alternative life styles emerging within the current social structure.

Traditional Marriage Partnership

The nuclear family composed of husband, wife, and children are represented in the traditional marriage partnership. Although the roles assumed within this family unit are those identified in the stages of the life cycle, the previously emphasized relationship is changing. Where once the major emphasis was economic well-being, this emphasis has shifted to include the high priority values of individual growth and self-fulfillment. Increasing emphasis is being placed upon companionship and mutual affection as integral components of husband and wife roles within the marriage.[27] Wives as well as husbands are encouraged to seek roles and avenues which will bring about personal satisfaction—whether these lie inside or outside the shelter sphere. As indicated in this and earlier chapters, the adult female's role within the traditional marriage is being modified. Although the traditional marriage partnership, its roles, and expectations bear only slight resemblance to those of your grandparents, it still composes a major portion of today's social structure.

Weekend Marriages

Inherent within weekend marriages[28] are dual careers, dual incomes, and the marriage roles. In the traditional marriage partnership the husband's career is generally the determinant factor in the geographical location of the family unit. In this marriage alternative the emphasis is upon the personal satisfaction of each partner regardless of geographical location. The capability of achieving personal satisfaction and professional fulfillment are two standards established by this couple as each seeks employment. If employment positions meeting these standards occur in the same community, then a traditional marriage partnership exists. However, if they do not, each member of the partnership resides in the community where his or her employment occurs. Throughout the week each is engaged and involved in career pursuits. Weekends, vacations, and such are spent together at the residence of one or the other of the partners.[29]

This marriage alternative eliminates the restrictions experienced by many traditional marriage partners. Career choices are made solely on the basis of personal satisfaction and professional growth rather than accepting employment positions based upon availability within a given community.

In the traditional marriage partnership, one marriage partner may accept a less desirable employment position so the other can satisfy personal needs and be fulfilled. There are instances when a promotion for one partner may necessitate the family unit moving to another community. The decision accepting or rejecting the promotion may be influenced by the other partner's employment. In order for one partner to take advantage of this opportunity, the other must leave a personally rewarding career. In these situations, one partner may experience frustration and resentment. Since the emphasis in alternative marriage partnerships is the personal fulfillment of both individuals in their career endeavors, the limitations imposed by the traditional marriage partnerships do not exist.

This does not mean, however, that there are no limitations. Decision making is done independently and collectively. Communications and personal relationships may be limited. The couple need to determine if there are to be children born to this union. If children are born, they must decide where and who will undertake the child care responsibilities. In general, managerial action is undertaken both individually and collectively.

This marriage form represents an alternative choice to the traditional marriage partnership. The weekend marriage is an ideal solution for some married couples where personal fulfillment in career endeavors is a high priority. Where the traditional concept of a marriage partnership is the highest priority, it is not.

Consensual Unions

Another life style may be referred to as *cohabitation, living together,* or *consensual unions.* It is a partnership in which two individuals of the opposite sex choose to live together as a mated pair without the legal sanction of state laws.[30] The rationale for this choice of an alternative life style varies. The decision may be based on a strong desire not to marry in order to avoid the legal obligations incurred in a traditional partnership. In other instances, one or both of the adults may have experienced an unhappy marriage ending in divorce. The detrimental effects of both the marriage and the divorce may have been so great that entrance into another legalized marriage partnership cannot be considered.[31] Others desire the freedom to terminate a relationship without having to undertake the legal process of divorce. To some couples, it is used as a trial period before determining whether a legally sanctioned marriage should take place. There could also be economic factors influencing choices.

Consensual unions are more readily accepted by today's society than they were by the previous generation. Some states recognize the rights and privileges of the female in these unions whereas others do not. Some population segments accept consensual unions as a viable alternative to the marriage partnership. Even though its existence is recognized, some people do not view it as being within the boundaries of acceptable social behavior. However, the selection of this life style (currently found on many college campuses and in large communities), is still, for the most part, considered to be outside the boundaries of acceptable social behavior. In choosing this alternative life style, you should be aware not only of the social but legal implications.

Management may be done in much the same manner as in the traditional marriage partnership or it may be undertaken through the independent action of each partner. In this alternative life style, decisions will be made to determine the procedures employed in the managerial action.

Single Adulthood Status

Some adults are deciding to live their life without forming either a marriage partnership or a consensual union. This decision may be based upon the desire to have the freedom to live as they choose without being forced to consider the wants and needs of another individual. Also, single adulthood status eliminates the necessity of a permanent commitment to another person and allows the single adult to establish a variety of relationships over a period of years.[32]

Although society still evolves around the concept of couples, there are evidences of changing attitudes toward the single adulthood status. The emphasis upon birth control, the declining emphasis upon the traditional obligations of the individual to marry and reproduce, and the increasing emphasis on personal growth and satisfaction has resulted in a more favorable acceptance of the single adulthood status.[33] However, there still exists a different attitude toward the single male as compared to the single female.

The choice of single adulthood status allows the individual to undertake management independent of input from other individuals. As a result the single adult determines resource allocation on the basis of personal wants, needs, and desires. However, the resource reservoir is limited to what is available to the single person only. This may mean that while resource allocation is done in the context of individual desires and needs, the extent of the resource reservoir may be different than that of a family unit. Although decision making does not necessitate consideration of others, it is done completely by the single adult without the input or support system of the family unit.

Described herein are alternative life style choices. Other available life style choices include communal living, group marriages, and the marriage contract. Your choice of a particular life style will be based upon your desired quality of life, your immediate and long-range goals, and your value structure.

The choice you make and the satisfaction you receive will be measured by your standards and reflect your values. As you examined the alternative life styles described herein you probably found at least one which was totally unacceptable and another one that could be a possible choice. There probably was one choice you would prefer.

These life styles and those of the single parent or dual income families represent alternative choices and have constraints as well as benefits. Some are considered more socially acceptable than others. In making your choice, recognition must also be given to the roles that must be assumed within each and the ultimate affect upon your management.

As the continual evolution of society takes place, other life styles may emerge. Regardless of the life style you choose or the choices made by your classmates, management will occur.

You as a Manager

Up to this point you have made decisions which have produced managerial action. Some of your decisions have been major ones dealing with your life style, career determination, and your life patterns. Other decisions have been minor ones concerning your daily living.

Although you may feel these were solely your own decisions—and indeed they were—whether major or minor ones, each was the result of input you received from your spheres of interaction. Ahead of you lie still more decisions that will be influenced by input.

You have experienced many demands upon your resources. These demands will increase as you change your role from that of a college student. Some of these demands will come from your family and shelter spheres regardless of the number of members and how each is defined. Others will originate as input from the remaining spheres. Each of these demands, regardless of their point of origin, will necessitate managerial action. This action, in turn, will produce new demands as you choose among alternatives and allocate resources.

Some of your resources will increase as others decrease. The qualitative and quantitative aspects of your resource reservoir will reflect the changes taking place in your life. Your decisions concerning the allocation of resources as you seek to minimize their use will be influenced by the input and the anticipation of future demands.

Undoubtedly you will experience periods of crisis, frustration, and stress as you life moves forward. Each of these in its own way will be a source of input upon your management and the future direction of your life.

At the moment you are aware of your values and their hierarchy. These values will continually be redefined and clarified by the flow of input. Those values that have become uniquely yours will be guides throughout your life and you will base your decisions and managerial action on them.

The society in which you live is composed both of individuals and of groups who collectively make decisions and undertake management action. The decisions and actions of these collective groups provide input upon your decisions and management just as your decisions and managerial action do upon theirs.

In the days, months, and years ahead you will assume many roles, just as you are currently doing. With the passage of time, some of the roles you are assuming, like your role of a college student, will be eliminated. Other roles that currently are major ones will be modified and become minor ones as new roles are assumed and take precedence.

Goals you have right now will be achieved and other goals will emerge to take their place. These new goals as they become a part of your goal hierarchy will be continually analyzed as you strive to attain your desired quality of life.

Management takes place on a daily basis. How effectively you manage from day-to-day will affect not only your daily life but your future as well. This means continual use of management principles and concepts. Effective management is an art. It doesn't just happen. Only you can make it happen.

Your management skills and competencies are as vital to your well-being as the skills and competencies you are learning in order to enter your professional career. Through the use of the tools of management you attain your desired quality of life.

The society in which you live is continually evolving. Technology is continuing to advance individual knowledge and capabilities. The life patterns of individuals and families are changing to reflect the benefits accrued from such technological advances. New social structures are emerging. High speed transportation and communication have enabled individuals of different nations to share their customs and cultures with each other. Each individual's spheres of interaction are extending and reaching outward.

As these boundaries extend outward the input continually increases. This increased input affects all of management.

You have made some decisions concerning your roles in society. Other decisions remain to be made. How you make these decisions and the satisfaction you receive will be directly related to the effectiveness of your management.

Neither you nor any other individual can live in isolation devoid of input from the spheres of interaction. Nor can you or any individual anticipate living a lifetime without undertaking modifications as a result of input received from the spheres of interaction.

Management will occur whether or not you choose to actively participate. You can decide to let things happen and then attempt to cope with the results or you can make things happen through effective managerial action. Ahead of you are many challenges. Your life can move in the directions you desire yielding satisfaction and fulfillment. Management principles and concepts are the tools to effective management. How effectively you manage only you, and you alone, can determine. The choice is yours.

ACTIVITIES

1. Advancing technology has had an influence upon your life. This will continue in the future. On the basis of your knowledge of the past and present, what technological changes would you anticipate occurring in the following?
   a. Your professional career?
   b. Your shelter sphere?
   c. Your life style?
2. Several science fiction movies, books, and TV programs have theorized and proposed concepts of the life style and living patterns of individuals and families in the next century. Assume that you were suddenly transported to the next century, what changes would you predict you would find in:
   a. Family and shelter spheres.
   b. Managerial actions and behaviors.
   c. Family structure and composition.
   d. Values, goals, and standards.
   e. Decision making.

3. Discussed in this chapter are some alternative life styles. Assuming that personal fulfillment, honesty, companionship, professional satisfaction, and independence are all high priority values. How would each of the following rank these values and why?
   a. Weendend marriage.
   b. Consensual union.
   c. Single adulthood status.
4. Compare and contrast the values, goals, standards, resources, and decision making for the following.
   a. Dual income and weekend marriage families.
   b. Single adulthood and the single-parent family.
   c. Single-parent family and the consensual union.
5. Throughout this course you have established and examined your management.
   a. What managerial aspects have you observed changing since the beginning of the course?
   b. Analyze the results of these changes.
   c. Define what management means to you and the benefits you have received.
6. When you graduate and enter your profession:
   a. What major decisions do you anticipate? What do you anticipate will be your alternatives?
   b. What do you anticipate will be your life style? Why do you feel this is the one you will choose?
   c. What changes do you anticipate will occur in your management? What are the causal factors that will necessitate these changes?

JAN AND DON

Jan and Don's wedding is one month away. Both have mid-management positions in different firms and good prospects for advancement in the future.

Don is 24 years old and an only child of older parents. His parents were in their mid-thirities when he was born. His mother, although a former teacher, has not been employed outside the shelter sphere since he was born. His father, who did not complete high school, is employed in the same job he has held for the last 15 years and probably will be until he retires. To a great extent Don's home is dominated by his mother. He has always felt a tremendous responsibility toward his parents. So much so that he attended the local university and has continued to live at home since his graduation. He will not consider employment with a company outside of this community.

Jan's parents are in their mid-forties. Her father's professional career has necessitated frequent relocations of the family unit for the last 15 years. Because of their frequent moves from one community to another, Jan has lived in a variety of communities and attended a number of school systems. Her family is a close one but in a different sense. Her mother and father are not only her parents but they are also her friends.

Don is a very forceful, domineering person. In his home everything centers around his wants, needs, and life style. His mother makes certain it does. Since he has reached college age, every decision in the family must have his approval. For the most part, he, rather than his father, is the head of the family. His personality and attitude are such that Don has the habit of commanding rather than asking people to do things. He has very definite and inflexible ideas on everything and expresses them quite openly. The men who are on a higher work level than him praise his skills and abilities in organization and management as well as his authoritative demeanor. This, however, does not apply to those who work with or under him. They see him as dominating, opinionated, and rigidly inflexible, someone who will not consider any ideas other than his.

Jan is a quiet, sensitive person who tends to keep her true feelings hidden most of the time. Her father joined a corporation shortly after she was born and has been an executive for as long as she can remember. His responsibilities and the corporation's expectations have been the family's primary guidelines. Since Jan was a young child she has been taught not to let others know what she is thinking or feeling and above all not to talk about the corporation except in general terms.

Jan is very good at her job and has received one promotion since joining the firm less than two years ago. She is well liked by those who work under her as well as the administrators. Her boss recently told her she is one of the individuals being considered for an executive position in a new branch opening in about six or eight months. This position would mean a real advancement for her but it would also mean moving to another community about 300 miles away.

With their wedding so close, Jan and Don are together almost every night except when one or the other has to work late. Although Jan has hinted to Don in general terms about the possibility of her new position, she hasn't really told him.

Jan is aware of Don's strong feelings concerning his responsibility to his parents. In the discussions they have had on this subject, Don has been honest, stating he will not move or even consider moving as long as his parents are alive. Consequently, he has refused two promotions because he would have to move out of state.

Knowing his feelings and his mother's vocal support of his position, Jan has been extremely reluctant to discuss either her job or the possibility of her promotion. Thus far she has rationalized that it may not happen so there is no need to worry Don now.

Discussion Questions

1. What are Don and Jan's individual values? Put each person's values in a hierarchy. How closely do their values correlate?
2. After Jan and Don are married, what would you assume will be the method of decision making, the goals established, and the life style?
3. As this new shelter sphere is established, what are the adjustments and modifications you foresee will need to take place? Who will make the most adjustments and why? Where would you anticipate this shelter sphere will be located?
4. On the basis of what you know about Don and Jan, would you assume they might consider a weekend marriage? Why or why not? If they do undertake a weekend marriage, what type of life style would you predict would occur for each of their separate shelter spheres?
5. Assume that Jan is offered the position. What do you anticipate will be her response to the offer? What is your basis for this decision? What would you anticipate would be Don's response?
6. Describe what you feel will be the future of this couple. What inputs will they be receiving and what will be the source of these inputs? Describe their future through the three stages of the life cycle, if you feel they will marry and remain married. If not, describe what you feel will happen to each of them in the next 25 years.

GLOSSARY

Consensual Union An alternative to a marriage partnership in which two adults of the opposite sex choose to establish family and shelter spheres and live togehter as a mated pair without the legal sanction of marriage according to state laws.

Pairing of Jobs An employment status whereby the duties and responsibilities of a single full-time position are equally divided into two half-time positions, each of which is assumed by a different individual. Each individual is employed for only a portion of the workday.

Single Adulthood Status An alternative life style in which the individual chooses not to enter a marriage partnership.

Split Level Jobs An employment status in which one single full-time position requires two different skills and competencies is divided into two half-time positions. Each half-time position is then assumed by an individual employed only a portion of the day.

School Shift A designation for the length and time of an employee's workday which coincides with opening and closing hours of the normal school day.

Traditional Marriage Partnership A nuclear family unit composed of husband, wife, and child or children all of whom reside within the shelter sphere established by the adult marriage partners at a single location.

Weekend Marriage A marriage partnership in which husband and wife due to employment location reside in separate shelter spheres during the week and in the same shelter sphere on the weekends.

Work Week The number of days per week an individual participates in employment in the labor force.

REFERENCES

1. Keith Melville, *Marriage and Family Today* (New York: Random House, Inc., 1977), pp. 427–430.
2. Ibid., p. 427.
3. Ibid., p. 428.
4. Ibid., p. 430.
5. Ibid., p. 429.
6. Ibid., p. 430.
7. Ibid., p. 429.
8. "America's Abundance" (Cedar Rapids, Iowa: ADM Corn Sweetners, 1979).
9. Normal L. Newmark and Patricia J. Thompson, *Self, Space and Shelter An Introduction to Housing* (San Francisco: Canfield Press, 1977), pp. 446–447.

10. Melville, op. cit., p. 415.
11. Ibid.
12. Ibid., p. 416.
13. Ibid.
14. "Working Women Joys and Sorrows," *U.S. News and World Reports, Inc.* (January 15, 1979), 64.
15. Melville, op. cit., p. 415.
16. Isabel V. Sawhill, "Homemakers: An Endangered Species?" *Journal of Home Economics* (November 1977), 20.
17. Ibid., p. 18.
18. Ibid.
19. Melville, op. cit., p. 415.
20. Ibid.
21. Ibid., p. 419.
22. Ibid., p. 417.
23. Max Lerner, "Is There A Future For the Family?" *Journal of Home Economics* (September 1974), 7–11.
24. Ibid., p. 7.
25. Melville, op. cit., pp. 418–419.
26. Ibid., p. 417.
27. Ibid., p. 420.
28. Ibid., p. 425.
29. Ibid.
30. Gail Putney Fullerton, *Survival in Marriage Introduction to Family Interaction, Conflicts, and Alternatives,* 2nd ed. (Hinsdale: Ill.: The Dryden Press, 1977), p. 90.
31. Ibid., p. 617.
32. Melville, op. cit., p. 42.
33. Ibid.

Bibliography

——, *America's Abundance.* Cedar Rapids, Iowa: ADM Corn Sweetners, 1979.

American Association of Agricultural College Editors, *Communications Handbook* 3rd. ed. Danville, Illinois: The Interstate Printers and Publishers, Inc. 1976.

Association of Home Appliance Manufacturers, *Meeting Changing Lifestyles.* Chicago: Association of Home Appliance Manufacturers, 1976.

Bernhardt, Kenneth L. and Thomas C. Kinnear, "Profiling the Senior Market" in Fred E. Waddell (ed) *The Elderly Consumer.* Columbia, Md.: Human Ecology Center, 1976.

Bigelow, Howard F. "What are Usual Family Patterns?" *Journal of Home Economics,* (January, 1950) 27–29.

Blood, Bob and Margaret Blood, *Marriage* 3rd. ed. New York: The Free Press, 1978.

Brickman, William W. and Stanley Lehner (eds) *Automation, Education and Human Values.* New York: Thomas Y. Crowell Company, 1966.

Brown, David L. "Women in the Labor Force", *Journal of Home Economics* (November, 1977) 21–22.

Bullen, Adelaide K., *New Answers to the Fatigue Problem.* Gainesville: University of Florida Press, 1965.

Burk, Margurite C., "Food Economics Behavior in System Terms", *Journal of Home Economics* May, 1970 pp. 319–326.

Burton, Robert H. and George J. Petrello, *Personal Finance.* New York: Macmillan Publishing Company, 1978.

Calhoun, Lawrence G., James W. Selby and P. Elizabeth King (eds) *Dealing with Crisis A Guide to Critical Life Problems.* Englewood Cliffs, N.J.: Prentice-Hall, Inc., 1976.

Calhoun, Mary Lynne, "The Handicapped Child" in Lawrence G. Calhoun, James W. Selby, and H. Elizabeth King (eds) *Dealing with Crisis A Guide to Critical Life Problems.* Englewood Cliffs, N.J.: Prentice-Hall, Inc., 1976.

Carson, Loren D. and Arnold C. L. Hsieh, *Control of Energy Exchange.* New York: Macmillan Publishing Company, 1970.

Catler, Neal E. and Robert A. Harrootyan, "Demography of the Aged" in Diana S. Woodruff and James E. Birren (eds) *Aging Scientific Perspectives and Social Issues.* New York: D. Van Nostrand Company, 1975.

Cottrell, Fred, *Aging and the Aged.* Dubuque, Iowa: William C. Brown Company Publishers, 1974.

Craig, Karen E. "Gainful Employment for Women: The Facts" *Journal of Home Economics* (November, 1977) 23–25.

Deacon, Ruth E. and Francille M. Firebaugh, *Home Management Context and Concepts.* Boston: Houghton Mifflin Company, 1975.

Dewey, John. *How We Think.* Boston: D.C. Heath and Company, 1910.

Diesing, Paul, *Reason in Society: Five Types of Decisions and Their Social Conditions.* Urbana: University of Illinois Press, 1962.

Dryer, Everett D., "Parenthood as a Crisis: A Re-study" *Marriage and Family* (May 1963) 196–201.

Eisebberg, Abné A., *Understanding Communication in Business and the Professions.* New York: Macmillan Publishing Company, 1978.

Fitzsimmons, Cleo, Dorothy A. Larery and Edward J. Metzen. "Major Financial Decisions and Crisis in the Family Span", North Central Research Publica-tions No. 208. Lafayette, Indiana: Purdue University Agricultural Experimental Station, 1971.

Fitzsimmons, Cleo and Flora Williams, *The Family Economy Nature and Management of Resources.* Ann Arbor, Michigan: Edwards Brothers Incorporated, 1973.

Flannery, Gerald V., Ralph E. Hillman, Jerry C. McGee and William L. Rivers, "Communication and Society" in James John Jelinek (ed) *Improving the Human Condition A Curricular Response to Critical Realities.* Washington, D.C.: Association for Supervision and Curriculum Development, 1978.

Folland, Laura, Eunice Pickett, and Ruth Hoeflin. "Adult Women in College: How do They Fare?" *Journal of Home Economics.* (November 1977) 29–31.

Fullerton, Gail Putney, *Survival in Marriage Introduction to Family Interaction, Conflicts, and Alternatives.* Hinsdale, Illinois: The Dryden Press, 1977.

Goodban, William T. and Jack J. Hayslett, *Architectural Drawing and Planning.* New York: McGraw-Hill Book Company, 1965.

Green, Kinsey B., "Coping Daily with the Handicapped and Elderly", *Journal of Home Economics,* (Fall 1978) 15–17.

Gross, Irma H., Elizabeth Walbert Crandall and Marjorie M. Knoll, *Management for Modern Families* 3rd. ed. New York: Appleton-Century-Crofts, 1973.

Havinghurst, Robert J. "Understanding the Elderly and the Aging Process", *Journal of Home Economics* (April 1974) 17–20.

Hobbs, Daniel F., "Parenthood as a Crisis, A Third Study" *Journal of Marriage and the Family,* (August 1965) 367–372.

Hoult, Thomas Ford, Lura F. Henze and John W. Hudson, *Courtship and Marriage in America.* Boston: Little, Brown and Company, 1978.

Hungerford, Nancy and Beatruce Paolacci, "The Employed Single Parent" *Journal of Home Economics* (November, 1977) 10–13.

Jackson, John H. and Roger L. Hayden. "Rationing the Scarcest Resource: A Manager's Time", *Personal Journal* (October, 1974) 752–756.

Janis, Irving L. and Leon Mann, *Decision Making A Psychological Analysis of Conflict Choice and Committment.* New York: The Free Press, 1977.

Jelinek, James John (ed) *Improving the Human Condition A Curricular Re-*

sponse to Critical Realities. ASCD 1978 Yearbook. Washington, D.C.: Association for Supervision and Curriculum Development, 1978.

Jones, Alpha H. and Lois O. Schwab, "Rehabilitation for Homemakers with Cardiovascular Involvements: Changes in Attitude and Abilities", *Home Economics Research Journal,* (December 1972) 114–118.

Kalish, Richard A., *Late Adulthood: Perspectives on Human Development.* Monterey, California: Brooks/Cole Publishing Company, 1975.

Keenan, M. K., "Models for Decision-Making," Long Beach, California: Department of Home Economics, California State University, 1969.

Kelley, Robert K., *Courtship, Marriage and the Family* 3rd. ed. New York: Harcourt Brace Jovanovich, Inc. 1979.

Kim, Paul K. H. and Kennard W. Wellons (eds) *On Aging: An Orientation To Social Gerontology.* Lexington, Massachusetts: Xerox Individualized Publishing, 1975.

Kimmel, Douglas C., *Adulthood and Aging An Interdisciplinary View.* New York: John Wiley and Sons, Inc., 1974.

Koehler, Jerry W., Karl W. E. Anatol, and Ronald Applbaum, *Public Communication Behavioral Perspectives.* New York: Macmillan Publishing Company, Inc. 1978.

Lerner, Max, "Is There a Future for the Family?" *Journal of Home Economics* (September 1974) 7-11.

——, *Make Your Kitchen Modern.* Iowa State Extension Service Bulletin P62. 1948.

Maloch, Francille and Ruth E. Deacon, "Proposed Framework for Home Management", *Journal of Home Economics* (January 1966), 31-35.

Manufacturing Chemists Association, *Air Polution Causes and Cures.* Washington, D.C.: Manufacturing Chemists Association, 1972.

May, Elizabeth Eckhardt, Neva R. Waggoner and Eleanor Boettke Hotte, *Independent Living for Handicapped and the Elderly.* Boston: Houghton Mifflin Company, 1974.

Maynes, E. Scott, *Decision-Making for Consumers An Introduction to Consumer Economics.* New York: Macmillan Publishing Company, 1976.

Melville, Keith, *Marriage and Family Today.* New York: Random House, Inc., 1977.

Micklin, Micheal, *Population, Environment, and Social Organization: Current Issues in Human Ecology.* Hinsdale, Illinois: The Dryden Press, 1973.

Miller, Roger LeRoy, *Economic Issues for Consumers* 2nd. ed, Saint Paul: West Publishing Company, 1978.

Moustakas, Clark E., *Creative Life.* New York: D. Van Nostrand Company, 1977.

Nagi, Saad Z., *Disability and Rehabilitation.* Kent, Ohio: Ohio State University Press, 1969.

Newgarten, Bernice L. "Grow Old Along With Me! The Best Is Yet To Be". in Trude J. Unger and Eugenia M. Parron (eds) *Growing Up and Growing*

Old Part II: Adulthood and Old Age. Lexington, Massachusetts: Xerox Individualized Publishing, 1975.

Newmark, Norma L. and Patricia J. Thompson, *Self, Space and Shelter An Introduction to Housing.* San Francisco: Canfield Press, 1977.

Nickell, Paulena, Ann Smith Rice and Suzanne P. Tucker, *Management In Family Living* 5th ed., New York: John Wiley and Sons, Inc., 1976.

Niss, James F. *Consumer Economics.* Englewood Cliffs, N.J.: Prentice-Hall, Inc., 1974.

Oppenheim, Irene, *Management of the Modern Home* 2nd ed., New York: Macmillan Publishing Company, Inc., 1976.

Overly, Norman V. (ed) *Lifelong Learning A Human Agenda ASCD 1979 Yearbook.* Alexandria, Virginia: Association for Supervision and Curriculum Development, 1979.

Peet, Louise Jenison, Mary S. Pickett and Mildred G. Arnold. *Household Equipment* 8th ed. New York: John Wiley and Sons, 1979.

Perry, John and Edna Perry, *Pairing and Parenthood.* San Francisco: Canfield Press, 1977.

Plonk, Martha A., "Exploring Interrelationships in a Central-Satellite Decision Complex", *Journal of Home Economics* (December 1968) 789-792.

Raths, Louis E., Merrill Harmin, and Sidney S. Simon, *Values and Teaching: Working with Values in the Classroom.* Columbus, Ohio: Charles E. Merrill Publishing Company, 1966.

Riebel, L. Jean, "Philosophy of Management" *Journal of Home Economics* (January 1960) 16-19.

Sawhill, Isabel V., "Homemakers: An Endangered Species?", *Journal of Home Economics* (November 1977) 18-20.

Seglem, Betty S. and Maggie P. Hayes, "Reasons for Early Divorce" *Journal of Home Economics* (November 1977) 32-35.

Simonson, Ernest (ed) *Physiology of Work Capacity and Fatigue.* Springfield, Illinois: Charles Thomas Publishers, 1971.

Steidl, Rose E. "Affective Dimensions of High and Low Cognitive Homemaking Tasks" *Home Economics Research Journal* (December 1975) 121-137.

Steidl, Rose E. "Complexity of Homemaking Tasks", *Home Economics Research Journal* (June 1975) 223-240.

Stien, Barry, Allan Cohen and Herman Gadon. "Flextime Work When You Want To", *Psychology Today* (June 1976) 40-43.

Szinovacz, Maximiliane, "Women Employed: Effects on Spouse's Division of Household Work", *Journal of Home Economics* (Summer, 1979) 42-45.

Thurber, Majda, "Goals, Values and Life Evaluations at the Preretirement Stage" in Kennard W. Wellons and Paul K. H. Kim (eds) *On Aging An Orientation to Social Gerontology.* Lexington, Massachusetts: Xerox Individualized Publishing, 1975.

Troelstrup, Arch W. and Carl Hall, *The Consumer in American Society and Family Finance* 6th. ed., New York: McGraw-Hill Book Company, 1978.

Unger, Trude J. and Eugenia M. Parron (eds) *Growing Up and Growing Old Part II: Adulthood and Old Age*. Lexington, Massachusetts: Xerox Individualized Publishing, 1975.

Waddell, Fred E. "Consumer Research and Programs for the Elderly: The Forgotten Dimension" in Fred E. Waddell (ed) *The Elderly Consumer*. Columbia, Md.: Human Ecology Center, 1976.

Waddell, Fred E. (ed) *The Elderly Consumer*. Columbia, Maryland: The Human Ecology Center, Antioch College, 1976.

Walker, Florence S. "A Proposal for Classifying Self-Imposed Housekeeping Standards" *Journal of Home Economics* (June, 1968) 456–460.

Walker, Kathryn E., "Homemaking Still Takes Time", *Journal of Home Economics* (October, 1969) 621–624.

Walker, Kathryn E., "How Much Help for Working Mothers?" *Human Ecology Forum* (Autumn, 1970) 13–15.

Woodruff, Diana S. and James E. Birren (eds) *Aging Scientific Perspectives and Social Issues*. New York: D. Van Nostrand Company, 1975.

——, "Working Women Joys and Sorrows" *U.S. News and World Report, Inc.* (January 15, 1979) 64–70.

Index